101

D1376002

Imperialism and Gender:

CONSTRUCTIONS OF MASCULINITY

Imperialism and Gender:

CONSTRUCTIONS OF MASCULINITY

EDITED BY

Christopher E. Gittings

Dangaroo Press

Acknowledgements

Christopher Lane's essay 'Passion's "Cumulative Poison": Colonial Desire and Friendship in Kipling's Fiction' is reprinted with kind permission from chapter one of his book *The Ruling Passion: British Colonial Allegory and the Paradox of Homosexual Desire*, © (Durham and London: Duke University Press, 1995). The lyrics to 'Magnificent Obsession' that appear in Barbara Rasmussen's essay 'Virginia Woolf: Masculinity as Imperial *'"Parade"'* are quoted by kind permission of Windswept Pacific Music Ltd. The short quotations from *Memoir of Mohammed el Adl* that appear in Joseph Bristow's essay 'Passage to E.M. Forster: Race, Homosexuality, and the "Unmanageable Streams" of Empire' are reproduced by kind permission of The Provost and Scholars of King's College, Cambridge.

Plate I is taken from George Catlin, *Illustrations of the Manners, Customs, and Conditions of the North American Indians* (1876). Plate II is published by kind permission of the National Museum of American Art, Washington D.C. Plate III is published by kind permission of the National Portrait Gallery, Washington D.C.. I am grateful to the Hogarth press for allowing me to reproduce Plates IV, V and VI from their 1938 edition of Virgina Woolf's *Three Guineas*. Plate VII from *Gunga Din* (RKO), © 1939 is provided by the British Film Institute Stills Collection and published by kind permission of Turner Entertainment Co., All Rights Reserved. Plate VIII is reproduced from *Young Australia* (1902-1903). Plate IX is reproduced from *The Australian Boys' Annual* (1912). Plate X is reproduced from *The Australian Boys' Annual* (1925). Plate XI is taken from *Worker* c.1916.

This publication was made possible, in part, by the generous·support of: the University of Birmingham's School of History and the Department of Byzantine Ottoman and Modern Greek Studies, and The Literature Board 6f the Australian Council, the Federal Government's art funding and advisory body.

We have done our best to ensure that we have included all the people and publishers who should be thanked. If we have inadvertently left anyone out we apologize.

Cover: 'Pieta' by Julie Burnett

© Dangaroo Press

First published by *Kunapipi* in 1996
This edition first published by Dangaroo Press 1996

Australia: P.O. Box 93, New Lambton, NSW 2305
U.K.:   P.O. Box 20, Hebden Bridge West Yorkshire, HX7 5UZ

ISBN 1-871049-33-4

Printed in Great Britain by Villiers Publications, London N3.

CONTENTS

Editorial

I thank the contributors for the keen insights their papers have leant to my own understanding of masculinities and imperialisms, and for their generous co-operation and patience during an expedited editing process.

Imperialism and Gender: Constructions of Masculinity in Twentieth Century Narrative, the conference from which this book developed, owed much of its success to the co-operation and support of the University of Birmingham's Faculty of Arts Gender Seminar Group, especially the encouragement and work of Margaret Callander and Marianna Spanaki. To all conference participants, my thanks for creating two days of rigorous engagement with concepts of gender and imperialism.

For granting me permission to use her painting on the cover, and for her support and interest in this project, my thanks to Julie Burnett.

I am indebted to Jan Penrose who first encouraged me to think critically about formations of masculinity while I was studying at the University of Edinburgh. My appreciation also goes out to Anna Rutherford whose interest in and enthusiasm for this project was instrumental in bringing it to publication. I am grateful to Glenda Pattenden for her unwavering commitment to the book in her many roles. Thanks also to Susan Burns for her work with permissions, publicity and administration. Faye Hammill's able assistance with some of the proof-reading is much appreciated. I am grateful to Stephanie Bird, Nicholas Cull, Matthew Fox, Brian Harding, and Barbara Rasmussen for their support, and useful suggestions during the May 1995 conference and throughout the editing process.

Christopher Gittings

CHRISTOPHER E. GITTINGS

Introduction

So there I was, suspended in mid-story, in 1951, and there I remain, sometime, waiting for the end, or finishing it off myself, in a booklined [sic] London study over a stiff brandy, a yarn spun to a few choice gentlemen under the stuffed water buffalo head, a cheerful fire in the grate, or somewhere on the veldt, a bullet in the heart, who can tell where such greedy impulses will lead?
Margaret Atwood, 'The Boys' Own Annual, 1911'[1]

Imperialism and Gender

This collection of essays developed out of a conference on imperialism and gender held in May 1995 at the University of Birmingham. Historically, Birmingham served as one of the armouries of the British empire; it was the site of a lucrative munitions industry, producing the canons, rifles, and pistols that helped to arm the men who, by 1897 had imposed British rule on approximately 387,400,000 people.[2] It is not the purpose of this introduction to summarize each paper, but instead to locate individual papers in relation to an overview of the concepts of empire, gender and race raised by the book.

Michael W. Doyle defines the process of empire-building as

> The relationship, formal or informal, in which one state controls the effective political sovereignty of another political society. It can be achieved by force, by political collaboration, by economic, political or cultural dependence. Imperialism is simply the process or policy of establishing or maintaining an empire.[3]

The contributors to this volume consider the roles British and French imperialisms, and American neo-imperialism have played in constructing masculinities. However, *Imperialism and Gender: Constructions of Masculinity* also includes, by way of an historical antecedent for the imbrication of empire and masculinity, Matthew Fox's essay on Hercules and representations of masculinity in the ancient world. Atlas, Hercules and Apollo, idealized images of masculinity found in classical literature and art, provided the paradigmatic texts that shaped western European concepts of masculinity and empire in the eighteenth, nineteenth and early twentieth centuries. And Fox's paper examines some original accounts which highlight ambiguities in gender construction even at this early stage.

The writers collected here investigate how the conquest of territory and the imposition of the imperial power's economic, political and cultural systems onto the colony have shaped gender identities. In many narratives of imperialism women remain at home in the centre of empire waiting for, and subordinate to the soldier hero who ventures forth for the benefit and protection of both the metropole and the passive woman.[4] Women, however, were involved in the British colonizing process; as wives of missionaries and military officers, as teachers, nurses, shop assistants, farmers, or travel writers, they helped to translate the alien landscapes of North America, Africa, the Caribbean, India, and Australasia into the British familiar. Considering white women's subordination to white men and the 'borrowed' power imperial women had over colonized men and women, Anne McClintock has argued that white women were 'ambiguously complicit both as colonizers and colonized, privileged and restricted, acted upon and acting'.[5]

Moreover, the sign systems of empire are replete with the bodies of women who have been imported into the visual iconography of patriarchal political systems to personify the imperial state; for example, Marianne in France, and Britannia in the United Kingdom. Britannia was modelled on Athena the Goddess of War, but Britannia herself was originally conceived of as a subordinate, half-naked woman at the feet of the conquering Roman Emperor Claudius.[6] The British empire allegorized its hegemonic relationship to its colonies in a mother-daughter image, a representation more palatable to nineteenth-century Victorians than the lascivious emblem of Roman imperialism, although perhaps not as honest. Mother or Britannia had hermaphrodite powers and could transform herself/itself into a penetrating phallic entity. This phallic potential was manifest in male colonists who were invited to inscribe their British authority on feminized overseas territories.[7] Julie Burnett's cover painting, *Pieta*, plays with this image of Britannia as a phallic mother. Burnett's Britannia conceives, births and nurtures the male war machine, infantilized here as a ridiculous child at play with a toy globe and an impotent phallic sabre. Barbara Rasmussen's essay avers that Virgina Woolf also responds with reductive parody to the ludicrous figure of the imperial soldier hero in *Three Guineas* and *To the Lighthouse*.

Gender identity is formed by many factors. In the epigraph to this introduction Margaret Atwood genders imperialism as male. 'Boys' Own Annual, 1911' interrupts the masculinized narrative of imperialism to ask questions about the production of a destructive and debilitating martial masculinity that is suspended in time: 'the issue with the last instalment had never come'(p.11). The legacy of imperial masculinity lives on for both men and women. Atwood's response to the colonizing British text *Boys' Own Annual* – a collection of narratives representing aggressive and frequently racist British boys plundering the 'playgrounds' of Africa and India – constitutes a postcolonial counter-discourse or decolonizing narrative.

Before venturing any further with a reading of Atwood, a few words on concepts of the postcolonial. Simplifying to the extreme, post-colonialism describes a critical practice dedicated to addressing the types of cultural marginalization propagated by imperialism. Problematically, the term is ascribed to both invader-settler[8] cultures such as Canada and Australia, and former European colonies in Asia, Africa and the Caribbean.[9] As one of the principles of postcolonial critique is the articulation of difference in resistance to imperial assimilation, the ascription of the term to a culture must be continually recontextualized and reconceptualized so as to avoid the potential for homogenizing the colonial experiences of diverse groups. Arun P. Mukherjee reminds postcolonial critics who 'erase differences' that 'we have not all been colonized in the same way. "Race" has made a tremendous difference in how the empire treated us'.[10]

The *Boys' Own Annual* serials disciplined an exclusive gender identity for white-settler Canadian boys, inculcating English values that equated masculinity and honour with military service and the sacrifice of life for the empire.[11] In Atwood's re-writing of imperial discourse, a Canadian female voice, a voice on the periphery of empire and power, assumes narrative control over the male space of the *Boys' Own Annual* from the centre of the British empire, refiguring narratives of imperialism as destructive and 'greedy impulses' that could place a bullet in the heart of their reader. The prose piece ends with the appearance of just such a damaged reader, the narrator's half uncle 'gassed in the first war and never right since'. We learn that 'the books had once been his' (p. 11). Here is a ramification for consuming *Boys' Own Annuals* and companion texts like *Chums*, and here also is the ending that Atwood writes for imperial power struggles. 'Boys' Own Annual, 1911' and the essays in this book deconstruct imperial systems, and the nexus between imperialism and masculinity, arguing that masculinity is socially engineered, and that imperialism is an agent of this process. Atwood's prose piece would suggest that the reading materials of young boys and girls help to determine gender identities. John Martin's paper develops this theme, examining the prescriptive role 'Boys' Own' Annuals played in forming Australian masculinities, while Peter Hunt's essay considers the texutalization of empire and masculinity in a range of English children's literature. Susan Bassnett also interrogates the stultifying influence of British imperialism's heroic male narratives for both men and women at home in the metropole.

Despite the efforts of Atwood and others, imperial formations of masculinity persist in the late twentieth-century. Individual societies continue to require the manufacture of soldier heroes to secure the interests of the state in conflicts such as the Falklands and the Gulf Wars. Investigations into historical formations of masculinity and imperialism can provide insights into contemporary constructions of masculinity. Ken Lukowiak, a veteran paratrooper of the Falklands conflict (an operation arguably designed to resurrect Britain's imperial past)[12], describes the process of making martial masculinity in a newspaper article entitled 'Break 'em, make 'em'.[13] As the title implies, Lukowiak delineates a systematic breaking down of civilian gender identity through humiliation, and physical exertion at the hands of the British military's paratrooper training personnel, 'then once you are broken they build you up the way they want you' (pp. 2.2-2.3). Lukowiak joined the Parachute Regiment 'because [he] wanted to be a man'(p. 2.2), and to accomplish masculinity he believed he had to learn aggression (p. 2.3). Paratrooper masculinity is constructed as a definitive and hierarchical gender identity, one that feminizes what it reads as inferior formations of masculinity. Lukowiak describes a group of soldiers not in the paras as 'a gaggle of crap hats. Chewing their little-girl sandwiches and sipping poofy Ribenas'(p. 2.2). Here, paratrooper culture abrogates the homosexual subject's male gender identity, and inferiorizes the feminine. The work of Graham Dawson[14] and R.W. Connell[15] argues convincingly that the military has been of fundamental importance to the definition of the soldier hero as a hegemonic and idealized form of masculinity in European and North American cultures.

Social Construction Theory and Gender

The discussions of gender formation articulated above, and the essays which follow this introduction, assume that gender is a social construction. Masculinity and femininity are not categories that exist organically, but are produced socially. Social structures like the family, and institutions such as the church and the military instil myths of gender which punish peripheral gender identities, and reward dominant ones.[16] Our understanding of ourselves and our world is shaped by the society in which we live.[17] Peter Jackson's and Jan Penrose's encapsulation of social construction theory provides a useful lens through which we can read the category of gender:

> social construction theory argues that many of the categories that we have come to consider 'natural', and hence immutable, can be more accurately (and more usefully) viewed as the product of processes which are embedded in human actions and choices.[18]

One other category inextricably linked, and sometimes mistakenly confused with gender is sex. Sex – male or female – has been read as a biological and therefore 'natural' category determined by anatomy, hormones, and physiology.[19] However, the research of endocrinologists, biologists and social scientists suggests that the chromosomal, gonadal and hormonal elements determining sex roles '"work in the presence and under the influence of a set of environments"';[20] they are tempered by the process of socialization. Socialization encompasses psychosexual development, the learning of social roles and the shaping of sexual preferences, processes constructing gender identity (Lorber and Farrell p.7).[21]

Sexual preference and choice of sexual object are closely related to gender identity. As Lorber and Farrell write 'Boys who consider themselves male and girls who consider themselves female are supposed to be sexually attracted to each other' (p.7). Same sex attraction is interrupted and disciplined by what Adrienne Rich calls 'compulsory heterosexuality'.[22] Connell defines the ruling or socially dominant heterosexual masculine as

> the configuration of gender practice which embodies the currently accepted answer to the problem of the legitimacy of patriarchy, which guarantees (or is taken to guarantee) the dominant position of men and the subordination of women. (Connell p. 77)

This totalizing masculinity oppresses women and other formations of masculinity: heterosexual 'nerds' or 'wimps' (p. 79) and all formations of gay masculinity:

> Oppression positions homosexual masculinities at the bottom of a gender hierarchy among men. Gayness, in patriarchal ideology, is the repository of whatever is symbolically expelled from hegemonic masculinity, the items ranging from fastidious taste in home decoration to receptive anal pleasure. Hence, from the point of view of hegemonic masculinity, gayness is easily assimilated to femininity. (Connell p. 78)

We can see this hegemonic masculinity at work in Ken Lukowiak's narrative of paratrooper masculinity, and in many of the texts investigated in the essays that follow, where behaviour that does not fit a ruling group's concept of masculinity is derided as feminine or homosexual. Susan Hayward's essay analyzes how French imperialism reads race and gender to construct a subordinate and feminized subjectivity for the African houseboy Protée in the film *Chocolat.* British imperialism also responded to racial difference in this way, subordinating African and Bengali men as feminine.[23]

Building Empire: Constructing Race

Western European imperial projects were predicated on the dominant white patriarchal construction of difference to itself as inferiority. This type of alterity or othering is sexual, gendered, racial and cultural. The European colonizer can, as Brian Harding's essay illustrates in the case of George Catlin, project a romanticized image of the male colonial subject as 'noble savage' onto the colonized, thereby identifying with this idealized indigene built from white materials. Frantz Fanon argued that the white male colonizer's relationship to the black colonized male subject, or extrapolating for our purposes here, the indigene, is always other – *black, red, yellow* – 'in relation to the white man'.[24] Diana Fuss's gloss on Fanon elucidates the colonizer's subjugating construction of racial otherness:

> The colonized are constrained to impersonate the image the colonizer offers them of themselves; they are commanded to imitate the colonizer's version of their essential difference.[25]

This problematic paradigm is traced here in Susan Hayward's essay on *Chocolat*, Nicholas Cull's analysis of *Gunga Din*, Graham Dawson's reading of *Lawrence of Arabia*, and Joseph Bristow's exploration of the relationship between E.M. Forster's autobiographical representation of his Egyptian lover, and the mixed race union in the author's late short story 'The Other Boat'. Gargi Bhattacharya's polemical essay ironizes and deflates the power of the white heterosexual masculine in the late twentieth century by revealing its decaying and impotent image as constructed in the eye of its other: the 'Mahogany Princess'.

Europeans could rationalize their invasion and conquest of Africa, the Americas, Asia and the Caribbean as *missions civilisatrices* designed to bring the 'light' of Christianity to 'benighted' peoples by replacing their cultural systems with European ones, to erase difference, and create 'Empires of the self-same'.[26] Of course, no matter what the success of cultural assimilation, the colonized would always be marked by race, a distinction that, within the imperial cosmology, perpetuated the perceived need for 'white fathers' to administer the lands and resources of 'dark children'.

Imperialism's White Homosocial Landscape

The martial and hierarchical terrain of imperialism is marked by white homosocial codes. In the case of the British army and empire, a racially homogeneous community (albeit one stratified by class and marked by region) of men in partial isolation from white women form strong homosocial bonds. Paradoxically, the potential for homosexual tension threatens the very ideal of ruling heterosexual masculinity that facilitates the formation of those bonds. These tensions are investigated here in my essay on Timothy Findley's *The Wars*, and in contributions from Joseph Bristow, Christopher Lane, Andrew Michael Roberts, and

Alan Williams. In turn homosocial relations, as Bristow, Cull, Lane and Roberts observe, are frequently represented as threatened by the presence of women.

Diana Brydon's essay delineates a correlation between the imperial narrative of Conrad's *Heart of Darkness* and the malignant homosocial world of Timothy Findley's Club of Men in *Headhunter*. The legacy of nineteenth-century Canadian colonial masculinity, Brydon argues is visited upon late twentieth-century Toronto in the form of a corporate masculinity.

Contributions from Peter West and Brian Matthews supplement the fictional and legendary representations of imperialism and masculinity hitherto discussed. West provides a history of male socialization in one colonial Australian town, while Matthews' autobiographical essay moves away from the theoretical to reflect on the lived experience of becoming a 'bloke' in the Australia of the last half-century.

This book contributes to understandings of the relationships between masculinity and imperialism, and the ramifications of these relationships for men and women. Formations of masculinity in the metropole are considered in relation to how these formations translate to the empire and onto the colonized. The anthology traces imperial and colonial formations of masculinity in the ancient world, twentieth-century Africa, Australia, Canada, England and India, as well as nineteenth-century America and England.

NOTES

1. Margaret Atwood, 'The Boys' Own Annual, 1911', *Murder in the Dark* (Toronto: Coach House Press,1983), p. 11. All further references are to this edition and are included in the text.
2. See *The Horizon History of the British Empire Vol. 2*, ed., Stephen W. Sears, (London and New York: McGraw-Hill, 1973), p. 315.
3. Michael W. Doyle, *Empires* (Ithaca: Cornell University Press, 1986), p.45.
4. See Graham Dawson, *Soldier Heroes: British Adventure, and the Imagining of Masculinities* (London: Routledge, 1994), p. 2.
5. Anne McClintock, *Imperial Leather: Race, Gender and Sexuality in the Colonial Contest* (London and New York: Routledge, 1995), p.6.
6. See Marina Warner, *Monuments and Maidens: Allegory of the Female Form* (London: Pan Books, 1987), Fig. 19.
7. For a discussion of imperialism and the gendering of colonized territory as female see McClintock, pp. 24-30, p. 354.
8. I am adopting Diana Brydon's reversal of settler-invader to invader-settler. Brydon reverses the term "to stress that the narrative of settlement in itself occludes and denies the prior act of invasion." See Brydon, 'Introduction: Reading Postcoloniality, Reading Canada', *Essays on Canadian Writing* 56 (1996), pp. 1-19 (16-17).
9. See Bill Ashcroft, Gareth Griffiths and Helen Tiffin, *The Empire Writes Back:*

Theory and Practice in Post-Colonial Literatures (London: Routledge, 1989), p.2.

10. See Arun Mukherjee, 'Whose Post-Colonialism and Whose Postmodernism?' *World Literatures Written in English* 30.2 (1990), pp. 1-9 (p.2). For further interrogations of how postcolonial signifies see: my essay, 'Canada and Scotland: Conceptualizing "Postcolonial" Spaces', *Essays on Canadian Writing*, 56 (1996), pp. 122-146; Linda Hutcheon, '"Circling the Downspout of Empire": Post-Colonialism and Postmodernism', *Ariel* 20, 4 (1989), pp. 149-175; Stephen Slemon, 'Unsettling the Empire: Resistance Theory for the Second World', *World Literatures Written in English*, 30, 2 (1990), pp. 30-41.

11. See Dawson p. 1.

12. See Dawson, pp.2-5.

13. *The Guardian*, 7 June 1995, pp. 2.2-2.3. All further references are to this issue and are included in the text.

14. See Dawson, p. 24.

15. R.W. Connell, *Masculinities* (Cambridge, U.K.: Polity Press, 1995), p. 213. All further references are to this edition and are included in the text.

16. See Erich Fromm, 'The Method and Function of an Analytic Social Psychology', *The Crisis of Psychoanalysis* (Hammondsworth: Penguin, 1973), p. 158. Qtd. in Horrocks, p. 16. Regarding gender and myths see Roger Horrocks, *Male Myths and Icons: Masculinity in Popular Culture* (Basingstoke, U.K.: Macmillan, 1995), p. 20.

17. See Peter L. Berger and Thomas Luckman, *The Social Construction of Reality: A Treatise in the Sociology of Knowledge* ([1966]; Garden City, New York: Anchor Books/Doubleday and Co., 1967).

18. Peter Jackson and Jan Penrose, 'Introduction', *Constructions of race, place and nation*, eds., Peter Jackson and Jan Penrose (London: UCL Press, 1993), pp. 1-23 (p. 2).

19. See Candace West and Don H. Zimmerman, 'Doing Gender', *The Social Construction of Gender*, eds., Judith Lorber and Susan A. Farrell, (Newbury Park: Sage in cooperation with Sociologists for Women in Society, 1991), pp. 13-37 (p. 13).

20. A. Fausto-Sterling, qtd. in Judith Lorber and Susan A. Farrell, 'Principles of Gender Construction', *The Social Construction of Gender*, eds., Judith Lorber and Susan A. Farrell, pp. 7-11 (p. 7). All further references are to this edition and are included in the text.

21. For a sustained discussion of sex as a discursive category, see Judith Butler, *Bodies that Matter: On the Discursive Limits of Sex* (London: Routledge, 1993).

22. See Adrienne Rich, 'Compulsory Heterosexuality and Lesbian Existence', *Signs: Journal of Women in Culture and Society*, 5 (1980), pp. 631-660.

23. On African men see McClintock, pp.54-55; on Bengali men see Mrinalini Sinha's *Colonial Masculinity. The 'manly Englishman' and the 'effeminate Bengali' in the late nineteenth century* (Manchester: Manchester University Press, 1995).

24. Frantz Fanon, *Black Skin, White Masks*, trans., Charles Lam Markmann ([1952]; New York: Grove, 1967), p. 110.

25. Diana Fuss, 'Interior Colonies: Frantz Fanon and the Politics of Identification', *diacritics* 24, 2-3 (1994), pp. 20-42 (p. 24).

26. See Christopher Lane's consideration of Britain's 'Empire of the Selfsame' in 'Passion's "Cumulative Poison": Colonial Desire and Friendship in Kipling's Early Fiction' in this collection.

MATTHEW FOX

Greek & Roman Hercules: Moments in Pre-Historical Imperialism.[1]

My title has a double meaning; Hercules as a figure representing imperialism both as a pre-historic forerunner for the subjects of imperial Rome themselves, and as a point of pre-historic reference for this collection. There is a danger in contributing an essay on classical material to a collection of studies of the contemporary world; a danger that the specificity of ancient society will be passed over in the urge to find similarities, or worse, to find origins and causes. However, it is a danger that can be productive, in that a recognition of similarity can restrain an unjustified sense of the uniqueness of modern conditions. And for the classicist to look at the configurations of ancient empire from a modern perspective is to look at an area traditionally characterized by its political irrelevance, and to find new possibilities in the details of how different imperial subjects related to each other. This paper will look at Hercules as the mythical founding figure of the Roman empire, in two very different accounts of his presence in pre-historic Rome. In one, Hercules acts as the bearer of an ideal civilization; in the other, he boasts of his credentials as a woman. In both accounts, the figure of Hercules can be read as the focus for conflicting interpretations of maleness, and these interpretations are themselves part of a larger discourse concerning the role of the citizen or subject within an imperial context.

But first some historical background. My two texts, Dionysius of Halicarnassus' *Roman Antiquities* and poem 4.11 of Propertius, come from the beginning of the Roman empire; empire in the sense of the rule of the emperor, in this case Augustus. Augustus, however, acceded to a realm that already included most of the Mediterranean world, since the expansion of the city of Rome to world rule had already been underway for several centuries. In terms of augmenting the empire with new territories, Augustus was not as active as some of his fore-runners, the generals at the heads of the republican armies. However, together with his remarkable achievements on the constitutional front, supplanting an oligarchic democracy with permanent rule by one man, Augustus did effect great changes in the way in which the Roman empire came to be perceived and understood. There had been sporadic indications throughout the course of Rome's expansion that her conquests required consolidation in the form of a new understanding of the justice of Rome's position in the world. Both in historical and literary works which propagated comprehension of Rome's rule, and in religious institutions which integrated its celebration among Rome's new subjects, Rome laid a reasonable basis for a stable imperial future. The Greek historian Polybius is the most significant apologist for the increase of Roman power, but even earlier, a Roman, Fabius Pictor, had written a history of Rome in Greek, intending thereby to explain and justify to her new subjects how Rome had reached her present prominence.[2] As well as these appeals to a small, literate audience, even if it was the elite-in-power, Rome's growth was accompanied by a growth in cults of the goddess Roma and similar institutions, which gave a focus in Rome's new communities for the profitable exercise of loyalty to central authority. Under Augustus, these two strands, the religious, and the literary/ideological were brought more closely together. Veneration of the person of the emperor became enhanced by a sense of the inevitable and divinely pre-ordained role of Rome in the world, both in Rome's provinces, and in the capital itself. In Virgil's *Aeneid* the nexus of an imperial presence, territorial expansion, and divine destiny fulfilled find their most subtle and wide-ranging expression, in a work of unparalleled influence on other forms of ideologically-loaded representation. Ideas which we encounter in isolation on monuments or in the work of other poets gain in their breadth of significance by virtue of the existence of the *Aeneid,* which functions as the expression of Roman imperial ideology in its fullest form, and as a repository of significance from which all other descriptions of Rome inevitably derive a greatly enhanced language of symbols and ideas.

Perhaps the most significant peculiarity of the Roman way of representing empire is its aetiological tendency. In common with much other ancient thought, the definition of empire itself was made by reference to an origin or a cause. You would not ask 'what is the Roman empire like?', but rather, 'what caused the Roman empire?', and thereby acquire an understanding of its character. So the origins of the city of Rome became a vital part of imperial ideology. For the opponents of empire, Rome's founders were barbarian shepherds, Rome's rule the manifestation of the randomness of the caprice of Fortune.[3] More commonly, at least in the sources which have survived, the foundation and early history of Rome demonstrate and guarantee the virtue and wisdom which is characteristic of the whole history of Rome, from the beginnings to the present day. In this discourse, it is difficult to make clear demarcations between history and myth, and indeed, important not to. But it should not be forgotten that for the Romans and their subjects, history was the dominant mode of explaining, and thus of understanding, the nature of Rome's empire.

Heracles

It would be an immense task to describe the multitude of manifestations which the figure of Hercules undergoes, and to give an introduction to the figure in the same manner as I have introduced the historical context would be incompatible with how I understand both Hercules and ancient myths in general. To prioritize any one representation of Hercules over another, or to suggest that any particular representation is more true to tradition or to the *real* myth, is to misunderstand the important fact that myths live only in their re-presentations, and that to interpret a myth necessitates looking at its representational context. Perhaps particularly with Hercules, in Greek Heracles, versatility is a defining feature, and if we are to chart the significance of particular representations of him, it will be an encumbrance to think in terms of original meanings or fixed identity. So the only introduction I shall make will be to point out that both Heracles and Hercules were very popular, had a long history, and could take on a wide variety of roles and characteristics.[4] From this multitude one episode had special significance in imperial Rome: the arrival of Hercules in Italy on his return journey from Spain, where he had stolen the cattle of the triple headed monster Geryon, and his battle with Cacus over the cattle on the Palatine hill. The story was an old one, appearing at least as early as the fifth century B.C.E,[5] but gained in popularity in the early empire, perhaps as a result of taking a central position in book 8 of the *Aeneid,* where Cacus is depicted as a fire-breathing monster. The first narrative I shall present gives us Heracles as a pre-historic civilizer. It comes from the *Roman Antiquities* of Dionysius of Halicarnassus, a Greek rhetorician and historian, who came to work in Rome shortly after Augustus had decisively installed himself as head of the Roman state.[6]

Dionysius' subject matter is the origins and early history of the Romans. His history ends at the point at which Polybius begins, and he clearly has the same aim, of mediating the Roman empire to its Greek subjects. Polybius' stress on autopsy in historical writing gives his work a heavy bias towards contemporary events. Dionysius, on the other hand, employs a variety of techniques to press mythical material into service. He goes back as far in time as he can to demonstrate the character and virtue of Roman rule. Indeed, his trump card in making Roman supremacy acceptable to a Greek readership is the claim that the earliest inhabitants of Italy were colonists from Greece. His zeal to reconcile his Greek readers to the virtues of Roman rule thus leads him to put forward a historical interpretation in which the good aspects of Roman rule can be seen to have their origin in the Greek origin of the Romans themselves. As part of his survey of pre-Roman Italy, Dionysius includes two versions of Hercules' visit, distinguished from each other in terms of their historical credibility. 'Of the things said about this god', Dionysius begins, 'some are rather mythical, others are more true'.[7] He takes the mythical material first, and describes how, in the course of one of his twelve labours, Heracles came to Italy, fought and killed a bandit called Cacus, who had tried to steal the cattle, and how the inhabitants commemorated the event in the establishment of one of the most important of Rome's public altars, the *Ara Maxima* in the Forum Boarium, which was still in use in Dionysius' own day. Dionysius concludes the account by reiterating 'this is the mythical story handed down about him'.[8]

There are two curious features of Dionysius' categorization of this narrative as mythical: the first its restraint; there is nothing remotely supernatural. The second is the emphasis upon the aetiologies; in discussing the *Ara Axima* Dionysius stresses the continuity of the traditions of the priestly families, the handing down of Greek sacrificial custom, and the spread of cults of Heracles throughout Italy. He also says that it was in premonition of Heracles' apotheosis that the local king, Evander, set up this altar. The mythical, then, does not in any sense exclude the believable. Indeed, Dionysius has reserved the category of mythical specifically to grant a particular kind of credibility to these aetiologies; a credibility which takes into account the possibility of apotheosis, and which stresses the sanctity of institutions central to Roman sacred practice.

What Dionysius is doing with the mythical elements becomes clearer when he comes to the truer story, introduced thus: 'The truer version, which is used by many of those narrating his deeds in the form of history, goes like this:'[9] Heracles was the greatest general of his age, and commanded a large army which was engaged in an expedition involving all the territories bounded by Ocean. If he encountered a tyranny, or a city that caused suffering to its neighbours, or any kind of hegemony of uncivilized and dangerous men, he would dispose of them, and replace them with monarchies operating within the law, states based upon wise constitutions and ways of life directed towards harmony and love of mankind. He resettled Greeks and barbarians, inland and coastal dwellers, who were traditionally distrustful of each other, so as to live together, and built cities in deserts, diverted rivers so as to stop them flooding, and constructed roads through inaccessible mountains, among other engineering feats. The battle with Cacus is transformed into that between the invading conqueror and the recalcitrant native warlord. After Heracles' successful defeat of resisting Ligurians, who seriously delay his entry into Italy, many cities voluntarily gave themselves up; especially the Greek ones. Cacus was a barbarian leader of an uncivilized people, and a plague to his neighbours. On his defeat, his territory, including the site of the future city of Rome, was divided up among the natives who had shown their loyalty to Heracles by participating in the expedition. Others who benefited from this resettlement programme were those whom Heracles had taken with him as prisoners from earlier campaigns. They had taken part in subsequent military actions, and were now rewarded with liberty and colonies. As a result of his actions in Italy, Heracles was awarded divine honours. The colonists he left behind near Rome maintained their own (Greek) form of government for a while, but gradually became wholly assimilated to the original inhabitants of the area, the Aborigines.

Dionysius' narrative displays concerns central to his mission of the justification and explanation of the empire of his own day. The division between barbarian and Greek is a major preoccupation. For Greeks it was normally a linguistic division between Greek and non-Greek speakers. The term barbarian also had pejorative associations based upon an evaluation of a way of life, and in a passage at the end of his survey of pre-Roman Italy, Dionysius extends these and argues against the linguistic distinction. The Romans cease to be barbarians because they live a civilized life. Likewise Cacus is described as completely barbarian (*komidé barbaros*); he not only did not speak Greek; he also behaved like a barbarian. The distinction acquires further depth in Dionysius' distinction between the different kinds of Italian inhabitants. Those that were Greek, in effect those to whose Greek origin Dionysius has devoted considerable attention earlier in the work, recognized their invading kin, and responded accordingly. So any distinction between the victim of aggression and the aggressor is submerged in the general vision of Greek supremacy over barbarians.

The native barbarians all live in remote mountain landscapes. Both the Ligurians and Cacus have a wildness which is a complement to their geographical location. Two other sections of the work provide resonance here: first a luxuriant description immediately before this episode of the fertility of early Italy, by which Dionysius seeks to explain the common conception of a golden age of Saturn;[10] second, the emphasis upon Heracles' manipulation of natural resources as part of his civilizing mission. Heracles here is certainly taming nature, but only in a clearly defined manner, and one which corresponds to the vision of Italy as essentially a land of plenty. His works are all designed to create better opportunities for human exploitation. The damage caused by unpredictable rivers is prevented. What was previously inaccessible is made available. But it would be wrong to distinguish between his effect on nature and his effect on people. His resettlement programme, like his political reforming, is designed to rid communities of undesirable characteristics, and install a uniform, Greek idea of civilization.

Jourdain-Annequin has amply documented the idea of Hercules as the civilizer and dispenser of culture, basing her account on Diodorus' more copious evidence for the rest of his adventures.[11] She employs structuralist dichotomies of nature/culture, and suggests that the urban community was essential to the appeal of the reiteration of this distinction in the form of a proliferation of Hercules' myths. What her analysis lacks, perhaps because she favours Diodorus Siculus as a source over Dionysius, is the sense of a political context to this vision of Heracles. The idea of the Greek civilizer imposing a uniform world order could only make sense within the empire; it is not the urban context, so much as the idea of world empire, which gives credibility to Heracles as the civilizer. For Dionysius, this version is the one more close to truth, more resembling history. Hercules is more believable as a civilizer than as a hero because in Dionysius' world, it was thoroughly possible to be granted divine honours for political reform, centralizing government, military campaigning and engineering projects, and less likely that without these you would be. And vitally, it is the explanation of Heracles' apotheosis which gives direction to both versions. Dionysius needs to explain how, as a result of his actions in Italy, Heracles became a god.

So a believable version of Heracles, one appropriate to a serious historical enterprise, shows the hero acting to modify the environment to make it more serviceable to humankind; destroying those natives who stubbornly adhere to their barbaric modes of existence, while bringing prosperity to those earlier victims who have now seen reason and can be trusted to perpetuate the civilized values for which the hero stands. To those who have studied the representation of European world conquests, this is all very familiar. It is crucial, however, not to misplace the mythical element in Dionysius' narrative and hasten to identify Heracles with the imperial ruler of his own day. Such identification was possible: Horace compares Augustus returning from Spain to Hercules in Odes III.xiv, and elsewhere Hercules is the prototype for Augustus' imagined deification.[12] Mark Antony actually claimed descent from Hercules, although this laid him open to criticism.[13] But in Dionysius' narrative it is precisely the differences established by the pre-historical setting which give Heracles his power. We should not look in Heracles for a kind of fore-shadowing of Augustus which is pointedly political in the sense of making direct reference to the living monarch. Rather, it is what Dionysius finds believable in his depiction of the ideal imperialist which can reveal to us his vision of the ideal foundation for Roman world rule. Because the Romans are Greeks, Heracles' Greek empire acts as a pre-historic foundation for comprehending Dionysius' own world. Heracles, then, the first person to do anything of note on the site of the city of Rome, provides a model for the glory which was to grow from that place.

Hercules

Set against Dionysius, the poem of Propertius which deals with a small episode from the same story is quite remarkable. It comes from Propertius' troublesome fourth book, the book in which the poet who has consistently asserted that the delicate poetry of love was all that he was capable of, moves to treat themes taken from Rome's epic pre-history.[14] Propertius' main point of reference for his encounters with pre-history is Virgil. Without Virgil's treatment of Hercules and Cacus, Propertius' would be almost incomprehensible, since brevity and stylistic compression are one side of the elegist's method for adapting the verbosity of epic poetry to his own slighter genre. The tone of the poem is difficult to place; there are clearly comic elements, but the poet is at pains to recreate a Virgilian sense of the wooded sanctity that characterized the site of Rome long before the foundation of the city.[15]

The challenge in taking this theme and adapting it to a different kind of poetry is the creation of a blend of epic elements with those which have characterized the passionate love-poet: a finely-wrought, delicate style; an exclusive and personal form of expression. All the poems in this book can be viewed as different versions of rising to this same challenge. Many of them are aetiologies; Propertius effectively establishes the idea that in looking for the origin of something familiar from contemporary Rome, a link can be established between the personal and the historical spheres. In contrast to Dionysius, and also to Virgil, the self-consciousness of the poetic *persona*, the awareness in the reader of a more or less uninterrupted dialogue with the poetic I, makes the relevance of the present in these aetiologies much more apparent.

In the Hercules poem, the elegiac rendering of Hercules in Rome boils down to the innovative adaptation of the story from Virgil, with many clear verbal echoes, and the addition of a new episode, building on Virgil's structure, but departing quite drastically from it in tone. The landscape is once more important: it features in the introduction, and in the transition from the Cacus episode to that concerning the sacred grove. We must bear in mind the contrast which would have been vivid to Propertius' readers, used to this convention, between the urban density of Rome, and this picture of what Propertius describes as the unconquered hill, the Palatine. The rivers which are commonly imagined to overflow the whole area recall Dionysius' picture of Heracles' beneficent actions with rivers; the Tiber neatly contained within its banks is clearly a potent image of civilization. So in this moist landscape we can read the symbols of an untouched, pre-urban idyll.

However, Propertius makes water into the focal point for his new addition: after dispatching Cacus and sending the cattle down to graze in what he names as the Forum in a moment of strange clairvoyance, Hercules is beset by a terrible thirst. He hears water flowing in a nearby grove sacred to the Bona Dea, the good goddess, who was tended exclusively by women, and pleads with the priestesses to let him enter and drink. He speaks what we are told are words not worthy of a god: the high point of his rhetoric involves disavowing his masculinity: he assumes that the reason for a women's cult is their fear of man, so he points out that he himself was once enslaved as a girl, taking servile tasks, spinning, wearing a fine silk frock, and enclosing his hairy chest in a soft bra. The priestess is unconvinced, however, and explains why no men may enter the shrine. This kind of question was a common topic of antiquarian investigation; the priestess equates her goddess with Athena, caught bathing by Tiresias; a ban on men was the result. This explanation is peculiar; but Hercules at any rate ignores the priestesses' admonitions and uses force to break in and quench his thirst. Almost as a curse, he then vows to set up the *Ara Maxima* to commemorate his visit, and in revenge refuses women the right to worship at it.

So we have the aetiology not just of the *Ara Maxima*, but of why these two cults are open only to one sex.[16] The cults have at their intersection the figures of Hercules and Tiresias, both of whom have lived as both man and woman. It is this congruency which explains the otherwise bizarre aetiology given by the priestess: as antiquarian conjecture it is noticeably bogus. The vision of transvestite Hercules was a familiar one to Propertius' readers. Hercules was sold as a slave to the Lydian queen Omphale, who became his mistress in both senses. His enslavement took the form of exchanging roles with the queen; she disported herself with his club and lion skin, he sat inside taking the clothes and the tasks of a domestic slave-woman. Representations of the couple, and of Omphale alone dressed as Hercules, were extremely popular subjects of sculpture, painting, and most especially, engraved gems worn as jewellery during this period.[17] However, it remains to observe what Propertius achieves by introducing this story to these aetiologies of Rome.

To begin with, Propertius imbues Hercules with more personality than any other version of these events; and as well as Omphale, he recalls the long-standing Greek interest in Hercules' inordinate appetites: that he should be driven by thirst to destroy the shrine clearly manifests the tradition of Hercules as insatiable. And his exploits too are scaled down, to divest them of the grandiose: instead of invading Italy, he invades this particular shrine; and his words of angry entreaty to the priestess have a formal similarity to the popular genre of poems written in the person of the excluded lover. All this helps to gloss the poet's comment that Hercules' words were rather less than a god's.

Hercules tries first to gain access by displaying his femininity; when this fails, he resorts to his strength. In one traditional vision of Heracles, this combination of gender transformation and gender reinforcement is very apparent.[18] Both forms of expression, like the inordinate thirst, seem incompatible with the aura of sanctity which the poem strives to create. Propertius' Hercules is absurd, comic, a travesty of the heroic founder; but the processes whereby he comes to be so are all carefully integrated into the aetiological mechanism which link Hercules to Rome in the first place. There is no clear point of conflict in the poem: Hercules bragging of his credentials as a woman is a vital stage in this dramatization of the foundation of the *Ara Maxima*; and by explaining not just the altar, but also the nature of its rites, Propertius justifies the apparent digression which this dramatization produces. No reader could suggest that the manipulation of gender here is just a device to produce amusement.

It would be ideal to be able to conclude that by focusing upon transformations of gender, Propertius strikes a blow at the bodily integrity of Hercules, with serious consequences for his role as the heroic forerunner of Roman imperialism. In the contrast between Dionysius and Propertius, we can observe that in Propertius' dramatization, in bringing Hercules to speak, he makes him considerably less monolithic than the objectified conqueror of the historical version. Indeed, by making thirst the motivating factor, the philanthropic selflessness that characterizes Dionysius' imperial reformer is disallowed from the start. This Hercules does articulate his desires, and it is they which lead him to fulfil his function in founding his altar. The central question is how far the poem actually presents the mutability of Hercules' gender as a problem.

Gender inversion is a frequent theme in Propertius' poetry; the most obvious manifestation is in the poet's subjection to his mistress, which provides the material for several poems on powerful women and subservient men. In the preceding poem in the book, this inversion takes the form of a pitched battle between the conquering mistress and the effeminate and defeated poet/lover. In that poem, the mistress is figured as a triumphant Roman general; perhaps she displays the triumphant features lacking in our Hercules; I argue elsewhere that she also provides the element of triumph lacking in Propertius' treatment of the battle of Actium.[19] The focus on Hercules and Tiresias as figures who have lived as both sexes picks up upon the vision of the poet as one whose sexuate identity questions the boundaries of female/male. Perhaps the broader question of identification can provide a link between both these versions of Hercules: as the first visitor to Rome, Hercules represents for Dionysius the ideal imperialist; he shows the way for Dionysius' own Greek culture to be assimilated to Roman world rule. In Propertius the identification with that first visitor produces a comic and desiring body, one who has experienced, in heroic form, the subjection to a woman and effeminization which the poet claims for himself, likewise with pride. Griffin has suggested the figure of the poet in Propertius bears a striking resemblance to Mark Antony.[20] Antony started by heightening his masculinity by associating himself with Hercules, and then slipped into being lampooned for effeminacy and subordination to Cleopatra, following the example of Hercules and Omphale. Finally he abandoned Hercules for Dionysus, the god whose gender was the most unstable of all. By taking Hercules at the point where he represents the first Roman, and making a display of his flawed masculinity, Propertius is integrating into history a constellation of gender attributes which belong to the counterculture of gender transgression which characterizes the world of love-elegy. We should not mistake the humour in Propertius, but in striving to combine historical aetiology with the gender inversion which characterizes the love poet, Propertius is careful to produce a version of Hercules which, like Dionysius' is believable in its own terms. And for both authors, this credibility involves a degree of personal ident-ification, but also identification in the plane of historical understanding.

I'd like to end by returning to an initial methodological point: we must be careful about awarding either of these versions, or indeed any narrative retelling of myth, the status of the right account. Dionysius has his own agenda, and it would be simplistic to claim that he represented a more traditional or more acceptable Hercules than Propertius', who after all looks in some ways a lot more traditional, in the sense of less modern, than Dionysius'. That said, I have the feeling that in both accounts we are dealing with reworkings aiming at greater verisimilitude. That Dionysius' Hercules is truer is explicit in the context of his history: he is truer because he is an object lesson in conducting a successful colonial venture, routing barbarism, instilling civilization, and rewarding his faithful and right-thinking subjects. Hercules represents, in other words, a paradigm of Greece's current salvation through Rome. Propertius' Hercules has a similar redemptive function: just as for Dionysius, he allows himself to be reformed in the ideal image of his narrator, but an image that gains in potency and appeal through exaggeration, grotesquerie, humour, all elements which give a sense of the greatness of the hero which is accessible, recognizable, but not mundane. The poet can identify with Hercules, but he isn't like him. Hercules' gender inversion may assimilate him to the elegist, but if we concentrate on what keeps Hercules an extraordinary figure in Propertius' poem, it is that his effeminization does not cause him shame; Hercules boasts of his womanly qualities even at the moment where his invasive imperialistic actions are the centre of attention. Its a model of conquest and power which builds upon the deferral of the Actium narrative to suggest that the poet can endorse imperial activity, if he takes the time to reconsider its emotional ramifications. And looking at the wider context of Propertius' last book, the account of Hercules is yet another reassessment of the poet's stance in relation to the affairs of the great world. So as a figure of the pre-historic colonist, Hercules, by virtue of his malleability and appeal, provides an ideal ground both for Propertius and Dionysius to work out their own versions of Roman pre-history, and although their accounts differ on predictable lines, it remains important to weigh up the attractions of their respective accounts with the contextual elements which make their narratives credible.

Propertius IV.9: A provisional translation

At the time when the son of Amphitryon had driven the calves from your stables, Erythea, he came to the unvanquished hills on sheep-covered Palatine, and halted his tired cattle (he was tired himself), where the regions of Velabrum were flooded in river water and where a boatsman was setting sail through the city waters. But they did not remain safe from the faithless host Cacus: by theft he dishonoured Jove. Cacus was a local inhabitant, a robber from a fearful cave, who made sounds divided from three mouths. To hide the clear signs of his obvious theft he dragged the oxen backwards by the tail into the caves, but not without the god seeing: the calves sounded out the thief, and anger destroyed the thief's terrible doors. Cacus lay smitten on his three foreheads by the Herculean branch, and the offspring of Alceus spoke thus: 'Go, oxen, go, oxen of Hercules, last labour of my club, sought twice by me, twice my prize, oxen, and sanctify the Bouarian fields by your lowing: the noble forum of Rome will be your pastures'.

He spoke, and thirst tortured his dry mouth, but the barren land did not provide water. But from afar he heard secluded girls laugh, where a copse's shady circle made a glade, a place closed off for the women's goddess and sacred springs, a shrine protected safely from any men. Purple wreaths veiled the hidden threshold, and in a shabby hut a fragrant fire smoked. A poplar decorated the shrine with it great leaves, its shady branches hiding song-birds. He rushed in, his beard dry and dusty, and hurled out before the doors these words not fitting to a god: 'You, I pray, who play in the sacred hollow of the grove, open your kindly doors to a tired man. I'm wandering in need of water around the sounds of splashing springs; a cupped palm filled in the stream would be enough. Have you heard of the man who lifted the world on his back? I am he whom all the world calls Hercules. Who has not heard of the brave deeds of Hercules' club, my arrows that never miss the great wild beasts, the one man who saw the shades of the Styx lit up? Now I bring my lot to this corner of the world, but, though tired, this country hardly welcomes me. Even if you prayed to bitter Juno, my step-mother, she wouldn't have closed off her waters. But if my face and lion-skin are scaring anyone, even I have played the part of slave girl in a silk dress, and done my daily spinning with a Lydian distaff. A soft brassiere held in my hairy chest, and in spite of my hard hands, I was a good girl'.

To these words of Hercules, the gentle priestess replied, 'Spare your eyes, stranger, and go away from the awesome shrine. Leave now, and flee safely from this threshold. The altar hidden in this hut is sanctified by a fearful law as forbidden to men. Tiresias the prophet, when he glimpsed Pallas as she bathed, putting down her Gorgon shield, paid a great price. Let the gods grant you other springs. This one flows alone for girls, secret and out of reach'. So the old woman: he battered the dark door-posts with his shoulders, as the closed door could not bear his angered thirst. And after he had quenched the heat in the drained river, he made this solemn vow through still-moist lips: 'Great Altar, vowed when I found my cattle, altar made great by these hands, never shall girls be suffered to worship here, so that Hercules' thirst will be eternally avenged'. This man, who had travelled the world and sanctified it with his hands, Tatius' men of Cures comprehended as Sancus. Holy father, greetings, now favoured by harsh Juno: Sancus, may you enter propitiously into my book.

NOTES

1. I would like to thank Chris Gittings for inviting this paper, the audience at the conference, and my colleagues at the West Midlands Classical seminar. Their helpful suggestions, even if I have not been able to incorporate them here, will enable me to take this work further.
2. Dieter Timpe, 'Fabius Pictor und die Anfänge Römischer Historiographie', *Aufstieg und Niedergang der Römischen Welt* 1, 2 (1972), pp. 928-96.
3. On these commonplaces of anti-Roman historiography see Erich Burck, 'Die römische Expansion im Urteil des Livius', *Aufstieg und Niedergang der Römischen Welt*, 30, 2 (1982), pp. 1148-89 (pp.1158ff); Hans Volkmann, 'Antike Romkritik, Topik und historische Wirklichkeit', *Gymnasium Beihefte*, 4 (1964), pp. 9-20; Harald Fuchs, *Der geistige Widerstand gegen Rom* (Berlin: de Gruyter, 1938).
4. C.K.Galinsky, *The Heracles Theme: The Adaptation of the Hero in Literature from Homer to the Twentieth Century* (Oxford: Blackwell, 1972) is still an excellent survey of Heracles' incarnations.
5. Dionysius cites Hellanicus' version in *Roman Antiquites* I.35.2. All references in this form are to the *Roman Antiquities*, translated by Earnest Cary, Loeb Classical Library (London: Heinemann; Cambridge: Harvard University Press, 1968).

6. On Dionysius see Emilio Gabba, *Dionysius of Halicarnassus and the History of Archaic Rome* (Berkeley: University of California Press, 1991) and Matthew Fox, 'History and Rhetoric in Dionysius of Halicarnassus', *The Journal of Roman Studies* 83 (1993), pp. 31-47.

7. 1.39.1

8. 1.40.6

9. 1.41.1

10. 1.36-38

11. Colette Jourdain-Annequin, *Héracles aux Portes du Soir: Myth et Histoire,* Annales Littéraire de l'Université de Besançon (Paris: Les Belles Lettres, 1989), p. 402.

12. Horace Odes III.3.9.

13. See Paul Zanker, *The Power of Images in the Age of Augustus* (Ann Arbor: University of Michigan Press, 1988), p. 57-65.

14. On Propertius, and particularly his last book, see J.Warden, *Fallax Opus* Phoenix Supplementary Volume 14 (Toronto: Toronto University Press, 1980) and Matthew Fox, *Roman Historical Myths* (Oxford: Clarendon Press, 1996), chapter 5. The present discussion of 4.9 extends that of pp. 169-175.

15. I include my own rough translation of the poem at the end. The translation of W.G.Shepherd, *Propetius: The Poems* (Harmondsworth: Penguin, 1985) is to be recommended to those who want a more elegant and faithful version of the Latin.

16. The poem ends with a further aetiology, linking a lesser local god, Sancus, to Hercules. This accumulation of anecdotal wisdom is typical of the refined style of Callimachus, Propertius' poetic mentor.

17. See Frank Brommer, *Herakles II: Die unkanonischen Taten des Helden* (Darmstadt: Wissenschaftliche Buchgesellschaft, 1984).

18. See Nicole Loraux, 'Herakles: The super-male and the feminine' in David M.Halperin, John J.Winkler, Froma I.Zeitlin, eds., *Before Sexuality* (Princeton: Princeton University Press, 1990), pp. 21-52.

19. See *Roman Historical Myths* pp. 166-169. Actium was Augustus' final defeat of Antony, the only obstacle to his sole domination of the Mediterranean. Virgil's account of Hercules and Cacus is widely believed to be an allegory of Actium. So that there is a double displacement: the battle of Actium displaced from its place in 4.6, only to be reworked as a battle of lovers in 4.8, and the displacement of Hercules' victory over Cacus into his conquest of the women's shrine.

20. Jasper Griffin, 'Propertius and Antony', in *Latin Poets and Roman Life* (London: Duckworth, 1985), pp. 183-197. See also Paul Zanker, *The Power of Images in the Age of Augustus* (Ann Arbor: University of Michigan Press, 1988), pp. 57-65.

BRIAN HARDING

White Medicine; Red Manhood: George Catlin's North American Indians

'American ethnology may be said to begin with Catlin', at least so far as the Plains tribes are concerned, according to Bernard DeVoto, in his celebration of American empire in *Across the Wide Missouri* (1947).[1] This judgment was restated in virtually the same words – 'American ethnology begins with Catlin' – in Michael Macdonald Mooney's introduction to an 1975 edition of the artist's *Letters and Notes*. Clearly associating Catlin with the expansionist ideology of the antebellum period, Mooney acknowledged that 'the picture books of Manifest Destiny were colored from Catlin's palettes'.[2] More recently, Brian W. Dippie, in his excellent *Catlin and His Contemporaries. The Politics of Patronage* (1990), stated that he was attracted to Catlin 'because of his surpassing importance to students of American culture ... his paintings and the vision behind them have become part of our understanding of a lost America. We see the Indian past through his eyes'.[3] Significantly, in his powerful and influential critique of Euro-American attitudes to Native Americans, *Facing West. The Metaphysics of Indian Hating and Empire Building* (1980), Richard Drinnon claimed that Catlin 'approached Indian cultures with respect', which made him 'a very rare white man indeed' and set him apart from contemporaries like Judge James Hall and Colonel Thomas L.McKenney, whose works on Native Americans blatantly revealed white prejudice and incomprehension.[4]

Certainly, Catlin saw himself as the champion of 'the Indian' in an age and culture whose dominant ideology justified the exploitation of the land and its indigenous peoples, allowing Euro-Americans to dismiss any scruples of conscience that might have troubled them had 'Indians' been considered fully human. If his white contemporaries were to be able to treat the Red Men fairly, Catlin believed that he had to make them divest themselves of 'their deadly prejudices ... against this unfortunate and most abused part of the race of their fellow men'. He announced his programme and stated his mission in the opening pages of his first book: *Letters and Notes on the Manners, Customs, and Conditions of the North American Indians*, which he published in

1841. His aim, he said, was to 'lend a hand to a dying nation' and thus to help snatch from oblivion what could be saved as a 'fair and just monument, to the memory of a truly lofty and noble race'. His own adult life had been devoted – so he claimed – 'to the production of a literal and graphic delineation of the living manners, customs and character of an interesting race of people, who are rapidly passing away from the face of the earth'.[5]

Catlin's clearest declaration of his faith in 'the Indians' was made in 1868, in his *Last Rambles Amongst the Indians of the Rocky Mountains and the Andes*. In a ringing statement of his admiration for the Native Americans he had encountered, Catlin structured his tributes on a series of implied contrasts with the whites. He declared his love for 'the people who have always made me welcome to the best they had ... who are honest without laws, who have no jails and no poor-houses ... who 'love their neighbours as they love themselves ... who worship God without a Bible ... who have never fought a battle with the white man, except on their own ground'.[6]

Last Rambles, though it contains much less information than his earlier productions, constitutes Catlin's most direct and bitterest denunciation of white exploitation of the native peoples of the New World, from Columbus' shocking ingratitude and cruelty to the indigenes of the Caribbean to Indian Removal and its consequences in the age of Jackson.

One theme of *Letters and Notes* was the bad faith of the white traders – and by extension of all whites – in their dealings with the Native Americans. In Catlin's narrative, the children of nature living on the Great Plains welcomed the first Euro-Americans to visit them with open-hearted friendliness and generosity, but in the years following their encounter with the Lewis and Clark expedition they learned to anticipate trickery and extortionate behaviour from *all* white traders. Catlin, of course, was not a trader. He could – and emphatically did – distance himself from the avarice of the fur trappers and traders,[7] but his venture into the territory of the Mandans and other tribes on the Upper Missouri was only possible because of the commercial enterprise of the American Fur Company's leaders.

The artist reached the mouth of the Yellowstone River in 1832 on the first steamer – the *Yellow Stone* – to make the ascent of the Missouri and so bring supplies to the company's trading post, Fort Union. Ironically, the artist-defender of 'the Indian' travelled as guest of the commercial enterprise that would undermine native American culture, expedite the march of white empire across the American West, and – in a very short time – physically destroy the tribes of the Upper Missouri by bringing smallpox to them on its steamer.

In Letter 5 of *Letters and Notes*, Catlin describes the scene at Fort Union, at the mouth of the Yellowstone River, in what is now North

Dakota, when – in the summer of 1832 – he arrived and began to paint the chiefs of the various tribes assembled to trade with the American Fur Company. During his one month's stay, Catlin used one of the bastions of the fur company's fort as his studio while he painted Crows, Blackfeet, Assiniboin and Ojibways. His aim was to record the lives of the still-untamed 'savages' who had not yet come into enough contact with white civilization to be contaminated by it.

The Indian heroes selected by Catlin for the portrait gallery he was beginning to construct, and later for the book he would write, are celebrated in the text of *Letters and Notes* for their 'manly' qualities. They are all men who have established their reputation and preserved their honour in battle. Most wear costumes ornamented with the scalp locks of defeated enemies; a detail that Catlin emphasizes in his text. The portraits for which Catlin persuaded the chiefs to pose were, as he explains, initially regarded with suspicion and fear by the natives, since they were considered to be 'medicine' that robbed their subjects of some power and might even threaten their lives. These primitive responses are – unsurprisingly – treated as absurd by the white artist, who quickly overcomes the objections of the sons of nature, working on them by flattery. To convert fear and anger into pride, the painter at first offers to portray only chiefs. To be painted, therefore, becomes a mark of distinction; an honour.

Chiefs pose in their finest costumes, which can include a head-dress of bulls' horns, buffalo robes or deer skins elaborately decorated. Not all are portrayed with weapons – the chief in the first portrait to be included in the book carries a pipe, not a tomahawk – yet Catlin calls attention to the scalp locks that fringe chief Stu-mick-o-sucks' (Buffalo's Back Fat's) deerskin costume: black hair 'taken from the heads of victims slain by his own hand in battle' (I, p. 30). Another of the subjects, Pe-toh-pee-kiss, is not a chief; he is one of the outstanding men of the Blackfeet: 'his dress is really superb, almost literally covered with scalp-locks' and – Catlin points out – he openly boasts that he took eight of his scalps from the heads of trappers and traders (I, p. 34). On a later excursion, to Fort Snelling, Prairie du Chien, and Dubuque, Catlin was sufficiently impressed by one chief whom he met at Camp des Moines, variously spelled by Catlin as Kee-o-kuck and Kee-o-kuk (Running Fox) of the Sacs and Foxes, to paint him twice: once on foot and once on horseback. 'He is a man of a great deal of pride, and makes a truly splendid appearance on his black horse', according to Catlin (II, p. 150). These images are terrifying. In the first of them, Running Fox, tomahawk in one hand, staff of office in the other, seems threatening and ferocious. Yet the text tells us that this chief helped end the Black Hawk War in 1833 by keeping his warriors out of it; that he was famous as an orator rather than a warrior.

In effect, then, Catlin's portraits of chiefs and leading men of the wild tribes, sometimes at odds with his prose commentary, insist that we respond to their subjects as men of blood, or as killers – as men whose manhood is constituted by their triumph over their enemies and the number of deaths they have caused. In painting them, I suggest, Catlin has exercised his 'medicine' in a way he never brought to consciousness: he has 'mastered' the savage in himself, projecting it onto the 'Other' and at the same time graphically representing it as subdued by his 'medicine' and thus at his command.

The hero who is given the fullest biographical sketch in Catlin's book is Mah-to-toh-pa (The Four Bears), a chief of the Mandans, with whom Catlin spent a month after leaving Fort Union. This chief appears first in the frontispiece of *Letters and Notes* [Plate I] and again, in a full-length portrait, later in the body of the work. In Letter 14 Catlin explains that The Four Bears was so distinguished a hero that he alone in the nation was allowed to wear buffalo horns as part of his head dress, as he does in the portrait that illustrates this letter.

In Letter 16 Catlin tells the story of the deed that won the Mandan chief the respect of his village and made him their leader in time of war. To avenge the death of his brother at the hands of a Riccarree warrior named Won-ga-tap, Mah-to-toh-pa waited four years, then travelled two hundred miles to the enemy village, entirely alone, entered that village in disguise, found the wigwam of his enemy, entered it, helped himself to food from Won-ga-tap's cooking pot, smoked a pipe, and – when the time was right – drove his lance through his unwitting host's body (I, pp. 150-1). He then took Won-ga-tap's scalp and escaped across the prairie. 'Readers', comments Catlin in a parenthesis, 'I had every word of this from his own lips, and every attitude and gesture acted out with his own limbs' (I, p. 150).

Mah-to-toh-pa is the perfect Indian 'knight' in Catlin's representation of him. From the early pages of *Letters and Notes* Catlin has dignified the tribal warriors by insisting on their 'chivalric' nature: on their knightly code of honour. In the story of this chief he finds the clearest and most inspiring example of chivalry. After the revenge story, we are told of the young Mah-to-toh-pa's man-to-man combat with a Shienne (Catlin's spelling) chief in front of opposing Mandan and Shienne war parties. The two heroes observe a ritual in which, when one has his gun and horse destroyed, the other renounces his, so that they may fight on equal terms. The bloody conclusion of the combat comes when the Mandan manages to seize his enemy's knife while grappling with him and plunges it to his heart. After this, he holds up both the weapon and the scalp of his foe to the view of the warrior spectators (I, p. 153).

In a footnote, Catlin adds that the knife, 'with the blood of several victims dried upon its blade' now (1841) hangs in his Indian Gallery. He returns to Mah-to-toh-pa's 'celebrated knife' later in his text. When

Plate I: Mah-to-toh-pa, Chief of the Mandans

describing scalping-knives and other Indian weapons, he adds another footnote claiming that it has become part of his own Indian Museum. This time he adds that 'it has been several times plunged to the hearts of his enemies by the hand of Mah-to-toh-pa' (I, p. 236). Catlin's pride in his ownership of the knife seems almost gloating. His attitude is fetishistic. It is as if he has stolen some of Mah-to-toh-pa's 'manly' medicine.

The portrait of Mah-to-toh-pa painted by Catlin while he was with the Mandans on the Upper Missouri is now in the Smithsonian. [Plate II] In it, the colour of the chief's robe is red, perhaps part of that 'colour of life' that, for Charles Baudelaire, 'flowed so abundantly ... that it was like an intoxication' in the Catlin Indian portraits he saw in the Paris Salon of 1846. To Baudelaire, there was an element of mystery in Catlin's use of colour: 'Red, the colour of blood, the colour of life'.[8]

If he had read Catlin's *Letters and Notes* Baudelaire would have known that when Mah-to-toh-pa stood for his portrait, on the blade of the lance of polished steel that he held in his left hand 'the blood of several human victims was seen dried ... one over the other' (I, p. 151). Again, the effect of Catlin's remark is to bring the bloody deeds – on which savage manhood depended – into the representation of that manhood, thus appropriating its power.

Two features of Catlin's account of the combat of the savage heroes are particularly remarkable. One is his excited, even frenzied, rhetoric: 'Like two soaring eagles in the open air, they made their circuits around, and the twangs of their sinewy bows were heard, and the war-whoop' (I, p. 153). The other is that, just before his account of Mah-to-toh-pa's heroic deeds, Catlin has described his attempt to paint the portrait of a beautiful young Mandan male who belongs to that small class of young Indian men who are *not* warriors but *beaux* or *dandies*. Catlin explains that his purpose was frustrated by some chiefs whose portraits he had already painted. They let the artist know that to paint a 'worthless fellow – a man of no account in the nation' would be an insult to the real men – the warriors – who have permitted him to take their images. The revealing aspect of the episode is the tone of Catlin's narrative. He writes contemptuously and with disdainful humour of 'these gay and tinselled bucks' who ride cautiously on beautiful and soft 'pleasure-saddles' to watch the games in which other young men 'are contending in *manly* [emphasis added] and athletic amusements' (I, pp. 112-3). The contrast between the *beaux* and the warrior-hero plainly suggests that the painter shares the tribal contempt for the effeminacy of the former.

It was not for nothing, then, that when James Hall, who was himself an 'authority' on the Indian (as co-author with Thomas L. McKenney of a multi-volume book on the Indians) wrote a favourable review of Catlin's Indian portraits in the November 1833 issue of his *Western*.

Plate II: Mah-to-toh-pa, Chief of the Mandans

Monthly Review, he stressed their 'manly' qualities.[9] In this he was not merely revealing his own prejudices; he was also responding to the tone of Catlin's work. Repeatedly, Catlin insists on the nobility, the honour of the Indian warrior who has killed his enemy, or enemies. More recently, in his *George Catlin and the Old Frontier* (1959), Harold McCracken devoted one chapter (Ch. 8) to 'The Magnificent Male', restating, in the idiom of the male chauvinist 1950s, what he took to be Catlin's valuation of Native American manhood. In McCracken's words, 'There was hardly an able-bodied tribesman throughout the whole Northwest who was not an enthusiastic hunter, as well as a bold and daring warrior and a magnificent male on constant parade.[10] Claiming that the Crow men were known for their fine physique and were 'virile, masculine', McCracken added that the Crow women, 'like all other Indian women' were the slaves of their husbands.

Civilized life is defined by contrast to the savage in *Letters and Notes*.[11] The natives, Catlin tells his readers, 'live without incurring the expenses of life, which are absolutely necessary and unavoidable in the enlightened world'. As a result, Indians direct their faculties and their inclinations solely 'to the enjoyment of the present day, without the sober reflections on the past or apprehensions of the future' (I, p. 85) that, it follows, characterise civilized life.

Catlin returns to the theme repeatedly in his narrative. The Mandans, Crows and other tribes on the Upper Missouri are not *'naked'* or *'poor'*, he explains. In a rambling and syntactically confused sentence Catlin contrasts poverty in the Christian world with lack of wealth among the savages. The Great Spirit has supplied the latter with an abundance of food to eat. Consequently, they are able to indulge 'in the pleasures and amusements of a lifetime of idleness and ease, with no business hours to attend to, or professions to learn'. Moreover, they have 'no notes in bank or other debts to pay – no taxes, no tithes, no rents, nor beggars to touch and tax the sympathy of their souls at every step they go' (I, p. 210). The implication is clear: 'civilized' life is dominated or defined by care; by anxieties about business, about one's profession; by financial obligations and commitments. Catlin's *Letters and Notes* appeared at the time when white American men were learning to measure their worth primarily through work; when – as David Leverenz has argued – the ideology of manhood emerging with entrepreneurial capitalism made competition and the power dynamics of the workplace the only source of self-value and self-assessment.[12] In the terms of this theory, which seems peculiarly appropriate to Catlin, manhood functioned to preserve self-control and to transform fears of vulnerability and inadequacy into a desire for dominance. In acting out the role of the artist who preserves Indian culture, in his works, Catlin can both preserve his white man's feeling of superiority *and* project his own suppressed (or repressed) conception of manhood onto 'the savage'.

Yet Catlin's use of the Indian as a means of escaping the pressures of white male middle class life can hardly account for the exhilaration with which he represents the warriors he chooses to honour with his magic-medicine. The process might be better described as one of subjection through admiration. The splendid, noble, knightly Indian is endowed with the destructive, murderous impulses that *he* (the savage) cannot control. In representing this threatening power, the artist-ethnographer establishes his authority, and while distinguishing his own culture from that of the savage, is enabled to enjoy the pleasure of vicarious 'manhood'. My contention is that Catlin projects on to the savage 'Other' those impulses that must be controlled or repressed in his white ('civilized') identity. His medicine, then, becomes that of 'mastering' the fierce manliness in his paintings. The artist's domination of his savage subjects is, to Catlin, nothing less than a 'mystery'. Early in his *Letters and Notes* he explains to his reader the significance of the word 'medicine' as used in his accounts of the Indians of the Upper Missouri. It derives, he says, from the French '*medecin*' and was introduced by the Fur Traders, most of whom were French speakers. Catlin goes on: 'The Indian country is full of doctors; and as they are all magicians, and skilled, or profess to be skilled, in many mysteries, the word '*medecin*' has become habitually applied to every thing mysterious or unaccountable' (I, p. 35). Catlin does not tell his readers what native American word or words were translated into French when the traders selected the term '*medecin*'; in fact he never uses the word translate. Instead, he says that each tribe has a word 'of their own construction, synonimous [sic] with mystery or mystery-man' (I, p. 36). Having said that, Catlin proceeds to apply the Anglicised French word to a variety of native American practices that are not explicable in terms of [white] rational discourse.[13]

In his use of the term, Catlin seems to take it as self-evident that the French speakers saw a connection between native reverence or awe (their sense of mystery) and the curative powers of the dignitaries who 'professed to be skilled'. As an example of the scope of the term, he refers to his own classification as a 'medicine-man', asserting that he is considered of the highest order of medicine man by 'these superstitious people' on account of 'the art which I practice' (I, pp. 35-6). The art is that of portrait painting. Catlin's tone here is less condescending than it often is when he discusses Indian 'superstitions'. It contrasts markedly with his contemptuous dismissal of the 'absurdity' of the rain-making ceremony and with his remarks on the 'ridiculous and disgusting' (I, p.168) aspects of the bull dance.[14] Obviously, the painter does not feel that the Indians' awe of his art is ridiculous; rather, it is a 'savage' tribute to his 'civilized' power.

While painting the portraits of the untamed chiefs at Fort Union,

Catlin was conscious, he tells us, of the enmities smouldering among the savages he painted. They were, he said, 'wild and jealous spirits' who had to control their mutual hatreds while in the Fort, where they were deprived of their weapons, but would mete out death and destruction to each other once 'free to breathe and act upon the plains'. Catlin also claimed that 'the operations of my brush are *mysteries* of the highest order to these red sons of the prairie' (I, p. 29), as if there were a connection between their pacific behaviour in front of his easel and the 'magic' of his art. In other words, there is a suggestion here that the artist sees himself as an Orpheus, whose power to tame the wild spirits of the Indian warriors is evidenced by the portraits they permit him to paint. Clearly, he regards his relationship to the fierce and impulsive savages as a delicate one (later, he semi-seriously considers the chance that he might be scalped before he can get back to St Louis), yet one in which his power is manifest in the portraits he paints.

When he returns to the theme of his magic (in Letter 15), Catlin gives a more dramatic version of his role as 'medicine man'. The Indians, he says, 'pronounced me the greatest *medicine-man* in the world, for they said I had made *living beings'* (I, p. 107). Here the tone is not easy to establish; the evident feeling of superiority to the naivete of the savages seems to go with an acknowledgment that their reverence for his 'magic' was appropriate and justified.

Catlin's verbal representation of his artist's role among the tribes of the Upper Missouri is part of a text that is lavishly illustrated, not only with portraits of chiefs, but also with portraits of medicine men and squaws, with Upper Missouri landscapes, and – in Letters 10 to 22 – with scenes of life in the Mandan village that became the artist's major subject for several weeks (July 20 to mid-August) after he left Fort Union and moved down river to Fort Clark. The first image offered to readers of the 1841 edition of *Letters and Notes* – the frontispiece – includes a full-length portrait of Mah-to-toh-pa, The Four Bears, spear in hand. [Plate I]. It also shows the artist in the act of painting the chief's portrait, in the presence of a crowd of gawping Indians. The caption, in the 1841 edition, reads: 'The Author painting a chief in an Indian Village'. In later editions Catlin changed this to 'at the base of the Rocky Mountains'.[15] In this composition the painter is dressed in a style that seems more appropriate to an East Coast studio than to the prairies. His dapper appearance suggests that the artist's relationship to his 'savage' subject is one of indulgent superiority.

Catlin's Indian portraits, together with his collection of Indian artifacts and native weapons, were exhibited in Pittsburgh and Louisville in 1833, in Albany in 1837. His 'Indian Gallery', as he called it, opened in the Clinton Hall, New York, 25 September 1837, and moved on to Washington, Baltimore, Philadelphia and Boston in 1838.[16]

On 25 November 1839, Catlin sailed for Liverpool with eight tons of materials and booked the Egyptian Hall, Piccadilly, for 30 December 1839. Hoping to make large profits from his 'Gallery Unique', Catlin did all he could to attract London audiences to his 'show' (for it was that) in 1840. In his *Notes on Eight Years Travels and Residence in Europe* (1848) the artist explains that one of the *tableaux vivants* he devised to entertain his London audience in 1840 showed the artist in the act of painting the chief while other natives watched admiringly. In the Piccadilly 'show' a tipi was used as a background for the portrait of the Mandan chief Mah-to-toh-pa, though tipis belonged to a tribal culture distinct from that of the Mandans, who lived in spherical earthen structures.[17]

In the light of Catlin's own remarks, the frontispiece to *North American Indians* can, then, be read as a graphic representation of the entertainment Catlin provided for his English public at his Indian Gallery in the Egyptian Hall, Piccadilly. It can also, I believe, be taken as a demonstration of the artist's 'medicine' or mysterious power over his savage subjects. The portraits and scenes that he has created are offered to his white readers (his book was on sale at the Gallery) as the historical record of the tribes Catlin had visited and observed. As he claims in his opening chapters, his function is that of the preserver of the Indian *past*. Since, like almost every white American of his generation, Catlin assumed that the native American was already doomed to extinction, he planned to immortalize 'the Indian' in his paintings.[18] He immortalised them by subjecting them to the power of his art. They were represented as 'Catlin's Indians'. Their portraits represented the qualities with which the artist's imperial gaze invested them.

In *Catlin's Notes of Eight Years' Travels and Residence in Europe, with His North American Indian Collection* (London, 2 vols, 1848), the author clearly presents himself as an impresario, a showman, rather than an ethnographer[19]. An indication of his new role is Catlin's brief association with P. T. Barnum, when the latter subleased the Egyptian Hall to exhibit Tom Thumb against the background of Catlin's Indian Gallery because the painter's receipts were too low to meet the rent unaided. In his memoirs (*Catlin's Notes*) Catlin explains that when he introduced *tableaux vivans* [sic] (I, p. 90) of as many as twenty figures to his Indian Gallery, the figures wore Indian costume but were white men and boys; the latter played the women. Among the *tableaux* were war scenes, with war whoops and war dances. Later, when a Mr Rankin arrived in Liverpool with nine Ojibways he had brought over 'on speculation' (I, p. 101), Catlin saw his showman's opportunity, did a deal with Rankin, and arranged for 'real Indians' to do their dances against a background of the Indian Collection. In Manchester, the Ojibways entered the hall in which Catlin's portraits of several hundred chiefs were hung amid wigwams, costumes, weapons, and in a 'truly exciting' moment (I, p. 107) they 'set up the most frightful yells, and made the whole neighbourhood ring with their howlings'. As the Indians 'exited through the crowd with war whoops, war-clubs, bows' and leapt onto the stage, a 'roar of applause' showed that they had made 'a hit' (I, pp. 114-6). Illustration no.7 to *Catlin's Notes* shows the Indians in costume, on a stage, surrounded by an audience dressed in top hats and bonnets. The 'savage' on display for the entertainment of the civilised – and obviously middle class – audience. The show culminates in the scalp dance. This 'terrifying dance' Catlin tells us 'seemed to come just up to the anxiety of the excited audience' and produced another 'roar of applause'. One old gentleman in the audience was so moved that he presented a chief with a silver tobacco box (I, p. 117). Payment seems appropriate for the thrills on offer. Ethnographer turned impresario, George Catlin sells the *'frisson'* the spectators desire. They pay their entrance fee and give 'valuable trinkets and money' which the 'Indians' 'receive with thanks'.

The idea of scalping obviously gave civilized white readers and audiences the supreme thrill in the 1830s and 1840s. In his London years, Catlin learned how to exploit the fascination of all classes with this exoticism. At the suggestion of his aristocratic English friend Charles A. Murray, they attended the Caledonian Ball dressed in costumes of Sioux and Sac warriors: props taken from the Egyptian Hall exhibition. They caused a sensation by pretending, through their supposed interpreter, that the scalp locks they wore were not yet dry, having been recently been taken in war from their enemies. 'This had a delightful effect' says Catlin (I, p. 74) in that it cleared a space around the 'savages' and allowed them to breathe more freely.

By this time Catlin has lost any claim to serious attention as the pioneer of sympathetic response to the Indian. He has become a showman who exhibits his wares (Native Americans and their costumes and weapons) in a constant struggle to profit from them. From his beginnings as the recorder and preserver of Indian life there had been an element of the entrepreneur in Catlin's attitudes, as Brian W. Dippie has conclusively shown, but before 1840 that had been restrained by the avowed purpose of achieving a revision of attitude in the white spectators/audience. William H. Fisk's 1849 portrait of Catlin [Plate III] seems to express the paradoxical nature of the artist's relationship to his Native American subjects and to illustrate some of the themes of this paper. In it, Catlin is shown in a tipi, with paint brush in one hand and palette in the other, staring towards the viewer and what can only be his easel. A Native American man, unidentified in the title, looks on over Catlin's right shoulder,[20] while behind him stands a squaw, her body hidden and only her face visible, it too gazing towards Catlin's subject. The 'savages' are in subordinate positions; their dark skin

Plate III: George Catlin, 1849

contrasts with the extreme pallor of the artist's face, though in fact Catlin was so dark-complexioned that he was considered to look like an Indian.[21] The clear-cut outlines of Catlin's features indicate his rationality and intellect, whereas the Indians' gaze is clouded, its significance obscure. By representing the 'manhood' that his own culture denied him – and by constructing that manhood in terms of its fierce and bloody nature, Catlin can enjoy the forbidden pleasures of 'the savage' without risking his idea of himself as the white man whose gaze dominates the wild, at the time when the course of empire was taking its way so vigorously that it was obliterating Native American culture. Compositionally, Fisk's portrait illustrates the power of the artist's 'medicine' through the prominently displayed palette and the phallically positioned paint brush, tinged with red, whose diagonal links the white artist with the shadowy figures he commands.

NOTES

1. Bernard De Voto, *Across the Wide Missouri* (Cambridge, Mass.: Houghton Miflin, 1947), p. 392. He adds that George Catlin's paintings and books have been immensely important to American ethnology ever since 1837. De Voto defines the West of the 1830s as more than a million square miles where there was no permanent white population and hence no federal law.
2. George Catlin, *Letters and Notes on the North American Indians*, ed., Michael Macdonald Mooney (New York: Clarkson N. Potter Inc, 1975), p. 2. If further evidence of the strength of the tradition were needed, it can be found in Richard D. Altick's assumption, in his masterful *The Shows of London* (Cambridge and London: Belknap Press of Harvard University Press, 1978), p. 275, that Catlin's role in the history of American art and ethnography is universally acknowledged.
3. Brian W. Dippie, *Catlin and His Contemporaries. The Politics of Patronage* (Lincoln, Nebraska: University of Nebraska Press, 1990), p. xvi.
4. Richard Drinnon, *Facing West. The Metaphysics of Indian Hating and Empire Building* (New York: New American Library, 1980), p. 497. Drinnon also asserts that, though Catlin hoped to make a living from his work, he 'never looked on native peoples as so many red objects to be consumed and exploited for economic personal gain'.
5. The full title of the two-volume edition, published by the author in 1841, was *Letters and Notes on the Manners, Customs and Conditions of the North American Indians Written During Eight Years' Travel Amongst the Wildest Tribes of Indians in North America, in 1832, 33, 34, 35, 36, 37, 38 and 39*. In later editions, Catlin altered the title. All further references are to the 1841 edition and are included in the text. The quotation occurs on p. 3.
6. George Catlin, *Last Rambles Amongst the Indians of the Rocky Mountains and the Andes* (London: Sampson Law and Son, 1868), pp. 354-5.
7. On this see Dippie, *Catlin and His Contemporaries*, p. 58. As Dippie states clearly, Catlin's article recommending enforcement of a federal government ban on alcohol in Indian country in the *New York Commercial Advertiser* , October 1834, earned him the hostility of the American Fur Company.

8. Charles Baudelaire, 'The Salon of 1846; VI, On Some Colourists' in *The Mirror of Art. Critical Studies By Charles Baudelaire*, trans., and ed., Jonathan Mayne (London: Phaidon, 1955), p. 74.
9. See William Truettner, *The Natural Man Observed. A Study of Catlin's Indian Gallery* (Washington, D.C.: Smithsonian Institute Press, 1979), p. 36. The James Hall and Thomas L. McKenney book was published in three volumes (Volume I in 1836) under the title *History of the Indian Tribes of North America.*
10. Harold McCracken, *George Catlin and the Old Frontier* (New York: Dial, 1959), p. 75.
11. That Catlin perceived Indian culture as antithetical to white culture has been noted by Patricia Nelson Limerick, in her *Legacy of Conquest* (New York: Dial, 1987) pp. 182-3. Limerick calls attention to Catlin's insistence that 'the Indian' (unlike the middle-class white man) lived the carefree life of the moment, with no anxious anticipations or regrets for past failures. Catlin's most scholarly and authoritative biographer – William Truettner – has suggested that the artist might have been motivated in his programme of travels into the wilderness by his desire to escape from the pressures and anxieties of life in the entrepreneurial white society of which he was a member by birth, education avocation and even vocation (portrait painter). Seeking to establish himself as a portrait painter at a time when the marketplace was assumed to be the American man's sphere, and entrepreneurial activity the means of proving manhood, Catlin might well have needed to escape from competition with other painters in the East (*The Natural Man Observed*, pp. 14ff). See also Dippie, *Catlin and His Contemporaries*, pp. 9-11, on the possibility that self-interest played a part in Catlin's dedication to Indian paintings.
12. David Leverenz, *Manhood and the American Renaissance* (Ithaca: Cornell University Press, 1989), pp. 73,85.
13. In his preface to his *North American Indian Portfolio* (London, 1844) Catlin repeats his emphasis on Indian 'medicine' though he does not use the word. This time he gives the 'mysteries' more explicit significance, claiming that he spent eight years 'mingling with the Red Men, and identifying ... with them as much as possible ... in order to better familiarize myself with their superstitions and mysteries'. Here, the mysteries, or *medicine*, is clearly taken to be the key to Indian culture.
14. *North-American Indians*, I, p. 168. Catlin gives a lengthy account of the 'bull dance', or the whole ritual that supposedly ensured that the buffalo would come, in Letter 22 (Vol.1, pp. 165-9). It disgusts him because of the phallic elements that are obvious even through Catlin's prim narrative. In the 1841 edition he shields his readers' sensibilities by giving his account of parts of the ceremony in the language of the Mandans, with no translation.
15. Kathryn Hight, '"Doomed to Perish": George Catlin's Depictions of the Mandan', *Art-Journal*, 49 (1990), pp. 119-24, states that Catlin identified the chief in the 1841 caption. Though the chief could easily be identified as Mah-to-toh-pa by anyone who read – and studied the illustrations in – Volume 1, I can find no explicit identification in the 1841 frontispiece and its caption.
16. See Truettner, *The Natural Man Observed*, pp. 22-36 and Mooney, *Letters and Notes* (1975), p. 61.
17. For penetrating commentary on the staged nature of the scene, see Kathryn Hight's article cited above. Noting discrepancies between Catlin's account of the occasion when he painted Four Bears and the scene depicted in the frontispiece, Hight argues that the 'event' shown in the latter is closer to what

occurred in Catlin's Indian Gallery at the Egyptian Hall, Piccadilly, than to any event that took place on the High Plains. See also Julie Schimmel, 'Inventing "the Indian"', *The West as America: Reinterpreting Images of the Frontier, 1820-1920*, ed., William H. Truettner (Washington and London: Smithsonian Institution Press, 1991), pp. 149-89. Schimmel draws attention to the 'attitudinizing' that permeated the relationship between white painters and Indian subjects. Catlin, in her view, 'paints the Mandan chief ... as a reflection of his own self-conscious controlling image' (p. 149); his relationship to his subjects comes straight from the drawing rooms of eastern society.

18. To be fair to Catlin, he did also make an impassioned plea for the preservation of territory as wilderness and as home for the surviving tribes (he was a pioneer in this), but his notion of national parks with resident Indians was patently a version of museum or theme park. In contrast to this gesture towards preserving 'specimens', Catlin's only hope for the Indian assumed that the savage could be civilized or the Indian 'Americanized', yet – as his text repeatedly affirms – he found the Indian interesting only when uncontaminated by white Anglo-American culture.

19. Brian W. Dippie, who has studied Catlin's London years more thoroughly than any other scholar, treats the artist sympathetically yet acknowledges that he was fighting a losing battle with the forces of commercialisation. His failure to get Congressional patronage of any substantial sort meant that Catlin needed to sell his works and his Indians in the marketplace. Since the publication costs of his *North American Indians* were so high that there was little return on his investment, he needed to attract viewers to his Gallery, yet in London his was one of a vast number of competing 'shows'. See, in particular, pp. 99,117. Dippie refers to Richard D. Altick's *The Shows of London* for an insightful account of Catlin's predicament as an impresario.

20. The male figure resembles Mix-ke-mote-skin-na (the Iron Horn), a Blackfoot warrior, painted by Catlin at Fort Union in the summer of 1832.

21. See McCracken, *George Catlin and the Old Frontier*, p. 18.

BARBARA RASMUSSEN

Virginia Woolf: Masculinity as Imperial *'Parade'*

This paper is a joke. Of course it is a *serious* joke and I'm haunted by Freud's suggestion in *Jokes and their Relation to the Unconscious* that 'a joke loses its effect of laughter' for the recipient 'as soon as he is required to make an expenditure of intellectual work in connection with it'.[1] So relax and envisage me agonizing over my paper when I should have been dealing with Second Year modularisation and suddenly urgently aware I had washing-up to do. So on go the radio and my rubber gloves and I gather that in a few moments Dr Karen Burke will be telling 'us ladies' how to have 'thin thighs for life'.[2] My ears prick up, suddenly cellulite is one of life's major problems. A few moments later the lyrics of 'Magnificent Obsession', as sung by Nat King Cole: 'You're my magnificent obsession, the greatest wonder on this earth. The Taj Mahal and other splendours to me really had no worth. You're my magnificent possession, a treasure left me from above. As long as I have breath within me, you'll be my one and only love ... ' have me tearing off my rubber gloves and scribbling them down.[3] Back to the washing-up with all the ironies in mind of reading Joan Riviere's 1929 paper on 'Womanliness as a Masquerade' which cites the case of the analysis of an intellectual woman who on one occasion dreamt of *'washing off* dirt and sweat, guilt and blood', the traces, according to Riviere's interpretation, of the 'sadism' involved in taking a masculine position as a public speaker, when I was doing just the same.[4] I might be consciously cynical but ideology was clearly at work.[5] I was washing up and worrying about cellulite while planning to give a paper referring to 'Womanliness as a Masquerade' and its discussion in particular of two intellectual women who, we might now say, were accomodating themselves to the male fantasy of the woman: one, as Rivere argues, by 'flirting' with 'father-figures' after public speaking and one by being defensively 'feminine' in her attire and disturbingly 'flippant' when lecturing to male 'colleagues'. The latter's usurpation of a masculine position, Riviere avers, had to be, defensively, a '''joke'''(pp. 36-39).

I was aware too of other ironies, of listening in 1995 to a black crooner singing lyrics which were both patriarchal and imperialist. Seduced by them, I too was under the spell of what Stephen Heath reminds us in his paper 'Joan Riviere and the Masquerade' is masculinity as *'parade'* which Heath translates as 'display' – a showing off of possession of the phallus. If men had the phallus, they would not need woman to figure it – or the Taj Mahal. Indeed, as Eugénie Lemoine-Luccioni, quoted by Heath just after a reference to Woolf's *Three Guineas*, avers 'if the penis was the phallus, men would have no need of feathers or ties or medals ... Display *[parade]*, just like the masquerade, thus betrays a flaw: no one has the phallus'.[6] Thus I at least was still within what Riviere terms 'womanliness as a masquerade' – still thinking I must have thin thighs to acommodate myself to that masculine fantasy of womanliness; to what Riviere accepts as, and terms, 'fully developed femininity' even as she declares it is always a masquerade. For her, 'fully developed femininity' involves most importantly: 'the renunciation (less intensity) of sadistic castration-wishes deriving from the later oral-biting level. "I must not take, I must not even ask; it must be *given* me"'(p.43).

So (suitably robed I hope), let me hide behind Professor von X. as Woolf pictures him in 1929 in *A Room of One's Own* after a day spent reading books *by* men *about* women in the British Museum:

> It was the face and the figure of Professor von X. engaged in writing his monumental work entitled *The Mental, Moral, and Physical Inferiority of the Female Sex* ... His expression suggested that he was labouring under some emotion that made him jab his pen on the paper as if he were killing some noxious insect as he wrote, but even when he had killed it that did not satisfy him; he must go on killing it; and even so, some cause for anger and irritation remained.[7]

In *A Room of One's Own* Woolf concludes that such an attitude supports male self-confidence:

> Women have served all these centuries as looking-glasses possessing the magic and delicious power of reflecting the figure of man at twice its natural size ... For if she begins to tell the truth, the figure in the looking-glass shrinks; his fitness for life is diminished. How is he to go on giving judgement, civilizing natives, making laws, writing books, dressing up and speechifying at banquets, unless he can see himself at breakfast and at dinner at least twice the size he really is? (pp. 32-33)

In *For they know not what they do: Enjoyment as a Political Factor* Slavoj Žižek points out that, 'the child from Andersen's tale who with disarming innocence states the obvious', that 'the Emperor has no clothes', does more than expose 'hypocrisy and pretence' since the whole 'intersubjective network' which depends on maintenance of that deception will collapse.[8] Yet in *A Room of One's Own* this is precisely what Woolf is (oh so urbanely saying) or rather, she is saying that the Emperor has only his clothes, his imperial gear; and she says it all the more emphatically and overtly in the later *Three Guineas*. In current terms she makes it clear that there is no substance to his or anyone's claim to have the phallus though it certainly has effects of power as long as we go along with it. The procession of 'educated men' from which 'the daughters of educated men' were for so long excluded,[9] employs clothes Woolf concludes in *Three Guineas*, 'to advertise the social, professional, or intellectual standing of the wearer':

> If you will excuse the humble illustration, your dress fulfils the same function as the tickets in a grocer's shop. But, here, instead of saying 'This is margarine; this pure butter; this is the finest butter in the market,' it says, 'This man is a clever man – he is Master of Arts; this man is a very clever man – he is Doctor of Letters; this man is a most clever man – he is a Member of the Order of Merit.' It is this function – the advertisement function – of your dress that seems to us most singular. In the opinion of St Paul, such advertisement, at any rate for our sex, was unbecoming and immodest; until a very few years ago we were denied the use of it. And still the tradition, or belief, lingers among us that to express worth of any kind, whether intellectual or moral, by wearing pieces of metal, or ribbon, coloured hoods or gowns, is a barbarity which deserves the ridicule which we bestow upon the rites of savages. A woman who advertised her motherhood by a tuft of horsehair on the left shoulder would scarcely, you will agree, be a venerable object. (p.137)

Meanwhile, excluded from the professions, women have had to dress to attract husbands and therefore dress their ideas to suit. Hence Woolf cites Lady Lovelace's reference to '"our splendid Empire" ... "the price of which," Lady Lovelace added, "is mainly paid by women"' (p.160). Placed in the context of such arguments, the photographs Woolf chose for *Three Guineas* [Plate IV] make us take an*other* look at masculine dress. The 'feathers', 'ties', 'medals' which for Lemoine-Luccioni, as we have seen, function as mere 'display', masking an ever-absent phallus, feature similarly in the photographs of *Three Guineas* as mere pomp and ceremony along with what appear to be quite fabulously (and no doubt quite unnecessarily) tall boots [Plate V]. The parade of boots is a topic to which I'll return but the way in which photographic and verbal texts interact to offer us an estranging view of the familiar may be illustrated by comparing the photograph of the bewigged judge [Plate VI] with Woolf's acidly interrogative commentary when she quotes 'the late Mr Justice MacCardie summing up the case of Mrs Frankau':

> 'Women cannot be expected to renounce an essential feature of femininity or to abandon *one of nature's solaces for a constant and insuperable physical handicap* ... In matters of dress women often remain children to the end. But ... the rule of prudence and proportion must be observed.' The Judge who thus dictated was wearing a scarlet robe, an ermine cape, and a vast wig of artificial curls ... what degree of social prestige causes blindness to the remarkable nature of one's own clothes? (p.279; my emphasis)

Adopting the defamiliarizing view of woman as 'outsider' Woolf

Plate IV: 'feathers', 'ties', 'medals'

Plate V: 'tall boots'

analyses empire in *Three Guineas* (itself as Heath argues, 'a strong social-political, feminist joke'[10]) on the home-front. The patriarchal home is at once seedbed of empire and fascism and a *front*, a deceit. It functions, one might say, as a fantasy scenario where male dress is a *'parade'*, a showing off of power, of the specious possession of the phallus and female dress is a masquerade of inferiority and dependence whilst also being a figuration of the phallus for men. Fantasy here, as Žižek suggests in *The Sublime Object of Ideology*, is an organization, a framing of desire but paradoxically also a masking of desire, of 'the abyss of the desire of the Other'.[11]

I started this paper at home, and Woolf analyses the logic of British imperialism from the home-front. Indeed with Mr Justice MacCardie and Professor von X. Woolf might well have been analysing her own paternal uncle, Fitzjames Stephen, who in *Liberty, Equality, Fraternity*, written during 1872 while he travelled back from being the appropriately named 'Legal Member of the Viceroy's Council in India', took issue with J.S. Mill's arguments for women's equality. For Stephen:

> Ingenious people may argue about anything, and Mr Mill does say a great number of things about women ... but all the talk in the world will never shake the proposition that men are stronger than women in every shape. They have greater muscular and nervous force, greater intellectual force, greater vigour of character.[12]

Plate VI: 'the bewigged judge'

Stephen goes on to aver that: 'Strength, in all its forms, is life and manhood. To be less strong is to be less of a man' (p. 199). Hence his necessary belief in inequality:

> I say the wife ought to give way. She ought to obey her husband ... just as, when the captain gives the word to cut away the masts, the lieutenant carries out his orders at once, though he may be a better seaman and may disapprove them ... No case can be specified in which people unite for a common object from making a pair of shoes up to governing an empire in which the power to decide does not rest somewhere; and what is this but command and obedience? (p.197)

The overall argument here is actually contradictory: men he avers are stronger both intellectually and physically but then he admits that the woman/lieutenant may be more able. Thus Stephen, an admirer of Hobbes, can only assert that a structure of command and obedience is as necessary for 'governing an empire' as it is for 'making a pair of shoes' and it is precisely the way he *dresses up* his argument that interests me: 'Government ... ought to fit society as a man's clothes fit him. To establish by law rights and duties which assume that people are equal when they are not is like trying to make clumsy feet look handsome by the help of tight boots' (p. 192).

Boots and shoes: Woolf's *Jacob's Room* ends as Mrs Flanders holds out a pair of the dead Jacob's old shoes; bloody shoes figure in *Between the Acts*. In both cases they are related to force and war. I want, however, to conclude with *To the Lighthouse* where Woolf negotiates her own patriarchal and imperialist past: her relations with her father, Leslie Stephen, – brother of Fitzjames and son of 'Mr Mother-Country Stephen', and with her mother Julia Stephen whose father was a doctor in India.[13] The home-front's connections with India are indeed clear in the novel, Mrs Ramsay significantly has a necklace 'which Uncle James had brought her from India' and 'had the whole of the other sex under her protection ... for the fact that they negotiated treaties, ruled India, controlled finance'.[14] But it is the Stephen family's obsession with boots that most concerns me here. Remember the scene where Mr Ramsay feels justified in forcing women 'he did not care how, his need was so great, to give him what he wanted: sympathy' and pressurises the resistant Lily, who sees he is parading his grief: 'he was acting ... this great man was dramatising himself' (pp. 165-166). She finally blurts out '"What beautiful boots!"', expects 'complete annihilation' for such a feeble response to his demand but, surprised, finds she has given Mr Ramsay what he wanted: 'Ah yes, he said, holding his foot up for her to look at, they were first-rate boots. There was only one man in England who could make boots like that' (pp. 167-168).

Here Mr Ramsay fetishizing his boots, Mr Justice MacCardie, Fitzjames Stephen, imperialism and masculinity as *'parade'*, come together. Freud in his analysis of fetishism ties it to male narcissism and fear of castration.[15] As Colin MacCabe has suggested, 'The fetishist inaugurates desire by the *replacement* of the mother's penis. This *replacement* involves an admission of the absence of the mother's penis ... and yet an assertion of its presence in the substitute'.[16] It is 'the forms of masculine authority' MacCabe goes on to argue, which, more generally than is often admitted, become 'invested' by the fetishist 'as a guarantee of the man's possession of the phallus'. Thus 'the transformation of the man's own penis into a fetish involves', MacCabe suggests, 'the designation of objects and institutions with phallic authority in the face of the evident failure of the real father (p.110). Hence Freud's comment in 'Fetishism', quoted by MacCabe: 'In later life a grown man may perhaps experience a similar panic when the cry goes up that *Throne and Altar are in danger*, and similar illogical consequences will ensue' (p. 110).

Fitzjames Stephen admits possible lack on man's part – the lieutenant/woman may be more able and the man less so – but disavows it: women are less strong intellectually and in every other way, hence a structure of command and obedience and women's inequality go without saying. The same structure of disavowal justifies absolute rule in India in Stephen's paper 'Foundations of the Government of India'.[17] India was won by conquest, does not have representative government, nevertheless absolute rule by 'educated Englishmen' is justified because of the perceived inferiority of Indian institutions. Likewise, Mr Justice MacCardie sees women as lacking but is blind to the lack masked by his own scarlet robe, ermine cape and wig, and Mr Ramsay, whose dependence on women is manifest, lights on his first-rate boots in the face of an unsympathetic woman and is reassured of his own superiority. He 'poohpoohed her [Lily's] feeble system' of tying knots, we learn (p. 168). Thinking of the judge in ermine and Ramsay's boots, it is of course 'the foot or shoe ... fur and velvet' that Freud observes as common fetishes supporting a split – that of both the admission and the disavowal of lack: ultimately the man's own.[18] In the scene of Mr Ramsay's boots, Woolf exposes the split, the disavowal; before his moment of triumphant reassurance she has already turned the narrative tables on him by parading those boots as farcically empty.

The joke of the empty boots, still walking, repeating the same old story even in Mr Ramsay's absence, is used to undermine a specific patriarchal construction of masculinity; showing it as just that: empty boots on parade with all their imperial and imperious vigour. If I started at home, with cellulite and Nat King Cole, it is because they precisely brought home to me the persistence of those boots: that structure of masculinity as '*parade*' and femininity as masquerade. For me at least those boots still keep on walking ...

NOTES

1. Sigmund Freud, *Jokes and their Relation to the Unconscious, VII: Standard Edition of the Complete Psychological Works of Sigmund Freud,* trans., James Strachey in collaboration with Anna Freud, assisted by Alix Strachey and Allen Tyson ([1905]; London: The Hogarth Press and the Institute of Psycho-Analysis, 1960), p.150.
2. Karen Burke, *Simple Steps to Thin Thighs* (U.K.: Hamlyn, 1995).
3. Fred Karger and Frank Laine, 'Magnificent Obsession'; recorded by Nat King Cole in May 1958. Quoted by kind permission of Windswept Pacific Musci Ltd.
4. Joan Riviere, 'Womanliness as a Masquerade', in *Formations of Fantasy,* ed., V. Burgin, J. Donald and C. Kaplan (London and New York: Methuen, 1986), pp. 35–44 (pp. 38–40) (first publ. in *International Journal of Psychoanalysis,* 10 (1929)). All further references are to this edition and are included in the text.
5. See Slavoj Žižek, *The Sublime Object of Ideology* (London: Verso, 1989), p.29.
6. Stephen Heath, 'Joan Riviere and the Masquerade', in *Formations of Fantasy,* pp. 55–56.
7. Virginia Woolf, *A Room of One's Own* (London: Hogarth, 1929) repr. in Michèle Barrett eds., *A Room of One's Own* and *Three Guineas* (London: Penguin, 1993), p.28. All further references are to this edition and are included in the text.
8. Slavoj Žižek, *For They Know Not What They Do: Enjoyment as a Political Factor* (London: Verso, 1991), pp. 11–12.
9. Virginia Woolf, *Three Guineas* (London: Hogarth, 1938) repr. in Michèle Barrett ed., *A Room of One's Own* and *Three Guineas* (London: Penguin, 1993) pp.

127-129. All further references are to this edition and are included in the text.

10. *Formations of Fantasy,* p.56.

11. *The Sublime Object of Ideology,* p. 118.

12. James Fitzjames Stephen, *Liberty, Equality, Fraternity,* ([1873]; ed., R. J. White (Cambridge: Cambridge University Press, 1967), p.194.

13. On James Stephen see Jane Marcus, *Virginia Woolf and the Languages of Patriarchy* (Bloomington: Indiana University Press, 1987), p. 83. Marcus points out: 'The press called him "Mr Mother-Country Stephen," for it was he who coined the phrase "the mother country." It was he who made the policies that bound the British colonies in a domestic metaphor that was to determine their relations for more than a hundred years, to yoke whole nations in a position from which to rebel was to insult sacred motherhood itself'.

14. Virginia Woolf, *To the Lighthouse* ([1927]; London: Penguin, 1992), p. 88 and p.10. All further references are from this edition and are given in the text.

15. Sigmund Freud, 'Fetishism' (1927) *Standard Edition,* 21 (1927) 147-157 (pp. 152-4). Interestingly, it was Joan Riviere who translated 'Fetishism' for *The International Journal of Psycho-Analysis,* 9, 2 (1928), pp. 161-6.

16. Colin MacCabe, *James Joyce and the Revolution of the Word* (London: Macmillan, 1978), p.110. Further references are given after quotation in the text.

17. James Fitzjames Stephen, 'Foundations of the Government of India', *Nineteenth Century,* 14 (Oct. 1883), pp. 541-68.

18. 'Fetishism', pp. 155-7.

SUSAN BASSNETT

Lost in the Past: A Tale of Heroes and Englishness

Let us begin with an obituary. Obituaries are interesting texts, for they often reveal a great deal more about the writer and about the readers designate, than about the subject of the text itself, the individual who has died. English obituaries are a distinctive genre, they are often highly personal, frequently ironic, at times even critical. They rarely eulogize, they seek to contextualize the life of the deceased and they offer far more than biographical information. One such obituary appeared in The *Guardian* on 16 June 1993, written by Frank Keating about James Hunt, the English racing driver who had died suddenly of a heart attack at the age of 45. Entitled 'Dashing to the flag', the text plays on the double meaning of those words: 'dashing' signifies both moving at speed and, as an adjective refers to exhuberance, charm and liveliness. Hunt had spent his life dashing, i.e. moving quickly, but had also been a dashing personality, flamboyant and spirited. The flag of the title also carries a double meaning: the flag is a fundamental signifier in racing, and victory is marked with a flag. But equally, the flag in question could refer to the British flag, the Union Jack, for Hunt had represented his country on the racing circuit as a British champion.

Keating's obituary plays on the double meanings and depicts Hunt in mock-heroic terms:

> James Hunt had a winning way with him both before and after his great successes on the racing circuits. Even in those comparatively supercharged and modern mid-70s, when his rear tyres were mischievously sluicing mud up into the windscreens of his snarling Continental rivals such as Nikki Lauda and Clay Regazzoni, people's perception in taproom Britain was that 'our James' was a throwback to sport's cavalier days, before even the bow-tie twirling Hawthorn of two decades before.
>
> Hunt was giving furious and technically trained Johnny Foreigners a hell of a beating, like it was an oldetyme sepia print of El Alamein or the Battle of Britain come to life ... and he was a Rockfist Rogan careering around in his leather helmet, short-sleeved cricket shirt, and pair of goggles, price 19s 11d from Timothy Whites and Taylors; and smelling the flowers and waving to the blondes in the crowd as he passed, and continuing to eye them through his wing mirror till he turned the next corner.[1]

This is a very curious text. Is it an ironic obituary, by a friend? A gently critical obituary of a man whose lifestyle appeared to belong to another age? Is the portrayal of Hunt as an old-fashioned comic book hero sympathetic, are we being asked to accept this portrait and these values, and look nostalgically back to a time when they were believed to be commonplace? The answer would seem to be that this text is highly ambiguous, just as the media treatment of Hunt in his lifetime was by no means straightforward. He was a racing star, but also someone whose lifestyle, particularly his relationships with women and his taste for the international jet-set scene frequently made headlines in the tabloids. Transforming Hunt into a caricature figure from a bygone age isolates him from the contemporary world, makes it possible to mythologize his life, turning the sensational stories of his alcohol and sexual problems into something anodyne and hence acceptable. Keating himself acknowledges the fictionalizing process in which he is engaged, pointing out that such an image might have been the ludicrous front that he was happy to go along with 'for promotional' purposes.

Underpinning Keating's mock heroic portrait is an ideal of English masculinity. The cool, calm English hero is set against the furious and technically trained Johnny Foreigners. This is the comic-book stereotype of Englishness, promoted by the boy's adventure story and the British cinema of the 40s and 50s, often parodied but basically taken very seriously. We have only to think of the current anti-European lobby, the Michael Portillos of today who uphold heroic English traits against unsavoury Continental ones to see how powerful that stereotype remains. In contrast with the victory-obsessed continentals, the English hero is not interested in winning, he is concerned just to play the game; he is somehow an innocent, with a boyish sense of mischief. 'Our James' Keating tells us, using a familiar appellative, was a throwback to the cavalier days of sport, the days before professionalism began to rear its head. Hunt is depicted as a figure from the past, 'like an oldetyme sepia print' and the text transports us back to the 1940s, to the Battle of Britain and El Alamein, to the last great moment of the English hero figure. It is a figure that we have come to know well, from the comics, the novels and above all from the cinema. This obituary firmly locates Hunt in the tradition of the idealized English hero figure.

The mythical English hero of the Second World War was always contrasted to the snarling, incompetent foreigners against whom he fought. It was a familiar pattern of contrasts, with foreignness set against the ideals of Englishness. Anthony Easthope has constructed a list of contrasts between Englishness and foreignness based on stereotypical representations expressed in a whole range of texts, most notably in political discourse: the English are objective, foreigners are self-obsessed, they are practical, while foreigners are (undesirably) theoretical, they are clear and plain speaking, not given to over-indulgence in rhetoric, they are endowed with common sense, in contrast to the fanaticism and dogmatism of foreigners, they are sensible, not silly, hard, not soft, sincere, not artificial. In love, they are reticent but true-hearted, in sport they are amateurs, not professionals.[2] This list of contrasts, which provides the skeletal framework of so many narratives of Englishness, is also gendered, for the ideal qualities of Englishness are equated with ideals of masculinity. Women, like foreigners, are inclined to be subjective, hysterical, emotional and silly. The values of masculinity are equated with the values of Englishness. Stuart Hall sums the situation up with his customary acuteness:

> To be English is to know yourself in relation to the French, and the hot-blooded Mediterraneans and the passionate, traumatized Russian soul.You go round the entire globe; when you know what everybody else is, then you are what they are not ... When I speak about this way of being in the world, being English in the world, with a capital 'E' as it were, it is grounded not only in a whole history, a whole set of histories, a whole set of economic relations, a whole set of cultural discourses, it is also profoundly grounded in certain forms of sexual identity ... A free-born English person was clearly a free-born English *man*.[3]

The qualities of the English hero were established in the nineteenth century, in the age of imperial expansion. J.E.C. Welldon, headmaster of Harrow from 1881-1887 was in no doubt that the training of the hero began at school and gave the Englishman a special quality that would differentiate him from Johnny Foreigner forever. Noting that Englishmen are not superior to French or Germans in brains or industry or science, or in techniques of warfare, Welldon declares that their superiority resides:

> in the health and temper which games impart ... The pluck, the energy, the perseverance, the good temper, the self-control, the discipline, the cooperation, the *esprit de corps,* which merit success in cricket or football, are the very qualities which win the day in peace or war ...[4]

Games, good sportsmanship was the key to imperial success, and the myth of the game played well even at the point of total defeat was a powerful one. Sir Henry Newbolt's famous poem, *Vitai Lampada,* reads like an anthem of a period, as the voice of a schoolboy rallies the defeated British army, reminding them to 'Play up, play up, and play the game'.[5] The honour of the school, loyalty to the team and self-discipline were the fundamental features of this world-view. Death was incidental, cowardice the ultimate horror. Sport and warfare are fused together, and the training and values of the one system elide into the other. The good sportsman is a good fighter, because although he aspires to win, he does not set winning above the game itself. Losing can therefore bring even greater honour, if the losing is done well.

Keating's obituary for James Hunt is full of irony and affectionate humour, but it clearly belongs to a tradition of obituaries for heroes who combine personal talents with ideals of Englishness. That tradition was consolidated during the age of empire, reaching its apotheosis during the First World War. A good example of the genre is Maurice Baring's poem, *In Memoriam A.H.*, written for Auberon Herbert, Captain Lord Lucas, a pilot in the Royal Flying Corps who was killed in action on November 3, 1916. The poem is full of references to the skies as both the place where he met his death and the symbol of the afterlife: 'a soaring death and near to heaven's gate'. Describing how the young man flew out of this life and into another, Baring depicts him arriving at a kind of Valhalla, a heaven for heroes where:

> Surely you found companions meet for you
> In that high place:
> You met there face to face
> Those you had never known but whom you knew:
> Knights of the Table Round,
> And all the very brave, the very true,
> With chivalry crowned;
> The captains rare,
> Courteous and brave beyond our human air:
> Those who had loved and suffered overmuch,
> Now free from the world's touch.
> And with them were the friends of yesterday
> Who went before and pointed you the way.[6]

Once in that place 'of freshness, light and rest', Baring imagines Auberon Herbert being welcomed by friends he knew and also, significantly, by knights of old, for the promised land is the place where 'Lancelot and Tristram vigil keep' over their dead king, Arthur. Into this warrior-heaven the newest comrade is welcomed as friend and brother, 'to that companionship which hath no end'.

Baring's heaven for warriors is a particularly English Valhalla. It is an Arthurian heaven, for very perfect knights. There are no women here, no Valkyries in the Germanic tradition, no houris to offer nights of endless pleasure, only men. It is also notable also that the two knights mentioned by name, Lancelot and Tristram both had deeply ambiguous relationships with women, having been involved in protracted and disastrous love-affairs with their kings' wives. Baring draws upon a particular nineteenth century version of Arthurian legend that stressed the ideal of comradeship among men, with the Round Table as a kind of team or club and King Arthur as the captain.

The nineteenth century Arthurian revival took many forms: there was a Celtic version that saw Arthur as a model of resistance against tyranny, a figure living in an age of violence and magic who provided a safe haven for those who chose to follow his path. This Arthur can be compared to a sort of guerilla leader or resistance fighter, in contrast to the German version which stressed his sanctity, his kingliness and his position as an elite warrior. The English Arthur was less of an elitist

— Harps on quests and knights etc.

figure, and appeared rather as a model of manliness and leadership. Countless retellings of the Arthurian legends, particularly those versions aimed at the schoolboy readership present him in this way. This Victorian repossession of Arthur is therefore linked to the creation of an idealized image of England and Englishness. The captain (King Arthur) and his team out on quests, fighting for good and searching for the Holy Grail, defending damsels in public but living good clean lives well away from the wiles of women tied in well with behavioural models taught in the public schools.

Women did not appear favourably in this version. They were seen principally as negative influences, as cruel and adulterous queens, betrayers or evil sorceresses. It is through women that the Round Table collapses, women such as Guinevere whose passion for Lancelot led her to betray Arthur, or Margawse, mother of Mordred who precipitated the end of the ideal order. Versions for schools tended in consequence to erase women, unless they were harmless damsels or suffering maidens like Elaine. There was no place in the chivalric ideal for women. They disrupted, they weakened and, like foreigners, they did not play the game.

The novels of Rider Haggard, the hugely successful writer of adventure stories for boys in the latter years of Victoria's reign are full of evil women and strong, resiliant men. When Allan Quartermain *Holly* looks for the first time on She-Who-Must-Be-Obeyed he sees her perfect beauty, 'only this beauty, with all its awful loveliness and purity, was *evil* or rather at the time it impressed me as evil'.[7] She is destroyed by the flame that has preserved her for thousands of years, and since She has also disposed of her rival, the heroes are able to return to England unencumbered. Likewise, in *King Solomon's Mines,* the noble Foulata dies trying to help the heroes escape the clutches of the evil old witch, Gagool. Haggard always manages to punish the bad women and kill off the good ones in time for everyone to get safely home again, womanless.

Haggard's characters are models of English masculine behaviour. *Allan Quartermain,* which appeared in 1887 was prefaced by a dedication that explicitly stated that the purpose of his novel was to educate boys in models of masculinity and Englishness:

> I inscribe this book of adventure to my son, Arthur John Rider Haggard, in the hope that in days to come he, and many other boys whom I shall never know, may, in the acts and thoughts of Allan Quartermain and his companions, as herein recorded, find something to help him and them, to reach to what, with Sir Henry Curtis, I hold to be the highest rank whereto we can attain – the state and dignity of English gentlemen.[8]

Sir Henry Curtis is the fictional embodiment of that ideal, a plain-speaking simple man, who enjoys shooting game, who gets 'as restless

as an old elephant who scents danger' when forced to live the life of a
country squire. Sir Henry is a 'a splendid looking man ... calm
powerful face, clear-cut features, large grey eyes, yellow beard and
hair-altogether a magnificent specimen of the higher type of
humanity'.[9] Allan Quartermain, Haggard's alter-ego narrator, declares
that he has 'never seen wider shoulders or a deeper chest'. In this
novel, Quartermain, Curtis and Captain John Good, the trio who
explored the Mines of Solomon in the earlier novel, unite again for
another journey to the African interior, accompanied by the noble Zulu
warrior Umslopogaas. This time they discover a hidden kingdom, ruled
by two sister-queens, Nyleptha, the golden-haired and Sorais the dark-
haired. Both women fall in love with Sir Henry, and when it becomes
clear that he prefers Nyleptha, Sorais wages war against her sister, with
catastrophic results. By the end of the book, Umslopogaas and
Quartermain are dead, and Sorais kills herself, leaving Sir Henry to rule
over the Zu-Vendi kingdom with his wife. Women have brought about
the downfall of the traditional order of the realm, and have led to the
death of heroes.

After Quartermain has died, Sir Henry takes up the narration, and
explains that he intends to protect his kingdom from the evils of the
modern world, which include gunpowder, telegraphs, steam, daily
newspapers and universal suffrage. As the reader is about to leave him
in this idyllic state, he suddenly adds a postscript that echoes
Haggard's dedication of the novel and gives him the opportunity to
note almost casually that he now has a son:

> I quite forgot to say that about nine months ago Nyleptha (who is very well
> and, in my eyes at any rate, more beautiful than ever) presented me with a son
> and heir. He is a regular curly-haired, blue-eyed young Englishman in looks
> and, though he is destined, if he lives, to inherit the throne of the Zu-Vendis, I
> hope I may be able to bring him up to become what an English gentleman
> should be, and generally is-which is to my mind even a prouder and a finer
> thing than being born heir apparent to the great house of the Stairway, and,
> indeed, the highest rank that a man can reach upon this earth.[10]

Sir Henry is strong and manly, and resolutely English – a model for
builders of the Empire. Joseph Bristow's splendid book, *Empire Boys*,
examines the way in which a literature for boys was also a literature for
Empire-makers, a form of training in imperial ideals linked to an overt
educational programme. He also examines how long that literature
endured, and how pervasive it was.[11] Sir Henry may be read as a
prototype, he recurs in other guises in comics, films and novels,
surviving two world wars. He is one of Baring's heroes, he is Biggles,
of course, and Dan Dare and the Wolf of Kabul, and Julian, the Enid
Blyton boy hero who took all the decisions for the Famous Five.

Like many women of my generation, I used to read the Famous Five
books and was filled with fury at the docile Ann who washed dishes

and the tomboyish Georgie who tried (and always failed) to take the control that Julian held. The model of gendered behaviour in those books continued the model found in nineteenth century boys' adventure stories. The hero was always a gentleman, women always had to be subservient and docile if they wanted to be admired and the aggressive ones always came out of things badly. Equally, like other women of my generation, I have not wanted that model of behaviour passed on to my children, neither to my daughters nor to my son. It is significant that the late 1960s – early 1970s, which saw the emergence of the feminist movement and a healthy questioning of establishment norms in all kinds of areas also saw the demise of many of the more xenophobic and racist comics and children's books. Despite such changes, the figure of the gentleman-hero remained visible, and as Graham Dawson has pointed out, the Falklands war of 1982 saw how close to the surface the old attitudes lay:

> A Task Force composed exclusively of men became the representative of the nation's will. British men and women were encouraged, as in the Second World War, to identify with it, and with them, through gendered inflections of the national myth. The 'feminine' narrative stance concentrated on the tearful goodbyes of girl-friends, wives and mothers; on their hopes anxieties and grief; on their sense of the terrible vulnerability of those they waited for, and pride in their suffering and loss. The 'masculine' version, by contrast, found the military technologies and strategies of the war fascinating, the prospect of battle exciting, and British soldiers, sailors and airmen heroic.[12]

One of the great difficulties for a cultural historian is to date change. Change involves process, and processes are never easy to map. The very understandable desire we all have to organize history coherently all too often leads to a distorted perspective. It has become commonplace, for example, to see 1968, the year of international student protest, as a year of great change in British society, just as it is equally commonplace to see 1956, the year of the Suez crisis, as a previous watershed, with 1945, the year of the end of the Second World War before that. Undeniably these dates have a certain signficance, but in terms of mapping the shifting patterns of continuity of a myth they mean very little. What we can say, however, is that the image of the English gentleman-hero began to lose its power sometime in the 1970s, accelerating in the 1980s. It was a process that did not happen on anything like the same scale as before, and appears to be related to a crisis of English identity on the one hand, and a crisis of heterosexual models of masculinity on the other. In a multicultural society, white middle-class models of behaviour can expect to be challenged; in a society that has seen radical redrawings of class lines in the age of Thatcherism and a new emphasis on consumerism and market forces, the old idea of playing the game ceases to have much impact. The English hero is now lamented as a lost ideal; since the 1970s there has been a discourse of nostalgia that pervades the British press, which crosses party lines and which has been specially in evidence in the 1990s with the fiftieth anniversaries of such events as D-Day, VE day and VJ day and with a series of scandals involving the England cricket team.[13]

One explanation for the continuity of such figures as the English-school-captain-hero figure resides in the power of the image at the time of its invention and the way in which it has been consciously manipulated ever since to serve a specific social purpose. For this hero figure *was* England, he epitomized Englishness and English values, and so long as the myth of England as a homogeneous state, a great world power, the centre of the Commonwealth stayed intact, then the hero remained unchallenged.

In the late 1940s – early 1950s the image of the English hero was still intact. Let us take, as an example, the story of one of those great hero figures, Captain Scott of the Antarctic. The bare facts about him are familiar: Scott set out to be the first man to reach the South Pole, but died in the attempt, accompanied by four members of his team: Dr Edward Wilson, Captain Lawrence (Titus) Oates, Petty Officer Edgar Evans and Lieutenant Henry Robertson Bowers (Birdie).The expedition was a failure, because when Scott and his men reached the South Pole, they found that their Norwegian rivals, led by Roald Amundsen, had been there before them. They had no option but to set off back across the Polar icecap, but ran out of supplies before reaching their nearest base.

Despite the failure of the British expedition, Scott and his men have consistently been seen as heroic figures. Indeed, so powerful is the myth of their heroism, that memory of the failure tends often to be erased. Quiz games, such as Trivial Pursuit, ask who reached the Pole first, Scott or Amundsen, because a common supposition is that Scott actually beat Amundsen to their goal, dying heroically on the way back. In the hugely successful *South With Scott,* first published in 1921 and reprinted six times within the first four months of publication, Captain Edward Evans summarizes the tragedy in language that reinforces the mythical ideal:

> The details of Scott's final march to the Pole, and the heartrending account of his homeward journey, of Evans' sad death, of Oates's noble sacrifice, and of the martyr-like end of Wilson, Bowers, and Scott himself have been published throughout the length and breadth of the civilised world.[14]

The myth of the martyr-like end of the British heroes began from the first announcements of the news on 11 February 1913. *The Times* praised the team's idealism, noting that

> This is the temper of men who build empires, and while it lives among us we

shall be capable of maintaining an Empire that our fathers builded.[15]

As he lay dying in his tent, Scott had written a message to the public, which contained a powerful, emotional plea for the English heroic ideal. This was published together with the news of their deaths. 'For my own sake', he wrote,

> I do not regret this journey, which has shown that Englishmen can endure hardships, help one another, and meet death with as great a fortitude as ever in the past.

He went on, using language that reflects the stiff-upper-lipped sporting heroism of the English gentleman, to declare that they had all taken risks knowingly, and

> things have come out againgst us, and therefore we have no cause for complaint, but bow to the will of Providence, determined still to do our best to the last. Had we lived, I should have had a tale to tell of the hardihood, endurance, and courage of my companions which would have stirred the heart of every Englishman.

Scott's message was reinforced later in the same year, 1913, when an edition of his journals, giving his account of the doomed expedition was published.[16] Then, when the First World War exploded on Europe in 1914, the myth of Englishmen dying uncomplainingly in appalling conditions was adapted to serve the war effort. 'We have so many heroes among us now, so many Scotts', wrote Agnes Egerton Castle in 1916, in a piece that reflected upon the 'splendour' arising from the bloody fields of Flanders and Gallipoli.[17] The story of Scott, the hero, had come at exactly the right time, and the mythologizing process that had begun before the war started, accelerated over the next few years.

The Scott myth stayed more or less intact for decades. The film version of 1949, starring John Mills as Scott illustrates how little the idealised portrait had altered. Scott is represented as a noble figure, a compassionate leader of men, speaking perfect officer-English, determinedly cheerful despite all the odds, rallying his desperate companions and dreaming, longingly, of his wife. As death approaches, the image of Scott and his wife walking together across an English beach momentarily cancels out the howling of the wind and the suffocating horror of the tent. In this version, women are helpmeets for heroes, and are rewarded with a love that transcends even death.

But the version of the Scott story told in Central TV's six-part series, *The Last Place on Earth* in 1985 was strikingly different. In this production, with a screenplay by the playwright Trevor Griffiths, based on Roland Huntford's book, *Scott and Amundsen*, and starring Martin Shaw as Scott, the idealism disappeared, to be replaced with a close, often cruel examination of the motivation of both Scott and his rival,

Amundsen.[18] Huntford's biography, which first appeared in 1979, was a no-holds-barred account not only of the two Polar expeditions, but also of the personalities of Scott and his Norwegian rival. Scott emerges from Huntford's book as a driven man, not particularly competent or well-organized, whose wrong-headedness led to the loss of his men and to his own death. But Huntford also shows the extent to which Scott was writing himself into a myth that would grant him posthumous fame during the expedition, carefully wording his reports and seeking constantly to offer an image of his own greatness and of his companions' final heroism. Huntford noted that one of Scott's last letters was to his friend, Sir James Barrie, better known as J.M.Barrie, creator of Peter Pan, in which he wrote proudly that they were showing 'that Englishmen can still die with a bold spirit, fighting it out to the end'. After his death, Scott's widow Kathleen asked Barrie to create an official reconstruction of the last hours in the tent, to ensure that there could be no doubts about Scott having been the last man to die. There had been suggestions that Wilson had outlived Scott briefly. Barrie's response, in a letter to Kathleen Scott was to create a stage picture with Wilson and Bowers dying first, and Scott awaiting death with his head flung back and his shirt unbuttoned. Barrie insisted on the veracity of his version, claiming that 'we know this because it was thus that the three were found'.[19] Huntford remarks in passing that Barrie was, of course, a practised playwright, well able to manipulate an audience. Kathleen Scott also had a vested interest in propagating the myth of her husband's heroism; Huntford reveals that 'by a melodramatic improbability' she had been having an affaire with Nansen, the other great Norwegian explorer. His portrait of the small-minded, ambitious Scott and his domineering unfaithful wife hardly accord with the idyllic couple in the John Mills version. Huntford's biography struck at the heart of a legend.

In an introductory interview to the published version of his screenplays, entitled *Judgement Over the Dead*, Trevor Griffiths discusses his own responses to the Scott story, the ambiguous feelings he had when first approached to dramatize Huntford's *lese-majeste* biography for television, and his initial refusal of the commission:

> I was very suspicious of those parts of my own response which I call Boy's Own, as it were. There was something vaguely ... that felt slightly comic strip or boy's comic. And I wasn't sure that I could find a politics within this piece that could be inserted into a contemporary discourse and the present struggle. So at first I refused the offer of the series.[20]

The solution to the problem came unexpectedly. Just as the advent of the First World War spurred the Scott myth on to become an iconic legend of English heroism, so Margaret Thatcher's decision to go to war in the Falklands in 1982 gave Griffiths the link he had been searching for. The resurgence of a jingoistic patriotism at that time, with its antiquated discourses of Englishness, sacrifice for one's country, imperial heritage and the importance of dying nobly could be linked to the Scott story directly, for it embodied the same values. Griffiths' last episode was entitled 'Rejoice!' a reference to the statement by Maragaret Thatcher when she heard of the sinking of the Argentine ship, *The Belgrano,* which then appeared as a headline in *The Sun.* Griffiths made the connection between war and patriotism that had led so many men to their deaths in the cause of the British Empire, in two world wars and now in contemporary Britain. His argument was a complex one: on the one hand, from his political perspective he presented that discourse as a continuing element in Conservative party thinking. On the other hand, by recognizing his own response to the myth, he also recognized the shaping power of that myth on generations of schoolchildren. Griffiths, as much as Margaret Thatcher, had been shaped by stories of English heroic endeavour. The difference between them lay in being able to distinguish a consciously constructed fantasy from reality.

One episode suffices to demonstrate the vast difference of perception from the post-World War II period to the post-Falklands period: the representation of the death of Captain Oates. This particular episode was presented by Scott as an example of supreme self-sacrifice. Oates, realizing that his limbs were so badly frostbitten that he had no chance of survival and would have slowed up his companions in their trek back to base, sacrificed himself by crawling out into the Antarctic winds. Wilson wrote a consolatory letter to Oates' mother, telling her how her son had died like a soldier. Scott, in his diary, recorded that Oates said simply 'I am just going outside and may be some time' as he staggered out to his death. He noted that Oates took pride in thinking his regiment would be pleased with his bravery, and added that although the others knew that he was going to his death, 'We knew it was the act of a brave man and an English gentleman'.[21]

The 1949 film preserves these words and this version of events. There is minimal dialogue, Oates wakes to see the tent flapping over him and despite the resolutely cheerful behaviour of his companions, crosses the tent and walks out into the snow. As he staggers into the howling blizzard, the music swells and we gradually lose sight of him. The camera focuses on the tearfilled eyes of Captain Scott.

Huntford argues that Scott presented Oates' death in this way to the world because he needed an alibi:

> A subordinate driven to the extremity of suffering would be damaging in the extreme, so Oates simply *had* to have a story-book ending. In any case, Scott, who always went by appearances, may well have interpreted Oates' action as the correct gesture.[22]

Griffiths seized upon the ambiguity in Huntford's interpretation of Scott's account. In his screenplay, Oates does not die well, he dies desperately. In the television version, the Polar explorers are shown with their hideously damaged bodies, disintegrating before our eyes, unlike the prettified film version showing frostbite and gangrene that is obviously make-up. In a sequence that mirrors the film version, and is clearly derived from it, the jovial cheerfulness of English gentlemen of the 1940s is replaced by a mocking sequence that opens with Wilson bending over Oates with a mirror to see if he is still breathing. When Oates crawls out of the tent he drags himself across the ground, and the camera shows us Birdie, the working-class member of the group mouthing a plea, with Martin Shaw's Scott stony faced and seemingly almost drugged, certainly not a man in control. As Oates crawls out, he responds to Birdie with one remark: 'Call of nature, Birdie'.

In this single sentence we can see the change of emphasis that has taken place in the myth of heroic Englishness. The famous heroic statement that Oates is supposed to have made, the stoical comment that Scott claims were the last words he uttered has been replaced. And the sentence Griffiths uses instead refers not to the accepted version of Oates' death but to the mythologizing process itself, for generations of schoolboys and boy scouts on camping trips have quoted Oates' words when going out of a tent to relieve themselves. The last words credited to Oates by Scott entered the psyche of several generations, and this is what Griffiths means when he refers to the comic book response within himself that the Scott myth occasioned. His Oates makes an in-joke for all those who have been brought up on the official version of the myth. In his adaptation of Huntford's book, Griffiths shows us the myth-making process in operation; he exposes the conscious construction of the myth even in extremis. These changes in representation of the Scott myth reflect the huge shift of perspective that has taken place in a relatively short time, compared to the period during which the myth remained intact. What has happened is that now it is being perceived as a fiction, an impossible image of masculinity that was bound up with the kind of patriotic ideals that have no place in a post-imperial world. The stoical English hero originated in educational policy in the C19th and served a specific purpose in an age of imperial expansion. It provided a powerful model, both of masculinity and Englishness. It had a formative influence on several generations, and the last of those generations is the one that holds power today and is determining the educational policy of the future.

Today we question that myth because we can see the myth-making as a consciously political act, just as we can see the hegemony of England and Englishness as political. The English gentleman hero was meant to personify order, coherence and British homogeneity. Today, that homogeneity is exposed as illusory, the history of British imperialism is being rewritten, the desirability of a model of heterosexual masculinity has been called into question. The English hero lies like a fallen Colossus, destroyed by forces from within and from without. The end of Empire, the changes to the political map, all the factors that have brought Britain to its present state of economic decline, the troubled relationship with Europe and the USA – these are some of the external forces wearing away at the stonework.

Internally, the repression of emotion, the deliberate suppression of feeling, the compartmentalizing of sexuality, the deliberate exclusion of the personal may have worked as fictional devices but failed utterly as life strategies. What we can see now is the terrible price paid by individuals who accepted the myth at face value and subordinated their own emotional lives to it.

Rider Haggard's *Allan Quartermain* is dedicated to his son, who in 1887 was 6 years old. The novel begins oddly, with Quartermain's sadness at the death of his own son, and ends with the birth of Sir Henry's son. Rider Haggard was only 31 when he wrote the novel, with the protagonist an old, tragic man, a curious alter-ego for a dynamic young novelist to chose. In 1891, only four years after the novel had first appeared, Haggard's own son died, probably of meningitis. Haggard dealt with this personal tragedy by refusing ever to allow his son's name to be mentioned in his presence. The intense grief he felt was ruthlessly suppressed, though during the First World War when many of his nephews and friends' sons were killed, including Kipling's only son, Haggard's diaries reveal a man tormented by unending personal pain that he could not allow himself to show in public or even to his own family. One shocking passage in his diary records the news he managed to obtain of how Kipling's son, reported missing in action, had died:

> Bowe says ... he saw an officer, who *he could swear* was Mr Kipling ... trying to fasten a field dressing round his mouth which was badly shattered by a piece of shell. Bowe would have helped him but for the fact that the officer was crying with the pain of the wound and he did not want to humiliate him by offering assistance. I shall not send this on to R.K.(Rudyard Kipling); it is too painful but, I fear, true.[23]

Haggard never saw the connection between the heroic myth, the English class system and the damage to the individual of repressing feeling, nor did he ever understand his own role in helping to shape that myth. Such was the ethic of the imperial hero. Constructed on a fault line, the hero, like the Empire was the instrument of and embodiment of repression. Today, looking back, we can see that English identity always was in crisis because it was artificially constructed on a false premise of homogeneity that erased ethnic, national, cultural and regional differences. Likewise, its symbolic hero was also a fictional creation. What we can marvel at is how long the myth endured, for how many decades the figure of the perfect Englishman of boys' adventure stories remained in the English imagination, that figure described so succinctly by A.A. Gill in a newspaper article 1993 about England, cricket, nostalgia and the dream:

> The England team of our imaginations, of our dreams, represents the whole of England from the top to the bottom ... The England team should be the personification of the nation, in white, playing in hierarchical harmony, with three leopards on their chests, not a brewery, showing Johnny Foreigner that it takes as much skill and greater reserves of phlegm ... to lose gracefully than to draw at all costs ... And the captain must be a young man from the traditional ruling class of our imagination. He should look like a captain, handsome but not beautiful. He should be intelligent but not brilliant ... He doesn't have to be any good, he can field at third man and go in at No.11. But he will be a chap we can admire. A chap who speaks softly, laughs with an easy grace in the face of a follow-on, is swift to offer a hand of congratulation, a man who walks without waiting for the finger. And he'll be a man with a floppy fringe and a smooth jaw.[24]

NOTES

1. James Keating, 'Dashing to the Flag', Obituary for James Hunt, The *Guardian*, 16 June 1993, p.7.
2. Anthony Easthope, unpublished lecture, University of Warwick, December 1993.
3. Stuart Hall, 'The Local and the Global: Globalization and Ethnicity', in *Culture, Globalization and the World-System,* ed., Anthony D. King (London: Macmillan, 1991), pp.19-41.
4. See Richard Holt, *Sport and the British* (Oxford: Oxford University Press, 1990), p. 205.
5. Vitai Lampada', in *The Collected Works of Henry Newbolt* (London: Thomas Nelson, 1931), p.131.
6. Maurice Baring, 'In Memoriam A.H.', *Poems of Today* (London: Sidgwick and Jackson, 1927), pp. 195-202.
7. H. Rider Haggard, *She* (New York: Dover, 1951), p. 118.
8. H. Rider Haggard, Dedication to John Rider Haggard, *Allan Quartermain,* (London: Longmans, Green and Co., 1887).
9. Ibid., p. 8.
10. Ibid., p. 10.
11. Joseph Bristow, *Empire Boys. Adventures in a Man's World* (London: Harper Collins, 1991).
12. Graham Dawson, *Soldier Heroes: British Adventure, Empire and the Imagining of Masculinities* (London: Routledge, 1994), p. 2.
13. Particularly interesting in this respect is (i) the case of the England captain, Michael Atherton, admitting to having dirt in his pocket which effectively meant he had tampered with the ball during a game in the summer of 1994 and (ii) the case of an article which appeared in *Wisden Cricket Monthly* in summer 1995 which suggested that 'negro' players lacked the proper patriotic commitment to play for England.

14. Captain E.R.G.R. Evans, *South with Scott* (London and Glasgow: Collins, 1926), p. 227.

15. *The Times*, 11 February, 1913.

16. See *Scott's Last Expedition being the journals of Captain R.F. Scott, R.N.C.V.O.* arranged by Leonard Huxley (London: Smith, Elder and Co., 1913).

17. Agnes Egerton Castle, 'The Precursor', *Treasury*, January 1916.

18. Huntford's book was originally entitled *Scott and Amundsen* when it appeared in 1979 published by Hodder and Stoughton. It was reissued in 1985 as *The Last Place on Earth* (London: Guild Publishing). This change of title was linked to the title of the Central TV series. However, when Trevor Griffiths' screenplay of the TV series came out, the title had changed again to *Judgement Over the Dead* (London: Verso, 1986).

19. Sir J.M. Barrie, letter to Kathleen Scott, 10 September 1913, quoted in Huntford, op.cit., p. 564.

20. 'Truth or Otherwise', Introduction to Trevor Griffiths, *Judgement Over the Dead*.

21. See Huntford, op. cit., p. 540.

22. Ibid p. 541.

23. See D.S. Higgins, ed., 'Entry for 28 December 1915', *The Private Diaries of Sir Henry Rider Haggard* (London: Cassell, 1980).

24. *The Sunday Times*, 31 July 1994, p. 12.

PETER HUNT

What Would Daddy Have Done? Overt and Covert Constructions of Masculinity in Twentieth Century Children's Literature

An axiom: children's books are different from adults' books; they do different things, in different ways, to a different audience. And yet, until recently, the theory and criticism of children's books has treated them as if they were the same. The reasons for this are obvious: in a literary/cultural matrix which is structured like the traditional family/empire, males are powerful, women dominated, and children both invisible and manipulated;[1] consequently, children's literature criticism has behaved as if it were the dominant WASP male criticism. It has, in theory, aspired to the universal; in practice, it has courted universities, performed at MLA, produced journals published by major universities (Yale, Johns Hopkins). It has, in short, had to adopt strategies to circumvent the imperialist hegemony of white male criticism. The original summary for this paper reflected this:

> The most potent cultural codifications may well not be the most overt. Children's literature, in the area of gender, is both very potent as a societal influence and very revealing as to the nature of the society.
> On the one hand it tends to show society as it wishes to be and to be seen; in retrospect, it often shows a less acceptable face – time (or a new reading) shows that society's subconscious through its children's books. Although often radical in form and apparently subversive, twentieth century children's literature has also been deeply conservative; in particular, its long 'shelf-life', and its transmission through education systems and families (as much as through the general culture) preserves and passes on cultural assumptions that are, on the surface, obsolete.

On reflection, I felt that this was not true to the way in which children's literature criticism is developing: the proposition simply could not be put in those terms. Rather than using 'macro' criticism, it is turning towards 'micro' criticism – predicated on the principle that what *matters* is one reading by one reader at one time: that this has always been all we have, but that this simple, obvious fact has been obscured (for educators at almost all levels) by the necessities of academic survival. (There is brilliant support for this view in John Harwood's *Eliot to Derrida: The Poverty of Interpretation* [2]).

I have recently been to conferences of children's literature 'practitioners', who are constantly in touch with readers, constantly confronting the problem of meaning made in other people's heads. They find much of deconstruction and reader response/reception theory blindingly obvious, and 'interpretation' – as commonly practised – rather curious. For if we concede, as we must, a plurality of meanings controlled as much by the skills and knowledge of the reader as of the text, we cannot prioritise (as we do, incessantly) the reading of one person – that is, the critic or the historian (or, occasionally, the teacher).

Thus this paper seemed to me to have an untenable title, as it appeared to be predicated on the premise of a meaning inscribed in, inherent in the text, rather than an infinitely fluid set of meanings being constructed in partnership with readers; and it implied just such a dominant, more 'correct' reading, by the critic. The question forced upon one is: what is interesting about children's literature and gender? Is it what we – as a specialist group – read in the texts; or what, say, a child in 1906 read in Kipling's *Puck of Pook's Hill*, or what a child in 1995 reads in *Puck*? (Bearing in mind that our definition of a child and childhood has changed generally and radically in those eighty-nine years – and, indeed, changes from child to child, day to day, house to house).

In short, the original – conventional – idea of this paper had to be revised in the light of the fact that children's literature criticism has learned the error of other people's ways.

And so I would like this to be a transitional paper, three papers in one, in which I would like to move from, as it were, generalist criticism to *childist* criticism[3] in the form of three readings of the title: a conventional reading; a revisionist reading; and, thirdly, a radical reading, a cline, from the many to the one.

The conventional reading would have to be based on Jeffrey Richards's excellent *Imperialism and Juvenile Literature.* Richards summarises the progress of imperialism, and its relation to gender, as the empire changed in the nineteenth and twentieth centuries:

> evangelism [and] the commercial and cultural imperialism [of the mid-century] ... gave way in the last decades of the nineteenth century ... to aggressive militarism ... as the evangelical impulse itself became secularised and fed into full-blown imperialism, which became in many ways a new religion blended of the Protestant work-ethic and the public school code. But in the inter-war years the empire changed again [and was] seen as a bulwark of peace ... What remains constant is the concept of manliness.[4]

Richards suggests, and I see no reason to disagree with him, that the older definition of masculinity – courage and endurance *plus* brutality –

was replaced with 'muscular Christianity' and the concept of the chivalric gentleman. The imperial idea was, in short, based on codes of 'proper' behaviour (as well as an innate sense of superiority). It was inculcated in the public schools, and (although this seems to be at least symbiotic) into public school fiction.

> It was read at every level of society and provided the dominant image of manliness. There has always been an alternative view of manliness, based on how much you can drink and how tough you are. It is racist, sexist, chauvinist, thuggish and hedonistic, but from the 1830s to the 1960s it remained a submerged and dissident view. In the 1960s it emerged to challenge and eventually eclipse the previously dominant model of masculinity – gentlemanliness. But by then the Empire had largely ceased to exist and the genres of imperial adventure and public school fiction which had sustained and justified it had undergone a similar eclipse.[5]

That seems to me to be substantially sound; through the lens of children's literature, it appears that as the Empire contracted, so the constructions of masculinity that it involved contracted with it. The idea of chivalry-plus-endurance was gradually eroded: the elements of machismo began to dominate.

However, this broad picture can obviously be refined.

Firstly, there is clearly a distinction to be made between mainstream and popular writing. Popular literature – the books and comics that replaced the 'penny dreadfuls' and not-so-dreadfuls, and which were read by the masses – sustained older, imperialist-masculine attitudes. Geoffrey Trease, for example, noted that – 'A new story in 1920 or 1930 tended to be a fossil in which one could trace the essential characteristics of one written in 1880 or 1890'.[6] George Orwell (*Horizon*, March 1940) famously attacked boys' fiction for 'being sodden in the worst illusions of 1910'.

Fossilised illusions they may have been, but they were potent nonetheless. They defined gender not only for children, but for adults: rather, they defined gender for children *through backward-looking adults*. And, of course, these books and magazines survive: thus *Biggles Defies the Swastika* is still in print and on tape, and *War Picture Library* and its siblings are still published in great numbers. (Of course, there could be a good deal of debate as to who reads these texts).

Secondly, there has not been a simple replacement of imperialist-masculine ideas with thuggery. The chivalric is preserved – and not necessarily with an increase in the 'macho' – in the 'Star Wars' series (which are themselves predicated on imperialism) and the 'Sword and Sorcery' books (which are predicated on romantic/Arthurian ideas). The thuggery may now dominate, of course – one thinks of Judge Dredd – and yet the 'newer' construction of the caring, artistic, sensitive male has established a presence, as in *Watership Down*, Disney's *Beauty and the Beast* or Dodie Smith's *The One Hundred and One Dalmatians* –

and even *Star Wars*.

Equally, thirdly, the class divisions are not quite straightforward. Jeffrey Richards cites the public-school-educated, middle-class Fred Inglis and the working-class Bill Naughton and Robert Roberts as responding to the same imperialistic male images.[7] This is precisely as one might expect: the macho male is admired at both ends of the class/political spectrum, where power is an issue: the 'new man' subsists in the middle-class middle – and his model is found in the middle-class, mainstream children's book.

The situation is further complicated by the dominance (certainly since the 1950s) of that very mainstream, by women as writers, publishers, educators, and parents, with whatever that implies – and what it generally seems to imply is balance, and the validation of a particular kind of masculinity.

Finally, children's books have always involved a certain (large) element of social engineering, and so 'political correctness' has accelerated the change from imperialistic concepts of the male to, as it were, female concepts of the male.

Thus the conventional reading: that imperialistic constructions of gender have survived in mainstream children's literature until very recently – and still survive in popular literature. One might call in evidence important and characteristic twentieth-century writers: Kipling, Ransome, Tolkien, C. S. Lewis, Blyton, W. E. Johns. In them, the masculine inscribed by imperialism seems to be sustained.

Let us begin with Kipling, and I would like to concentrate on what I think is his masterpiece, *Puck of Pook's Hill* (1906), a book which in many ways seems to set the tone for the century.

The empire – both in decline and in danger of decline – is his theme, and his heroes – Sir Richard and Sir Hugh of the new England, and Parnesius and Pertinax of the Roman Empire – exemplify the virtues of friendship, loyalty, honesty and chivalry (together with keeping your wits and your sword sharp). In fact, the whole might be summed up by the poem 'If-' (from the sequel to *Puck*, *Rewards and Fairies*) with its closing line: '... you'll be a man, my son'.

And that is, of course, a line that nearly crops up in Arthur Ransome's masterpiece, *We Didn't Mean to Go To Sea* (1937), in which the fourteen-year-old John Walker sails a yacht, against the odds, across the North Sea. Here, John is surrogate head of the family, his elder sister is 'mate' and cook, his younger sister a fairly ineffectual (in maritime terms) mystic – and his younger brother an aspiring ship's engineer. John sails always with his father's advice at the back of his mind: 'What was it Daddy had said? "Never be ashamed to reef in the dark"'. When they arrive in Holland, they meet their father (in a rather more subtle and effective encounter than it sounds in summary); Ted Walker is a Commander in the Royal Navy, on his way back from the outposts of Empire, and he places hands on John's shoulders and says, 'You'll be a seaman yet, my son'.[8]

(Throughout Ransome's books there is reference to a literary tradition of the nineteenth century – Richard Jefferies's *Bevis*, itself part of the imperial tradition by word and deed, is one of their antecedents). [9]

Ransome structures his families with men in control (even the first expedition onto the lake in *Swallows and Amazons* (1930) cannot be authorised by Mother alone), and with a manifest destiny to go into the Navy, they behave according to the 'code' and maintain England and Empire.

Even the post-second world war retreat into secondary-world fantasy produced work with much the same old message. In Middle Earth, Tolkien's kings and knights defend their empires by chivalry and mutual support, and a fair amount of macho muscle and (literally) flag-waving.

In popular literature, it is obvious that W. E. Johns's 'Biggles' knows his place in the world of foreigners (on top), that Enid Blyton constantly privileges the male (and not the 'sensitive' male) and the middle-class, and that C. S. Lewis is fighting the wars of England once again in Narnia, where the girls may cry, but not onto their bowstrings.

This, then, is children's literature, lagging, as always, behind adult literature, purveying a masculine image which is apparently outdated, but which it in fact helps to perpetuate.

My second reading might be called 'revisionist'.

Cultural maps always require re-drawing and re-reading, and while it is undoubtedly true that people like Capt. Brereton and Percy F. Westerman continued the gung-ho approach to adventure stories through the 1920s and 1930s (with what now seems appalling taste), in the influential mainstream of children's literature there are some distinctively different sub-texts to be read.

Here it seems that, after the first world war, what we are seeing is a requiem. Mark Girouard, talking of the horrors of the trenches of the first war, in *The Return to Camelot: Chivalry and the English Gentleman*, observes that the middle classes set out to war with chivalric ideals:

> There most of them died; and there chivalry died with them. Or at least it received its death-wound. For it is in fact easy enough to find chivalry at work in the years after the war. In fiction, especially, bands of brothers abounded, chivalrously protecting the weak and doing down villains, under the leadership of Bulldog Drummond, Major-General Hannay, Group Captain Bigglesworth and others. Bertie Wooster continued being doggedly and disastrously chivalrous into the 1960s ... [But] as a dominant code of conduct it never recovered from the great war ... because [the war] helped to produce a world in which the necessary conditions for chivalry were increasingly absent ... Chivalry, along with patriotism, playing the game, and similar concepts became not so much devalued as simply irrelevant.[10]

It is interesting that Girouard's examples are all books which have slid down the age range towards children's literature: in short, the use of the chivalric ideal in marginal or marginalised genres – fantasy, comedy, and, most obviously, in children's literature (itself often escapist and nostalgic for adults) – demonstrates that this side of masculinity was not in step with the times

Kipling, perhaps surprisingly, can be recruited in support of this: the hooligan-imperialist's reputation might be reconsidered.

Let us return to *Puck*. In that book, who are the role models, the really influential men – the men who set the standards, and who seem to be admired by the narrator? They are the Norman knight, de Aquila, the shrewd councillor who thinks 'for England', and Kadmiel, the Jew who does everything outside the law and makes the law of England. These men are not Empire builders. Kadmiel, having broken the power of the King, retires:

> 'And you? Did you see the signing of the Law at Runnymede?' said Puck, as Kadmiel laughed noiselessly.
> 'Nay. Who am I to meddle with things too high for me? I returned to Bury and lent money on the autumn crops. Why not?'.[11]

These men are individualists, new thinkers, outsiders. And the whole book is underpinned by the ageless Hobdens (who have been poachers and hedgers time out of mind), and the amoral, unjudgemental Puck. These figures all look inwards, towards stasis, towards craft and initiation – not out to conquest and Empire.

Even Pertinax and Parnesius, the subalterns on the Roman Wall, who are in direct line to Stalky, are essentially their own men; in their valuing of friendship over power, of integrity over imperialism, of home over empire, they are mavericks. (And Pertinax, in rejecting the ruthless imperialism of Maximus, pleases his father).[12] He is not even part of the imperial power:

> 'But you're a Roman yourself, aren't you?' said Una.
> 'Ye-es and no. I'm one of a good few thousands who have never seen Rome except in a picture'.[13]

Similarly, Sir Richard is a reluctant conqueror, who would not have been comfortable in a G.A. Henty novel, and his story is about reconciliation and home.

Kipling is celebrating the end of one kind of culture – one kind of masculinity – while celebrating another, that of the craftsman who does not wish to conquer or to fight, but to create and preserve – a point echoed in what is probably the century's single best children's book, Alan Garner's *The Stone Book*.

I would argue that *Puck* is essentially a requiem, an acknowledgement that the days of imperialism are gone, and with them certain aspects of gender. Dan, the boy at the centre, is not a Bevis – he is a new man, of home and craft: he understands the past only in terms of skill and loyalty – not Empire.

We can even reconsider that hymn to imperialism, 'If-': as Kipling (wryly) said,

> Among the verses ... was one set called 'If-', which escaped from the book, and for a while ran about the world. They were drawn from Jameson's character [Dr. L. S. Jameson of the 1895 raid] ... Schools, and places where they teach, took them for their suffering Young – which did me no good with the Young when I met them later. ('Why did you write that stuff? I've had to write it out twice as an impot').[14]

And Ransome? It is as well to remember that *Swallows and Amazons* was Ransome's twenty-ninth book, written after the author had been for several years at the centre of world politics in the Russian Revolution and later in China. I bring up this unfashionable biographical note because his children's books, despite some superficial imperialistic male features are in fact focused elsewhere.

Swallows and Amazons properly belongs with the group of retreatist, quietist post-first world war books like *Winnie-the-Pooh*, Dr. Dolittle, and the later Masefield: books written, often, by men in retreat from the horrors of war. In the 1920s and 1930s there is hardly a mention in 'mainstream' children's books of the upheavals in Europe and elsewhere.[15] Thus Ransome's books are a recreation of a childhood *that emphatically does not value imperialism*. His most famous books are all enclosed by the comfortable hills of the Lake District; and where the children venture out, they take with them the security of their ships, or, as in *Peter Duck*, their attitudes undercut the values of the imperialistic adventure story.

Further, Ransome had little time for class-superiority. For him there were 'no lower orders' in the Lake District – no need for domination: like Kipling's craftsmen, his sailors and fishermen are quietists, insiders: they share a freemasonry in which child, adult, male, and female, are all equal.[16] Thus his alter egos are the studious Dick, or the retired traveller, Uncle Jim; his role models are fishermen and writers and doctors: his imperialist ornithologist in *Great Northern?* is a villain, his military father figure very much off-stage. (The very existence of this character, biographically speaking, is due to Ransome's need to lay the ghost of a disapproving father.) [17]

In Tolkien's books, for all the large-screen heroics, who are the heroes? Bilbo is a home-loving, old-England man; Frodo is a mystic non-combatant. Around them, imperial empires rise and fall, sway and totter, and are forgotten: the constructions of masculinity which matter are, like Sam, essentially gentle and home-loving.

Literary history is not as neat as we might wish, and if we can't re-

read Blyton or Lewis in this way, then we might look to the second most successful children's writer of all time, whose heroes and heroines are all either victims or guizers: Roald Dahl. The most successful writers of the day, like Ann Fine, or Jan Mark, or Gillian Cross, valorise the female, the balanced – and a construction of masculinity very remote from post-imperialist thuggery (one might think of the actor husband in Ann Fine's *Madame Doubtfire*), while my discussions with secondary-school pupils suggest that the historical novel has virtually disappeared from sight.

Even Biggles needs rather more subtle handling than he has often received. It is as well to remember that in his first incarnation Biggles is a sensitive, war weary young veteran – 'slim, rather below average height, and delicate'[18] – and that he came from the pen of a man who had been a shot-down fighter pilot and a prisoner of war, and whose interest in the military was one of defence, not expansion. (His later decline is not relevant to this argument: as Margery Fisher observes: 'Biggles as the enemy of the Hun can be accepted in historical perspective: as the bloodthirsty, self-righteous opponent of thriller-villains, he deserves no critical charity').[19]

All of that argues, I think, that the majority of mainstream children's writers, at least from 1918, and arguably since 1900 (with Nesbit, Kipling and Grahame) decisively rejected imperialistic constructions of the male. The first world war may have been the first major influence: it produced a generation of writers, throughout the 1920s and 1930s, and beyond, who turned to childhood (and nostalgia) for security, and retreat. Under the guise of protecting (or creating) childhood, they were protecting themselves; in doing so, they created a concept of the children's book which constructed gender in a way which, at a profound level, rejected the constructions of the past. These constructions have persisted, ignoring the second world war, and producing a female dominance of the mainstream, middle-class children's book.

Thus the imperialist construction of the male in children's books may have covertly been rejected long before it was overtly rejected, and the books which have been validated by the critical establishment have tended to be those which show the male in retreat – to nostalgia, to security, to a world without women.

I hope that you have found that persuasive, but I fear that we must honestly doubt how far the text of history which you and I have so adultly decoded ever meant any of that to younger readers – or that it could mean any of that to any one child reader now. For in my third reading of the history, I would like to close the gap between the theoretical reader (or the self-confident reader) and the actual readers.

Thus if we generalise about the probable constructions of masculinity resulting from *actual* readings of children's (or any) books, then we might reasonably conclude that it is the covert rather than the overt which will have power. We can recognise and react to (and influence the response to) what is commonly agreed to be an 'incident' in a text: but the subconscious meaning must come more potently from the sub-texts – and those absorbed over a period. Equally, those sub-texts are increasingly not borne by books (and, I would suggest, have very rarely ever been borne predominantly by books).

Affect has to be seen in a vastly complex sociological-historical continuum, and, intractable though it may be, as academic readers we need to consider the virtues of 'micro' readings. Thus, for example, it could be argued that even popular literature has not had the affect that a general deduction might suggest. Did working-class readers of public school books believe them, or actually always see them as *other*? Were popular war comics read simultaneously as exciting heroics, and as recognised fantasy in a stoic, grittily realistic realisation of actuality? There is plenty of evidence to suggest, for example, that feminists or sociologists do not have to worry about adolescent girls being entrapped or influenced by 'romances': on the whole, even the least articulate can understand that fantasy is fantasy.

But, most fundamentally, what of the characteristics of the way in which children read? They are, by definition, developing readers, inclined to have a freer, if less wide-ranging associative reading strategy (or technique); and they are likely to react *against* both covert and overt adult constructions of gender (and, indeed, of reality). And thus I would argue that while we as analysts might suggest that there have been certain gender constructs throughout the period, we have to be infinitely careful about deducing anything from our image. For all the long 'shelf-life' of a children's book *as object*, that 'book' *as subject* must change; *Puck of Pook's Hill*, for example, is a different book to a generation deprived of, ignorant of, or, indeed, incredulous of imperial attitudes or gender constructions, and therefore will have quite a different potency *for each reader.*

And we have to place this in the context of the future. As a generation of children begin to 'surf the internet', their attitudes to text, to gender, to narrative, indeed, to intellectual structures generally will change. As a first step in understanding this, we shall have to take on board the fact that whereas John Walker, in 1930, may well have asked 'What Would Daddy Have Done?', the real answer for several generations of children and adults would now be: 'OK: so we'll do something else!'

NOTES

1. See Lissa Paul, 'Enigma Variations: What Feminist Theory Knows About Children's Literature', *Signal,* 54 (1987), pp. 186-201.
2. John Harwood, *Eliot to Derrida: The Poverty of Interpretation* (London: Macmillan, 1995).
3. Peter Hunt, *Criticism, Theory, and Children's Literature* (Oxford: Blackwell, 1991), pp. 189-291.
4. Jeffrey Richards, ed., *Imperialism and Juvenile Literature* (Manchester: Manchester University Press, 1989), pp. 5-6.
5. Richards, pp. 6, 7.
6. Quoted in Peter Hunt, *An Introduction to Children's Literature* (Oxford: Oxford University Press, 1994), p. 106.
7. Richards, pp. 8-9.
8. Arthur Ransome, *We Didn't Mean To Go To Sea* (London: Cape, 1937), pp. 170, 292.
9. Peter Hunt, '*Bevis* and the tradition of adventure', *The Henty Society Bulletin,* 21 (1982), pp. 7-11.
10. Mark Girouard, *The Return to Camelot: Chivalry and the English Gentleman* (New Haven: Yale University Press, 1981), p. 290.
11. Rudyard Kipling, *Puck of Pook's Hill,* ed., D. Mackenzie ([1906]; Oxford: Oxford University Press, 1993), pp. 70-71, 173.
12. *Puck,* p. 93.
13. *Puck,* p. 85.
14. *Puck,* p. 441.
15. Peter Hunt, ed., *Children's Literature: An Illustrated History* (Oxford: Oxford University Press, 1995), pp. 193-202.
16. Peter Hunt, *Approaching Arthur Ransome* (London: Cape, 1992), p. 20.
17. Hugh Brogan, *The Life of Arthur Ransome* (London: Cape, 1984), pp. 357-8.
18. Quoted in Margery Fisher, *The Bright Face of Danger* (London: Hodder and Stoughton, 1986), p. 365.
19. Fisher, p. 363.

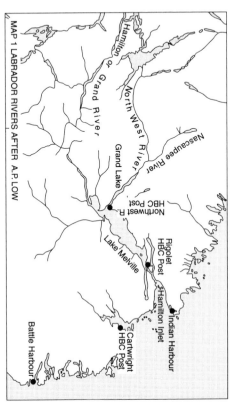

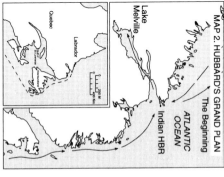

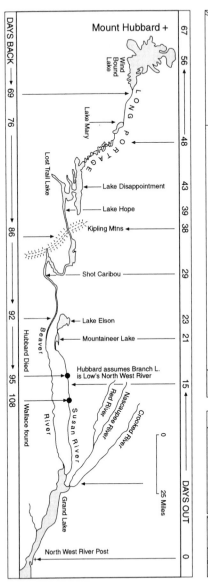

ALAN F. WILLIAMS

Explorers Wild: The Hubbards in Labrador

Brought up in Michigan, blooded as a newspaper reporter in Detroit and New York, and not long married to a Canadian (Mina), Leonidas Hubbard Jr. was a writer for the leisure magazine *Outing* when he conceived the idea of exploring unknown Labrador.

'How would you like to go to Labrador, Wallace?' was the question posed in November 1901 while Hubbard and his friend were tramping through the snow in the Shawangunk Mountains of southern New York State. 'Labrador!', Dillon Wallace is supposed to have exclaimed, 'Now where in the world is Labrador?'. Hubbard pencilled an outline: 'Think of it Wallace! A great unknown land right near home, as wild and primitive today as it has always been! I want to get into a really wild country and have some of the experience of the old fellows who explored and opened up the country where we are now'. A year later, Hubbard's plans were made: 'It will be a big thing, Wallace, it ought to make my reputation'.[1]

Well, it did, but not in the way he imagined. It would be his friend who would write a best-seller on their trip and become known as a significant author on the great outdoors. Dillon Wallace wrote *The Lure of the Labrador Wild* in 1905. It was not a tale of happy adventure but of endurance, love and tragedy. For the expedition compounded its mistakes and there were errors of judgement. Hubbard lost his life. Wallace was found within a day or so of the same fate and he owed his rescue to the durability of the third member of the party. This was George Elson, described (in the language of the times) as a 'half-breed' Cree Indian.

The main purpose here is to review the problems of the expedition and to explore the personal relationship between Hubbard and Wallace. Wallace's first book went to eleven editions by 1913. The promise made by Wallace to Hubbard to complete the work in Labrador led to a second work by Wallace: *The Long Labrador Trail* (1906).[2]

Hubbard and Wallace pitted their wits against a very hostile and unrelenting environment. With the coast of Labrador familiar to European fishermen since the early sixteenth century, little was known about the interior until the nineteenth. The indigenous peoples, long-

established but few in number and widely-scattered, consisted of both
Inuit ('Eskimos') and 'Indians'. Along with more of mixed blood (the
'Breeds'), many were trappers and hunters for the long-established
Hudson's Bay Company.[3] The HBC posts were scattered peripherally
between Ungava Bay, the Labrador coast and Lake Melville. Because of
the sea ice, Labrador could not be approached until late spring-early
summer. Expeditions could only be mounted in summer if the aim be
to study rocks and ecology. Any expedition overtaken by winter had to
exchange canoe and tent for komatik and snowshoes. Dog teams could
offer rapid travel, but they were only fully effective beyond the forest
zone in the north and along the barren, fjord-like eastern fringe.

In the southern interior, Labrador's own Niagara, the Grand Falls of
the Hamilton, were first seen by a European in 1839. The 1880's and
90's brought new knowledge through the work of the Canadian
geologist A.P. Low.[4] He explored the Hamilton and major tributaries as
well as the lakes from which they were fed. Importantly in the tale of
Hubbard, these waters included the vast sheet, over 90 miles long and
up to 25 miles wide, called Michikamau.

Michikamau (Big Water) featured as Hubbard's first goal. Its
treacherous and potentially deadly surface had been first crossed in the
winter of 1838 when frozen.[5] Hubbard would search for it in summer,
his motives being scientific (he would make known the geography of
the interior) and romantic (he would have a good tale to tell). By going
up the Naskaupi River rather than the more travelled Hamilton or
Grand, he was deliberately plunging into a region where no European
footsteps would be found to guide him.

While he was planning his expedition in New York, Hubbard's first
mistake was to rely upon Low's maps. Low's summary (Map 1)
showed the Hamilton system well, but it represented Grand Lake
merely as an elongated widening out of the large river called the
Northwest, which flowed from Lake Michikamau to Grosewater Bay
after being joined about 20 miles above Grand Lake by the Naskaupi.
Hubbard's plan was to prove these streams to their source. He would
reach the Northwest River Post early in summer, ascend the Naskaupi
and Northwest Rivers to Lake Michikamau and then, from the northern
end of the lake, cross the drainage divide to the north-flowing George
River. His overall plan was even more ambitious, for it involved
choosing alternative ways out, one, a winter journey of several
hundred miles by komatik to a harbour in southern Labrador, the other
by arduous snowshoe travel to the St. Lawrence.

Hubbard's second mistake was to rely upon the coastal boat
schedules of the Reid Newfoundland Company whose *Virginia Lake*
had left St. John's, Newfoundland, for Labrador and was days late in
returning.[6] Thereby, his expedition failed to reach Labrador at the
earliest opportunity. When the vessel's second spring trip brought

them to Labrador uncomfortably (there were many 'stationers' aboard, fishermen who came to Labrador each season) Hubbard could not wait for the Reid vessel to visit Nain before returning south to Rigolet, so he disembarked at Indian Harbour at the entrance of Hamilton Inlet, up which he must go.

The captain told him that Dr. Simpson's little steamer (the *Julia Sheridan* of Grenfell's Mission to Deep Sea Fishermen) would arrive the same afternoon to go to Rigolet and Northwest River Post with the mails. Simpson arrived the following day to say he would not go down the inlet until *after* the return of the *Virginia Lake* from the north. With every hour precious, Hubbard hired a young 'livyere'[7] to take his team and equipment 50 miles by small boat. A ragged sail and hard sculling took them only 35 miles before the *Virginia Lake* caught them up. A pantomime activity delayed them next. Simpson arrived, but as he had forgotten the mail for Northwest River that the *Lake* had left at Indian Harbour, he had to return at once: 'Dr. Simpson not being permitted by his principles to run his boat on Sunday ... we were told not to expect the *Julia Sheridan* back from Indian Harbour until Monday noon'.[8] At Rigolet, 'Skipper' Tom Blake told Hubbard that Grand Lake offered good conoeing to its upper end where the Naskaupi would offer more paddling for 18 or 20 miles to the shallow Red River. Blake's son Donald confirmed that the had sailed his boat as far as the Red and he had heard from the Indians that the Naskaupi came from Lake Michikamau.[9] This convinced the Americans that the Naskaupi was the river that A.P. Low had mapped as the Northwest.

The delays meant that a further 9 days were consumed in reaching the take-off point. The trio left the Northwest River Post on July 15 and, reaching the upper end of Grand Lake, they paddled straight to the obvious extremity where they found a wide stream which they took to be the Naskaupi. Indeed, why not? Low's map showed but one river flowing into Grand Lake. Hubbard was never to know that he spent the next several weeks ascending the wrong river:

'we were mistaken. We had passed the Naskaupi five miles below, where it empties into a deep bay extending northward from Grand Lake. At its mouth the Naskaupi is divided by an island ... so thickly covered with trees ... that when we crossed along in front of the bay no break ... was perceptible. Perhaps it will be said that we should have explored the bay'.[10]

They did not because Hubbard was already driven by the fear that he would be beaten by the short summer. The river they began to ascend was the Susan. They worked their way with painful slowness, each carrying loads of 100 lbs or more suspended by headbands. But great *bonhommie* was always expressed in front of a bright fire. '"Boys", said Hubbard, after we had made a good supper of trout ... "this pays for all the hard work"'. Aboard ship, Hubbard had heard the

Newfoundlanders address each other as 'B'y' and this stuck, even to the very end. Hubbard entertained his good companions with quotations from his favourite author, Kipling, while they puffed on their pipes. One verse seemed so appropriate to their position:

When first under fire, if you're wishful to duck,
Don't look or take heed of the man that is struck;
Be thankful you're living and trust to your luck,
And march to your front like a soldier [11]

Hubbard might be living out a *Boys' Own* adventure, but by riverbed, swamp and gully the going got tougher as they progressed up the Susan, which they thought was the Naskaupi. Days began at a cool 33 degrees, but rose to 92. Nothing could protect them from the flies and they had to sacrifice food and gear. Scouting with a broken compass, Wallace got lost, emerging from the bush 18 miles below their last camp. Hubbard became depressed at their slow progress and a pattern of feeding emerged which persisted even until there was little left. If the day went well (miles covered, partridge shot, trout caught) they celebrated success; if it went badly, they cheered themselves up from their depleting stores.

On day 13 out of Northwest River the rhythm and the solitude began to play upon the minds of the Americans, each admitting that they felt they were the only people left in the world. But what of the 'English-Indian' George Elson who was born at Rupert's House (the HBC Post on James Bay)? Wallace recognised that to him their feelings must seem 'highly artificial, if not affected'. They told themselves they would find caribou on the moss-covered barrens to the north. But a new problem emerged which must be reckoned Hubbard's third mistake: neither of the Americans had a change of footwear. Their mocassins began to break up when they had travelled only 80 miles. Wallace confided to his readers that already he dreaded the prospect of being required to retrace their steps.[12] But they came across a new branch where the rotten poles of a wigwam were quickly accepted by Hubbard as a sign that they were on the aboriginal route to Michikamau.

From 'Mountaineer Lake' they portaged to 'Lake Elson' and found a new riverbed which Wallace, at the end of it all, was to know as the Beaver. Their labours, and their diet, seem already to have disoriented them; both Hubbard and Elson got lost, like Wallace before. Again, however, trials by day are contrasted with the comfort of spruce boughs before a roaring fire with the Northern Lights sweeping in fantastic shapes across the sky. And from Hubbard, more of his favourite verses:

Now the Four-Way Lodge is opened, now the Hunting Winds are loose –
Now the Smokes of Spring go up to clear the brain;
Now the Young Men's hearts are troubled for the whisper of the Trues,
Now the Red Gods make their medicine again![13]

As the Red Gods called Hubbard, Wallace built on his romanticism to convey an image of the younger man as sensitive, steadfast and vulnerable. Kipling is recalled to shape their adventure even as we begin to detect Hubbard's difficulty in coming to terms with the harsh realities. When Wallace and Elson climb high to find the way, the Imperial imprint is to be left upon the face of Labrador:

> the mountains we estimated rose about 2,500 feet above the country ... ice and snow glistened in the sunshine. Barren almost to their base ... they presented a scene of desolate grandeur placed there to guard the land beyond. As I gazed upon them, some lines from Kipling's *Explorer* that I had often heard Hubbard repeat were brought forcibly to my mind:
>
> 'Something hidden. Go and find it. Go and look behind the Ranges – Something lost behind the Ranges. Lost and waiting for you. Go!
>
> Let us call these ranges the Kipling Mountains'[14]

This while they lived off trout – but not enough – until Hubbard and Wallace brought down a big stag (inexpertly: George was the best shot). Incredibly, it was the only caribou they were able to kill on the whole journey. Only George thought they might need to eat its skin, which he carried as part of his load from Day 30 to Day 42. Geese, trout and ptarmigan saw them over the Kipling Mountains, but they could find no way forward:

> 'Do you remember' asked Hubbard, 'the slogan of the old Pike's Peakers? – "'Pike's peak or Bust"'.
> 'Yes', said I, 'and very often they busted'.
> 'Well', said Hubbard, 'we'll adopt it and change it to our needs. "Michikamau or Bust" will be our watchword now'.[15]

Now the terrain became even rougher and they met a maze of water. On 'Lake Hope' they believed they could connect directly with Lake Michikamau. But because they ascended the wrong rivers they were many miles from the Big Water. They paddled into 'Lost Trail Lake', then into 'Lake Disappointment', where in three days they covered 60 fruitless miles. Hubbard now decided that since he was not, after all, on the Naskaupi-Northwest system which would lead to the Big Lake, they must portage north to find it and, if they could not, turn west where then it must be.

This was Day 44 (August 27). A careful reconstruction of the expedition's progress, rations carried, fishing and shooting and the terrain crossed, indicates that they had already passed the last point of safe return. Hubbard was ill, their footwear had failed, their trousers hung in strips, the venison was going, their flour almost gone. Winter would probably overtake them before they could descend the George River; there might be little more game. Wallace knew, too, that were

they to turn around, they did not have provisions to take them half
way to Northwest River Post. But none wanted to be first to admit
failure: Hubbard could not give up his dream, Wallace could not be
disloyal to the friend with whom he had shared so much and Elson
could only go whither they went.

That they still went on – 'Michikamau or bust!' – was madness, but at
the same time powerful confirmation of goodwill undimmed between
fast friends who had agreed to test their manliness together. Hubbard,
we are told, ached for the company of Mina as his body began to fail
him. The older man had by this time been a widower for three years.
As both men slowly starved, Hubbard told Wallace a private tale of his
marriage day, not shared before because it was so personal and because
it had happened 'before he and Wallace had shared camp together in
the great outdoors'. How far did this homosocial context provoke
homosexual tensions? In his book, Wallace underlined Hubbard's sense
of blood brother linkage between men who both saw nothing but
adventure in the search for Kipling's 'Something lost behind the
Ranges. Lost and waiting ...' There is no doubt that the unseen bonds
which united them were strong and genuine, reaching beyond the
grave. But Mina Hubbard took no pleasure either in the portrayal of her
husband in *The Lure of the Labrador Wild* or in the presentation of his
bonds with Wallace. The book was dedicated to 'L.H. Here, b'y, is the
issue of our plighted troth. Why I am the scribe and not you, God
knows: and you have His secret'. And when Wallace wrote his second
Labrador book he began it by quoting Hubbard:

> It's always the way, Wallace! When a fellow starts on the long trail, he's never
> willing to quit. It'll be the same with you if you go with me to Labrador. When
> you come home, you'll hear the voice of the wilderness calling you to return,
> and it will lure you back again.[16]

If these two were white Americans of the brotherhood of the
wilderness, city clubmen yearning for the camp fire and intoxicated
with the pure forest air laden with the scent of firs, what of George
Elson, the 'English-Indian' who knew only the lands of the Cree? He
was second choice, recruited at arm's length by the HBC agent at
Missanabie, Ontario. George had never seen a city before he entrained
for Hubbard's office in New York and he had never seen Labrador. He
owed nothing to the Americans other than his agreement to be
woodsman and cook. Yet they were all fully aware that in going on
they were taking a long chance. Earlier described as impetuous,
Hubbard was now described as 'nervously active' and haunted by the
spectre of an early winter. Their fate would be sealed if they met with
more delays; they would be too late for the caribou migration and,
therefore, too late for the Indians at their hunting. Every camp
conversation turned to food: restaurant meals in Manhattan, domestic

cook-ups at Congers, burnt cakes once thrown away. To Wallace (but not to George) Hubbard confessed to strong contrary thoughts which were testing his will. On the last of August he admitted he would be glad to get to Michikamau and leave: 'I'm afraid', he added slowly, 'I've been a little homesick today'. A few days later he was ashamed that he looked like a walking skeleton. But even the first snowfall would not deflect him because he felt that if he did not reach the caribou grounds he would not have enough material for a story.

We can believe that by now the balance of Hubbard's mind was disturbed. In 'marching to the front like a soldier' he was risking death for glory. Amazingly, Wallace thought the two could still hide the true extent of Hubbard's condition from George. Having portaged another 40 miles, on Day 56 they reached a great lake backed by a great grey mountain to which they paddled. The next day Hubbard and George succeeded in climbing 'Mount Hubbard' from which they gained their first and last sight of Michikamau.[17] Windsqualls then kept them on a little island with only berries to eat for four days. To Wallace (but not to Hubbard) George now told stories of Indians who had starved to death. If this was his way of influencing decisions, Wallace was only interested in trying to dissect the condition of a personality (as we might say) split by genes: 'Apparently two natures were at war within him. One – the Indian – was haunted by superstitious fears; the other – the white man – rejected these fears and invariably conquered them'.[18]

If George was perceived as a white man, Wallace was more sensitive to the changes wrought in Hubbard: 'he was only a young fellow, you know, with a gentle, affectionate nature that gripped him tight to the persons and objects he loved'. And still the gales howled through the trees. On September 16, for the first time Hubbard heard George's stories of Indians that starved. After contemplating the still lowering skies that hid the way to Michikamau, he turned to the camp fire: 'Boys, what do you say to turning back?'.[19] It was Day 64 from Northwest River, Day 88 from New York.

Hubbard's natural optimism persuaded him that good fishing and shooting would see them through. Not only that, but he repeated 'Plan B':

> If we kill some caribou I think we'd better turn to and build a log shack, cure the meat, make toboggans and snowshoes, wait for things to freeze up ... We can get some dogs at the post, and we'll be in good shape to push right on without delay to the St. Lawrence. It'll make a bully trip, and we'll have lots of grub.[20]

This was, of course, quite unreal. While the gales continued to tie them down, Hubbard extolled the virtues of his marriage; now he was bothered that he had given too much attention to glory. On Day 72 a goose provided giblets, entrails and broth; the next day it provided wings and feet, and the morning after they scrorched and ate the bones. Each saw his companions now as scarecrows with eyes deep in sockets. Wallace still maintained that Hubbard remained bright and stable; in his book. we might say, it would not serve him to report otherwise and only George Elson could tell differently. Over one camp fire, Hubbard was reconfirmed at the centre of their partnership:

> Thanksgiving, he said, must be our reunion day always ... We must never drift apart. We were brothers, comrades – more than brothers. We had endured the greatest hardships together, had fought our way through that awful country together, had starved together; and never had there been a misunderstanding, never a word of dissension.[21]

As Hubbard became weaker, we are told, his spirit grew brighter and the more he suffered. On Sunday September 27 he was studied closely yet secretly:

> As he sat there in the red glow ... I took note of his emaciated form and his features so haggard and drawn. I seemed for the first time to realise the condition to which the boy had been brought by his sufferings. And while I stood there, still unobserved, I heard him softly humming to himself:
> 'Rock of Ages, cleft for me,
> Let me hide myself in Thee'[22]

They recrossed the Kipling Mountains but were still 150 miles from Northwest River. They regained Camp Caribou and knew they must choose between the 'big river' (the Beaver) or abandon the canoe to follow the Susan on foot. Wallace and Elson favoured the 'big river' (which all thought must enter Goose Bay rather than Grand Lake; see Map) because by canoe they would move faster. Hubbard favoured the way they had come because they had left food behind (a little flour, powdered milk, lard) and knew where the trappers cabins were. George now told of his dream that the 'big river' led directly to Grand Lake and safety (another example of George giving his leader veiled advice?).

With Hubbard hopeful and the others fearful, they began to struggle down the Susan River. It was Hubbard's last big mistake. They were nourished by so little now they were beginning to feel indifference. The Bible replaced Kipling and Hubbard was completely worn out 'but withall a great hero, never complaining'. His condition was pitiable 'but he bears himself like the hero that he is ... How can we save him!'[23]

There could only be one way: for Wallace and Elson to reach the abandoned flour 25 miles downriver, for Wallace to return with some for Hubbard while Elson went on another 30 miles to reach Donald Blake's hunting *tilt*. Wallace tells that Hubbard requested him to write up the story of the trip and to place his diary in Mina's hands. Wallace and Elson wrote last notes. All embraced and Wallace turned to embrace again. It was Day 96, Sunday October 18.

Down the trail, Wallace and Elson ate raw partridge; the mouldy flour was found and divided, George to go on, Wallace to go back through the deep snow. By October 24 he thought he had gone too far. Smoke-blinded and starving, he made his fire within 200 yards of Hubbard's camp, although he was unaware of it. Near his end, he staggered on stockinged feet, suffered delusions, listened to his dead wife. Meanwhile George Elson took seven days to reach Grand Lake where he found a house newly-built by Donald Blake. Blake, his young brother Gilbert (Bert), Allen Goudie and Duncan McLean found Wallace by sniffing the remains of his night fire on the morning of October 30.[24] Hubbard had not left the tent; he died ten days before George Elson could raise the alarm.

There was no quick way out for Wallace, who turned down the last trip of the year by the *Virginia Lake* to bring out Hubbard's body. With Elson, he embarked on the *Aurora* (Capt. Abraham Kean) for St. John's, May 14 and arrived in Brooklyn on the *Sylvia* May 27. They carried the diaries from Hubbard's last tent, including Hubbard's last words (which Wallace cannot quote; they belong to Mina Hubbard). Wallace noted:

> Your hand was firm when you wrote, b'y speaking eloquently of that which most of all was you. 'It is a man's game', you said one day, in referring to our desperate struggle to reach those we loved. You played it to the limit, b'y, and it was a man's death[25]

This was Wallace's last confirmation of faith in his friend's code of masculinity as found in Kipling.

Hubbard yearned to become one of a select new group of explorer media heroes, whose adventures were eagerly awaited by a huge new American public.[26] But when his end was known, newspaper critics said he was fool-hardy and ill-prepared. Wallace would have his readers believe that Hubbard had consulted the best authorities (in the United States) and it was a bad year; the old men of the country (Labrador) had never known game to be scarcer. Hubbard was not just ambitious for success as a writer on the great outdoors, he was the most conscientious man Wallace ever knew. But even from Hubbard's tale as revealed by Wallace, we can see that he arrived late, would not be dissuaded by the best authorities in Labrador, did not employ a local trapper to take them into the Naskaupi, could not live off the land with rod and gun, did not know when to admit defeat, went too far and endangered all their lives. We can see that Hubbard seriously underestimated the unyielding nature of Labrador. He undertook to explore its bleak interior because he was aware that the American Empire was explored, filled out, settled. 'Manifest Destiny' had been achieved and Frederick Jackson Turner would tell of the closing of the American frontier. Hubbard sought the northern wilderness to relive the old colonial experience of his forebears, but was arrogant to reject the contemporary, and still colonial, voices of those who knew Labrador better.

Men who have shared great danger on the battlefield, upon the high seas or in captivity will so often experience deep and lasting feelings for their comrades. There is no doubt that Hubbard and Wallace shared very special feelings for each other which were heightened by their dependence in isolation. Wallace made no secret of their bonding. Echoing words given to Hubbard earlier, he wrote that 'Only men that have camped together in a lonely, uninhabited country can in any degree comprehend the bond of affection and love that drew Hubbard and me ever closer to each other as the Labrador Wild lured us on and on'. Yet, as O'Flaherty suggested, Hubbard's sentiment seems out of place in Labrador: 'There is nothing pretty or gentle or "nice" about this "frayed edge" of the North American continent. The land and ocean here have been through history intolerant of weakness and miscalculation ... Hubbard's adventure reminds us of this, and thus the haunting story of his encounter with the Labrador hinterland is a parable of enduring significance'.[27]

Can distance and hindsight give this parable another slant, if not a different ending? Hubbard was branded a hero by the magazine of the Alumni Association of his alma mater: 'the man who is born with the insatiable desire to do something, to see what other men have not seen ... belongs, however great his success or complete his failure, to that minority which has from the first kept the world moving on ...'[28] Sentiments of masculinity like this were not unusual in a period which saw so much unendurable privation experience in polar exploration. But we also have Hubbard Canonized. An 'unknown friend' wrote that 'To dare and die so divinely and leave such a record is to be transfixed on a mountain top, a master symbol to all men of cloud-robed human victory, angel-attended by reverence and peace ...', while another wrote that 'Mr. Hubbard ... failed, but God spelled "Success" of "Failure" ... The life given up in the wilds of Labrador was not in vain'.[29] If these comments seem mawkish today, they were conventional at the beginning of the century and attractive to those in such as Congers and Poughkeepsie who selected the Sunday School prizes. We may constantly redefine heroism, yet many will still believe there is no quicker way to become a hero than to expire as victory dawns (Wolfe at Quebec; Nelson at Trafalgar). Hubbard of Labrador died, like Scott of the Antarctic later, as failure dawned. It was clearly Wallace's aim to persuade his readers that this circumstance could uplift even while it destroyed.

At the last we must turn to Mina Hubbard who would take nothing offered by Wallace. Mina last saw her husband at Battle Harbour on July 5, 1903; in New York, his death was not confirmed until January

22, 1904. Her determination to redeem his reputation led to her own expedition to Labrador in 1905 with four young assistants, including Wallace's rescuer Bert Blake, and George Elson. She would not combine with Wallace, for whom she had developed the most virulent antipathy. At the same time Wallace launched an expedition to accomplish Hubbard's original plan. Both expeditions left Northwest River *on the same day* (June 27, 1905). Mina's party reached Michikamau August 2 and Ungava Bay August 27. With Wallace's group left behind, the press claimed that 'Mrs. Hubbard's party won the race'; but Wallace (with one companion) journeyed on through the winter by dog-sled journeys of a kind Hubbard would have approved.

Mina Hubbard's book, *A Woman's Way Through Unknown Labrador*,[30] included an account of the last days of her husband's ill-fated expedition by George Elson. Wallace's *The Long Labrador Trail* came to press nearly two years earlier. This made no reference to Mina or her parallel expedition or to George Elson; and Mina made no reference to Wallace. A fictionalized account focussed on the Hubbards, called *Great Heart*, written by James West Davidson and John Rugge in 1988, is to become an American-made, feature-length movie partly shot in Newfoundland and Labrador in 1996. After *Great Heart*, it is probable that while the memory of Hubbard still stands in one corner, it is the diminutive yet determined, 35-year old Canadian woman from Bewdley, Ontario, and the 'English-Indian', George Elson, who will occupy the others.

Real-life endings are seldom tidy. In 1913, with Bert Blake and a Connecticut Judge, Wallace reached the place where his friend had died in the 'wrong' valley. He cut a loving inscription into the boulder which had reflected Hubbard's last campfire and withdrew. Wallace wrote further books on Labrador, including stories for children. He died in 1939. Mina Hubbard moved to England in 1907 and, marrying into a wealthy family, her subsequent life included work with the Suffragettes. In 1956, when she was 86, Mina wandered into the path of a speeding train.

NOTES

1. Dillon Wallace, *The Lure of the Labrador Wild* (New York: Fleming H. Revell Co., 1905). The text used here is the Breakwater Books edition (St. John's, 1977).
2. Dillon Wallace, *The Long Labrador Trail* (London: Hodder and Stoughton, 1907).
3. Labrador history to the beginning of the present century was summarised in W.G.Gosling, *Labrador: Its Discovery, Exploration and Development* (London: Alston Rivers, 1910) and by Wilfred T. Grenfell et al., *Labrador: The Country and the People* (New York: Macmillan, 1910).
4. A.P. Low, Report on Explorations in the Labrador peninsula, *Canada*

Geological Survey Annual Report, Vol.8 (N.S.) (Ottawa: Govt. of Canada,1895). Low's northern career is summarised in Chapter VI 'Low and Labrador', in F.J. Alcock, *A Century in the History of the Geological Survey of Canada* (Ottawa: Dept. of Mines & Resources, Govt. of Canada,1948), pp. 55-59.

5. John McLean, *Notes of a Twenty-Five Years Service in the Hudson's Bay Territory* (London: Hudson's Bay Company, 1849). An HBC agent, McLean made a cross-country dash with Amerindians from Fort Chimo to Northwest River. It is not clear which way he took, but like Peary in the Arctic, his party ate their dogs to save themselves.

6. The vessel's timetable was at the mercy of sea conditions on the Labrador ice shelf. Ice dispersal differs considerably from year to year. An earlier modern survey of the problem is Pierre Biays, Le courant du Labrador et quelques-unes des consequences geographiques, *Cahiers de Geographie de Quebec,* 8 (Avril-Septembre 1960), pp. 237-301.

7. A *livyere* was a settler on the coast of Labrador as opposed to a migratory summer fisherman from Newfoundland, the *stationer,* who came each season by the coastal boat, and the *floater* who came as crew aboard a fishing vessel.

8. Wallace, *The Lure of the Labrador Wild,* p. 45.

9. Ibid., p. 47.

10. Ibid., p. 55.

11. Ibid., p. 63.

12. Ibid., p. 82.

13. Kipling: *The Feet of the Young Men;* Wallace, *The Lure,* p. 90.

14. Wallace, *The Lure,* p. 95.

15. Ibid., p. 105.

16. Dillon Wallace, *The Long Labrador Trail* (New York: Hodder and Stoughton, 1906), p. 11.

17. Wallace, *The Lure,* p. 126.

18. Ibid., p. 131.

19. Ibid., p. 138. The pages of *The Lure* leading to these words are included in Peter Neary and Patrick O'Flaherty eds., *By Great Waters: A Newfoundland and Labrador Anthology* (Toronto: Toronto University Press, 1974), pp. 123-132.

20. Wallace, *The Lure,* p. 140.

21. Ibid., p. 155.

22. Ibid., p. 158.

23. Ibid., p. 195.

24. Bert Blake told the tale to Elizabeth Goudie, who wrote *Woman of Labrador* (Toronto: Peter Martin Associates, 1973) (edited with an Introduction by David Zimmerly). Elizabeth was Bert's niece. She explains that the Goudies and Blakes intermarried. Bert married a McLean and they named their first daughter Mina Benson after Hubbard's wife. Bert met *all* the participants linked with the Hubbards in their Labrador expeditions; in great old age, he lived in Happy Valley, Labrador.

25. Wallace, *The Lure,* p. 238.

26. For this general context, see William H. Goetzmann, *New Land, New Men America and the Second Great Age of Discovery* (New York: Viking Penguin, 1986).

27. Patrick O'Flaherty, Introduction, Breakwater Edition, Wallace, *The Lure,* p. 16.

28. Wallace, *The Lure,* p. 273, quoting James A. LeRoy.

29. Ibid., Preface to the Sixth Edition, printed in Breakwater Edition, p. 281.

30. Mrs. Leonidas Hubbard, Junior *A Woman's Way Through Unknown Labrador: An Account of the Exploration of the Nascaupee and George Rivers* (New York: The McClure Co.; London: John Murray, 1908).

NICHOLAS J. CULL

America's Raj: Kipling, Masculinity and Empire

The posters for *Gunga Din* promised much: 'Thrills for a thousand movies, plundered for one mighty show'. That show was a valentine to the British Raj, in which three sergeants (engagingly played by Cary Grant, Victor McLaglen, and Douglas Fairbanks, Jr.) defeat marauding hoards of 'natives' with the aid of their 'Uncle Tom' water bearer, Gunga Din (Sam Jaffe)[Plate VII]. Audiences loved it. Its racism notwithstanding, even an astute viewer like Bertolt Brecht confessed: 'My heart was touched ... I felt like applauding and laughed in all the right places'.[1] Outwardly the film had little to do with the United States. Most of the cast were British-born and its screenplay claimed to be 'from the poem by Rudyard Kipling'.[2] Yet the film was neither British or faithful to Kipling, but solidly American: directed by George Stevens for RKO, with a screenplay by Oxford-educated Joel Sayre and Stevens's regular collaborator Fred Guiol.[3] The screenplay also displayed the handiwork of the masters of the wisecracking script, Charles MacArthur and Ben Hecht, and a few (uncredited) sombre touches from the first writer to work on the project: William Faulkner.[4]

That Americans could produce such a film raised few eyebrows at the time. *Gunga Din* stood at the end of a long-standing American interest in Kipling and the British Empire including numerous films with Imperial themes. However, the gap between what Kipling wrote and American readings of his work – exemplified in *Gunga Din* – is highly significant. It reveals much about that country's psychological needs as it struggled to define its role in the world during the first half of the twentieth century. Similarly, the later career of *Gunga Din* and the wider Empire film genre offers a commentary on the United States' own experience of Empire and its price.

Kipling in America

Kipling fascinated all levels of American society.[5] President Theodore Roosevelt maintained a long correspondence with him, and nicknamed his second son Kermit Roosevelt 'Kim' as a result.[6] The doomed American explorer Leonidas Hubbard, quoted great chunks of Kipling

Plate VII: In Hollywood's version of Kipling's India, the three inseparable Sergeants – Cutter, Ballantine and MacChesney (Cary Grant, Victor McLaglen and Douglas Fairbanks Jr.) – cheerfully defend the Raj with the aid of 'native' troops. Their loyal water-bearer Gunga Din (Sam Jaffe) looks on, positioned (in keeping with the film's implicit racial hierarchy) to the right of Cutter's boot. Gunga Din (RKO), British Film Institute Stills Collection, © 1939, reproduced by kind permission of Turner Entertainment Co., All Rights Reserved.

to his starving companions during their ill-fated expedition to Labrador, and named a range of mountains in his honour.[7] Boys with military ambitions, including the future generals Ridgway and Patton, found their home in his work; Patton later wrote his own, quite dreadful, poems in the style of Kipling.[8] With Kipling's poems regularly appearing in the American newspapers, the Irish-American satirist, Finley Peter Dunne pointed to an absurd Kipling cult and had his comic creation Mr. Dooley proclaim that 'Roodyard [sic] Kipling' wrote 'the finest pothry [sic] in the wurruld [sic]'.[9] But Kipling had caught the spirit of the age.

Kipling filled a niche in the American imagination of the 1890s as no indigenous writer could. His novels and poems seemed to offer a lively portrait of military and Imperial life at odds with the old American mistrust of standing armies, but in tune with the brazen rhetoric of men like Theodore Roosevelt. As the US embraced an empire of its own in the Pacific and Caribbean, Kipling was read as propaganda off-the-peg. Yet in their enthusiasm Americans neglected the element of warning in Kipling's work. The most obvious misreading was of Kipling's poem: *The White Man's Burden*. This bitter verse carried within it a clear statement of the futility of Empire in which 'the best ye breed' could expect only thankless suffering and the 'savage wars of peace'. Nevertheless the poem immediately became part of the American language, surfacing in numerous Imperial tracts.[10] The United States had to learn of 'savage wars of peace' the hard way – in the jungles of the Philippines and Central America.

Kipling's Empire in 1930s Hollywood

The massive trauma of the Great War forced a radical reassessment of American foreign policy. In its aftermath, as anti-war novels and films abounded, the US government turned its back on alliances and Kiplingesque military forays to right the wrongs of Asia.[11] Hollywood, however, felt differently. Throughout the 1930s the Empire prospered in film. The genre had much to offer. First of all the films took place far away and long ago, and provided a welcome escape from the depression. Moreover, they offered welcome reassurance at a time of renewed challenges to the old certainties of race, class and gender. The hegemony of the white American male was challenged as never before by the collapse of American industry and agriculture. The post-war years had brought new competitors in the job market – including Afro-American migrants from the South – and new challenges closer to home as women rejected their old position of vote-less subordination. In such a world it was no wonder that a genre of films in which the common white man consistently triumphed should prosper. It is, however, surprising that Hollywood was unable to meet these psychological needs with its traditional fare: the western.

Western films and novels had flourished in the boom-years of the 1920s. During the 1930s the genre went into relative decline. The big budgets drained away and westerns became the staple of 'B' movies and serials, surviving largely because such films were so cheap to make.[12] It is easy to see why. The agricultural depression sat uneasily along side narratives of triumph in the west. By translating the action to the British Empire, Hollywood was able to retain the same themes and to use the same locations in the California Sierras.[13] An Empire setting also enabled the studios to employ their roster of British stars and to tap the steady market for 'army pictures' without evoking unpleasant memories of the trenches. Finally, Hollywood needed to make a profit. With the additional cost of 'talkies', the studios found that they could only break even on the US release of a film. Profits required a lively export market. It soon became apparent that Europe had no objection to seeing its imperialism restaged by Americans.[14] Having found a formula that would sell internationally, Hollywood stuck to it.

The success of Henry Hathaway's *Lives of a Bengal Lancer* in 1934 unleashed a barrage of imitators.[15] Soon the setting of British India was familiar enough to be satirized by Laurel and Hardy in *Bonnie Scotland* (1935) and safe enough to be the basis for a Shirley Temple vehicle: *Wee Willie Winkie* (1937).[16] While only the latter was actually based on a Kipling story, Kipling's India was never far below the surface in these films. Kipling's death in 1936 leant further topicality and soon plans were afoot to remake *The Light That Failed, Captains Courageous* and, of Kipling's Indian works, *Kim* and two episodes from *The Jungle Book*.[17] At the time of his death Kipling himself had been working on treatments of his story 'Thy Servant a Dog' and *Soldiers Three*.[18] In this atmosphere it is hardly surprising that first MGM and then United Artists should consider an epic film based on Kipling's poem *Gunga Din*. RKO finished the job.[19]

The Movie

Gunga Din makes an immediate claim to its origins in Kipling. The film begins with a narrator reading the second half of the opening stanza of the poem – perhaps the best known of his *Barrack-Room Ballads* of 1892. In the finale of the film Kipling himself is portrayed writing his poem in response to events that he has witnessed. It is then read as a eulogy at Gunga Din's grave-side. The opening of the film also claims historical veracity, with titles reading: 'the portions of this picture dealing with the worship of the goddess Kali are based on historic fact' and credits acknowledging three British army technical advisers. Such credits are misleading. The notion of a Thug revival in the 1880s is fantasy and Kipling's poem provides little more than the character of

Din. The body of the film is a free-wheeling adventure very loosely based on the characters of Kipling's cycle of military short stories featuring the 'Soldiers Three': Privates Mulvaney, Ortheris and Learoyd.[20]

Little of the original 'Soldiers Three' survived into the final screenplay. They are promoted Sergeants and their names changed to Cutter, Ballantine and MacChesney. In the original they are wry antiheroic figures, ironic inversions of Dumas' *Three Musketeers*.[21] They represent both working class and regional foundations of the British Empire, and speak in thick Irish, Cockney and Yorkshire dialects.[22] In order to be comprehensible in an American screenplay, they speak an uneven Hollywood cockney. Their adventures are 'up-graded' and sanitised for the film. Rather than just weathering scrapes around the barracks, they now hold the fate of India in their hands as they battle to avert its re-conquest by the Thugs. Similarly the tragedy that pervades their lives is utterly absent. One does not see in RKO's India the 'madness, alcoholism, self-doubt, and suicide' that, as Zoreh Sullivan has written, 'haunt the characters' in Kipling's Indian short fiction. Victor McLaglen's MacChesney has none of the 'inextinguishable sorrow' that marked Kipling's own Private Mulvaney.[23]

The plot interweaves three stories. The first is the challenge to British India from a revival of the Thug murder cult. The second, is the desire of the loyal water-bearer Gunga Din to become a fully fledged member of the Regiment. The third is the struggle to preserve the team of three, in the face of Ballantine's decision to leave the army to get married. These three stories overlap playfully. It becomes clear that MacChesney and Cutter find Ballantine's marriage as distasteful as being prisoners of the Thugs. All three strands of the film deliver powerful affirmation of the white working man's race and class and gender. Accents and manners establish the heroes as working class, but it is in the areas of race and gender that the film really goes to work.

Like many films of this era, *Gunga Din* privileges male friendship above all other bonds.[24] The opening barracks fist-fight and first battle with the Thugs show the three sergeants working together. They co-operate instinctively like members of a first-rate cricket team. The three-man friendship lends itself well to exploring the love between men. There is safety in Kipling's triangle of the 'Soldiers Three' that is absent from his other stories dealing with close male friendship, such as *The Light That Failed* or *The Man Who Would be King*. Here at least the screenplay of *Gunga Din* reflects Kipling. The protagonists of *The Man Who Would Be King* acknowledge at the beginning of their adventure that the intrusion of a woman could threaten their plans to conquer a kingdom in the Himalayas and write a prohibition on marriage into their contract. The breaking of this clause in the contract shatters their partnership and costs them their kingdom. Ballantine's marriage in *Gunga Din* is no less threatening.[25] The scenes in which Ballantine

(Fairbanks) courts his fiancee Emmy (Joan Fontaine) are oddly
ambiguous. Close-ups dominated by teeth establish their relationship as
rather grotesque, animalistic and oddly unnatural. Ballantine's desire
for marriage is cast as un-masculine. He is humiliated when his
comrades meet him in a drapers shop, choosing curtains for his 'den'
with his wife-to-be. When Ballantine marches away dragging a skein of
cloth behind him, Cutter and MacChesney joke that his 'petticoat is
showing'. Once Cutter has fallen into the hands of the Thugs,
Ballantine acts. He tells Emmy:

> The trouble is you don't want a man for a husband. You want a coward who'll
> run out on his friend when he's in danger. Well that's not me, and never has
> been, and never will be. I don't care how much I love you – and I do, very
> much – I'm a soldier ... I mean I'm a man first.

With manhood defined, Emmy effectively disappears from the film.
Ballantine resolves to remain in the army and the joyful reunion at the
end of the film is wholly male.

The racial message of the film is equally clear. It takes a hoard of
Thugs to overpower a single white man. The Indians die without
dignity. Their efforts to run from sticks of dynamite are presented
comically as though in a cartoon. Although the Thug Guru (played by
Edward Ciannelli) is allowed to explain his cause and gives his life for
it, he is first represented as a madman, and photographed so as to
accentuate glinting teeth, fanatical eyes and an exaggerated black face.
In contrast Gunga Din initially appears only as comic relief, like
MacChesney's pet elephant, Annie. Yet while the elephant is nurtured
as a 'little elephant girl', Gunga Din is merely patronized. When Cutter
(Cary Grant) discovers him secretly drilling, he attempts to help him to
master the basic moves. The scene is played for laughs, the man,
dressed only in a *dhoti*, is urged to place his thumbs down the seams
of his trousers. Yet Gunga Din makes choices throughout the film. He
declares to the Guru that he is supporting the British of his own free
will, and is not a slave but a soldier. Ultimately, he sacrifices his life to
raise the alarm. He is the catalyst who advances the action of the film.[26]
Hoping to become a soldier, he tells Cutter of the existence of a golden
temple in the hills ripe for plunder, he frees Cutter from prison,
summons Ballantine and MacChesney to his aid and then raises the
alarm to avert the massacre of an unsuspecting British regiment. Yet he
is implicitly less of a man than the British. He is diminished by the
camera angles, by his limited ambition (he tells Cutter that he has no
wish to be a Maharajah: 'Bugler would be very satisfactory'), and by
the visual humour of the film which depicts him as symbolically
impotent. In the first battle he mimics the sergeants by waving a broken
sword. Later he offers Cutter a fork to dig his way out of prison.
Arguably, the film seeks to move the audience into the same position as

the narrator of Kipling's poem, and to question the certainties of white supremacy with the line: 'You're a better man than I am Gunga Din', but given the racial thrust of the film, the compliment is rendered meaningless.

Gunga Din does have an ethical framework, and, indeed, the script flirts with a critique of imperialism. Cutter, like Dravot in *The Man Who Would Be King* is undone by greed. His eagerness for plunder leads him straight into the arms of the Thugs. For Cutter, India is just the venue for his jolly army life, to be exploited as necessary. He considers blowing up the Taj Mahal and starting a war just to keep his friend Ballantine in the army. The screenplay does not endorse such behaviour. Cutter survives the film only by a whisker.[27] But potentially anti-Imperial messages are diluted by the portrayal of the Indians. They are sneaky. They torture their captives. They are fanatical devotees of a blood-thirsty religion. They feign obsequiousness, and only attack in strength. The British, in contrast, are open. They march along singing loudly and are prepared to face terrible odds.[28] The British are also oddly discriminating in battle. The three sergeants use their fists on unarmed Thugs, but shoot at Thug snipers. Fair play wins the day.

In writing such scenes the American authors give a fair idea of the elements in Kipling's work that they find appealing. These omissions are not less telling. The ambiguities of Kipling's Empire are missing altogether. In such poems as *Piet* or '*Fuzzy-Wuzzy*' Kipling gives his soldiers a grudging respect for their enemies.[29] Moreover, in the poem Gunga Din was admired by the British narrator not for rescuing the regiment at the cost of his own life, but for simply risking his life by attending to the wounded under fire.[30] Finally, there is a dark underside to Kipling's poem, which emerges in its final stanza:

So I'm meet 'im later on,
At the place where 'e is gone –
Where it's always double drill and no canteen.
'E'll be squattin' on the coals,
Givin' drink to poor damned souls,
An' I'll get a swig in hell from Gunga Din![31]

Although these words are read in the film, their bleak implications are negated by the images that accompany them. As Gunga Din is piped-to-rest posthumously appointed to the rank of Corporal, he appears in an ellipse in the centre of the screen as a contented heavenly figure dressed in full uniform, and salutes. Unlike the damned Din of Kipling, the Hollywood incarnation is clearly redeemed.[32]

In sum the film that appeared in 1939 was a virtual negation of Kipling's work. Where Kipling found complexity, tragedy, hybridity, and futility, *Gunga Din* presents simplicity, facile masculine posturing and easy answers in violence. The film's cultural distortions make

Kipling's own highly problematic writing seem like the most carefully balanced ethnography. As *Gunga Din's* box office success made clear, no one in the United States minded. In Britain, Kipling's widow, Caroline, had her reservations. She claimed that the representation of her husband in the final reel exposed his memory to ridicule. RKO obligingly cut the offending scenes from later released prints.[33] The film was, however, banned in Japan, Malaya and British India.[34]

The Later Career of Gunga Din.

The release of *Gunga Din* in January 1939 coincided with the deepening crisis in Europe. While the film doubtless provided welcome escapism at the time, it had apparently been shaped to promote pro-British feeling in the US in the face of the totalitarian threat. Yet by 1941 the film had outlived its political usefulness.[35] The United States joined the war with the expectation that the peace would include decolonization. The US government's Office of War Information took care not to offend their new ally India. As Clayton Koppes and Gregory Black have noted, the OWI prevailed on RKO not to re-release *Gunga Din* and persuaded MGM to abandon their plans to film Kipling's *Kim*.[36]

The Empire film also suffered by default from the revival of the Western.[37] The genre offered the ideal vehicle to celebrate America's new-found self-confidence. Now westerns could be packaged as westerns again, and Empire movies became westerns also. As Jeffrey Richards has noted, *Lives of a Bengal Lancer* (1937) became *Geronimo* (1939), *Four Men and a Prayer* (1938) became *Fury at Furnace Creek* (1948). *Gunga Din* resurfaced as a western *Sergeants Three* in 1961, remade by John Sturges (who edited the original) with Frank Sinatra, Dean Martin, Peter Lawford and Sammy Davis Jr. as their faithful bugler.[38]

Kipling and the Empire bubbled away under the surface for a while. In 1950 MGM finally filmed *Kim* and a flurry of lacklustre Empire pictures followed.[39] The shadow of Kipling was barely discernible in America's own Empire. In the later stages of World War Two, American officers in Teheran nicknamed their mess servant Gunga Din.[40] Teddy Roosevelt's grandson, Kermit Roosevelt, the head of CIA operations in the Middle East retained the Kiplingesque family nickname Kim.[41] But literary tastes were elsewhere. With an Ian Fleming novel on his bedside table and a confidence unmeasured by the experience of European Empire, John F. Kennedy committed his troops to war in Vietnam.[42]

The experience of Vietnam left its mark on both westerns and Empire films. In both genres the protagonists became alienated victims who found vindication in buddy relationships and death in Mexico *(The Wild Bunch)* or Bolivia *(Butch Cassidy and the Sundance Kid)*[43] or high in the Himalayas in John Huston's film of Kipling's *The Man Who Would Be King*. Huston's film, like Kipling's text displayed Empire as a profane scramble that brings death and madness to its two would-be rulers Dravot and Carnehan (played by Sean Connery and Michael Caine). Yet, the old spirit of *Gunga Din* is never far away. In Huston's version the 'native' ally of the two adventurers, nicknamed Billy Fish, becomes a Gurkha (played by Saeed Jaffrey), the sole survivor of a lost expedition who is still loyal to the British Crown. In character and costume he takes up exactly where the ghost of Gunga Din left off. But above all the myth of male friendship is reinscribed and the Imperial project is shown to be, for the most part, tremendous fun, and the audience is left with the suggestion that but for the intrusion of a woman, Carnehan and Dravot could have kept their kingdom.[44]

British India remains a perennial presence in movies whether British-made end-of-Empire epics, or such lively pieces of American escapism as Disney's 1994 offering: *Rudyard Kipling's The Jungle Book*. Old themes endure. In Hollywood's India, even Thugs may still be found as in Spielberg's monumentally tasteless *Indiana Jones and the Temple of Doom*.[45] Debate about Empire is elsewhere. The United States may have ignored the inner-warnings of Kipling, but the same messages were learned in Vietnam. As Kipling feared that the glory of the British Empire might someday fade to become 'one with Nineveh and Tyre',[46] so the United States now grapples with the prospect of Imperial decline. Filmic treatments of the Vietnam war regularly show respect for an enemy who could fight on 'a handful of rice and a little dried rat meat' and portray the Veteran as every inch as exploited as Kipling's 'Tommy Atkins'.

> For its Tommy this, an' Tommy that, an', Chuck him
>   Out, the brute!
> But it's 'Saviour of his country' when the guns begin
>   to shoot; [47]

In *Apocalypse Now* Francis Ford Coppola highlights the degree to which Vietnam was an Imperial war, by borrowing elements from Conrad's great critique of empire, *Heart of Darkness*.[48] The Vietnam War seemed to vindicate Kipling's epigram: 'A fool lies here who tried to hustle the East'.[49] There is a coda. In the aftermath of the publication of Robert McNamara's memoirs, with its shocking admission that this architect of the war in Vietnam believed the cause to be lost but remained silent, at least one commentator turned to the disillusioned Kipling, broken by the loss of his only son in Great War, for his conclusion:

> If any question why we died,
> Tell them, because our fathers lied.[50]

NOTES

The author is grateful to Prof. Jeffrey Richards of the University of Lancaster for his helpful comments on an earlier version of this work, and to the Department of History at the University of Maryland, College Park, for their hospitality during its completion.

1. Jeffrey Richards, 'Boy's own Empire: Feature films and Imperialism in the 1930s', in *Imperialism and Popular Culture*, ed., John M. Mackenzie (Manchester: Manchester University Press, 1986), p. 144.
2. McLaglen, Grant and the other actors in British army roles were all British-born, with the exception of Douglas Fairbanks Jr.
3. Sayre graduated from Exeter College, Oxford in August 1922 with a BA in English. Contrary to Philip French, 'Kipling and the Movies' in *Rudyard Kipling: The Man his Work and his World*, ed., John Gross (London: Weidenfeld & Nicolson, 1972), p. 166, he was not a Rhodes Scholar. He co-wrote the screen play for George Stevens, dir., *Annie Oakley* (RKO, 1935). He served as *New Yorker* war correspondent in Persia.
4. The development of the screenplay for *Gunga Din* is documented in Rudy Behlmer, *Behind the Scenes*, (Hollywood: Samuel French, 1990), pp. 88-90. Hecht and MacArthur (authors's of *The Front Page*) were hired by Howard Hawks. Faulkner's contribution was the device of ending with a final heroic sacrifice by Gunga Din and a scene in which the British gather at his grave and intone 'You're a better man than I am Gunga Din'.
5. In 1892 Kipling married an American and lived in the US for the next four years: for a summary see Norman Page, *A Kipling Companion*, (London: Macmillan, 1984), pp. 17-20. Such works as his poem *An American: 1894* and his account of his American travels *From Sea to Sea*, touched on American themes. His verse *The White Man's Burden* of 1899 was subtitled *The United States and the Philippine Islands*. Rudyard Kipling, *Rudyard Kipling's Verse: The Definitive Edition* (London: Hodder and Stoughton, 1977), pp. 184-185, 323-34.
6. I am grateful to Kermit Roosevelt III and Corinne Roosevelt for confirming this connection.
7. See Dillon Wallace, *The Lure of the Labrador Wild*, (New York: F. Revell Co., 1905), as cited in Alan Williams, 'Explorers Wild: The Hubbard's in Labrador', in this collection.
8. *The Poems of General George S. Patton Jr.: Lines of Fire*, ed., Carmine A. Prioli (Lewiston, NY.: Edwin Mellen Press, 1991), p. vi. Matthew B. Ridgway, *Soldier: The Memoirs of Matthew B. Ridgway* (New York: Harper, 1956), pp. 16, 21, 78, 305, 309.
9. Finley Peter Dunne, *Mr Dooley in the Hearts of his Countrymen* (Boston: Small, Maynard and Co, 1899), pp. 13-17.
10. For a selection of usage and parodies of the poem see Nell Irvin Painter, *Standing at Armageddon: The United States, 1877-1919* (New York: Norton, 1987), pp. 141-69.
11. As was clear from the Hoover administration's response to the Manchuria Crisis.
12. Edward Buscombe ed., *The BFI Companion to the Western* (London: Deutsch/BFI, 1988); on the 1920s: pp. 33-35, on the 1930s: pp. 41-43. For production figures see pp.427-28. In 1933 Westerns constituted only 13% of all films made in the US as against 28% in 1926. This was the lowest ebb for the genre until the 1960s. 'A' represented only 1 film in every 80 produced between

1930 and 1939. In 1934, the year in which both *Lives of a Bengal Lancer* and *Clive of India* were made, no studio released a single 'A' Western.

13. In order to persuade Gary Cooper to appear in *Lives of a Bengal Lancer* the director urged him 'to think of it as a western set in India'. Richards, 'Boys Own Empire', p. 145.

14. For a break down of revenues at MGM see H. Mark Glancy, 'MGM Film Grosses, 1924-1948: The Eddie Mannix Ledger', *Historical Journal of Film, Radio and Television*, 12, 2 (1992), pp. 127-144. On Warner Brothers' bid to maintain export revenue in wartime see Nicholas J. Cull, *Selling War: British Propaganda and American 'Neutrality' in World War Two* (New York: Oxford University Press, 1995), pp. 51-52.

15. Henry Hathaway, dir., *Lives of a Bengal Lancer* (Paramount, 1934); Richard Boleslawski, dir., *Clive of India* (Twentieth Century, 1934); Michael Curtiz, dir., *The Charge of the Light Brigade* (Warner, 1936); John Ford, dir., *Four Men and a Prayer* (Twentieth Century Fox, 1938) and Sidney Salkow, dir., *Storm Over Bengal* (Republic, 1938). For an earlier example of the genre see John Ford, dir., *The Black Watch* (Fox, 1929). The British were able to send a number of successful Empire pictures over to the United States, the most famous being Zoltan Korda, dir., *The Four Feathers* (Alexander Korda, 1939).

16. James Horne, dir., *Bonnie Scotland* (MGM/Hal Roach, 1935) is set in a Scottish regiment in India; John Ford, dir., *Wee Willie Winkie* (Twentieth Century Fox, 1937).

17. The original story provided little more than the name of the title character (originally a boy) and the general scenario for the film: *Wee Willie Winkie and other Stories* (Allahabad: A.H. Wheeler & Co, 1888). The other Kipling projects were all accomplished between 1937 and 1941: Victor Fleming, dir., *Captain's Courageous* (MGM, 1937); Robert Flagherty and Zoltan Korda, dirs., *Elephant Boy* (Korda, 1937); William Wellman, *The Light That Failed* (Paramount, 1939); Zoltan Korda and André de Toth, dirs., *The Jungle Book* (Korda, 1941). MGM first announced its plan to film *Kim* in 1938, the film did not appear until 1950. *The Light That Failed* had been filmed three times in the silent era, as had a version of Kipling's poem 'The Vampire' which appeared as *A Fool There Was*. For a survey of Kipling in film see French, 'Kipling and the Movies', pp. 162-69.

18. French, 'Kipling and the Movies', p. 162; Jeffrey Richards, *The Age of the Dream Palace: Cinema and Society in Britain, 1930-1939* (London: Routledge, 1984), p. 49. The failure of Gaumont British to complete *Soldiers Three* is documented in Jeffrey Richards, '"Soldiers Three": The "Lost" Gaumont British Imperial Epic', *Historical Journal of Film, Radio and Television*, 15, 1 (1995), pp. 137-141. Kipling was also quoted in movies. It is a love of Kipling that persuades a young soldier to join-up in John Ford, dir., *The Lost Patrol* (RKO, 1934), cited in Jeffrey Richards, *Visions of Yesterday* (London: Routledge, 1973), pp. 148, 174.

19. For the 1928 MGM plan and the development of the RKO project see Behlmer, *Behind the Scenes*, pp. 88-101. On the un-produced UA film and a 1935 screenplay by R.J. Minney see Richards, *The Age of the Dream Palace*, p. 140.

20. The three first appeared in short stories written for the *Civil and Military Gazette* from 1887. Their stories were included in *Plain Tales From the Hills* (Allahabad: A.H. Wheeler & Co, 1888), and a second volume of their own: *Soldiers Three* (Allahabad: A.H. Wheeler & Co, 1888). Related stories appeared in *Life's Handicap* (London: Macmillan, 1891), *Many Inventions* (London: Macmillan, 1893), and *Actions and Reactions* (London: Macmillan, 1909). For

bibliography see Kipling, *Soldiers Three and In Black and White* (Harmondsworth: Penguin Twentieth Century Classics edn., 1993), p. 208.

21. The three are introduced in *Plain Tales from the Hills* in a story called 'The Three Musketeers'. RKO's sergeants are placed in the Royal Engineers and are responsible for such things as repairing telegraph wires. Kipling's soldiers are mere 'privates in a regiment of the line'.

22. Mark Paffard has suggested that this echoes Shakespeare's four regional soldiers in *Henry V*. See Paffard, *Kipling's Indian Fiction* (London: Macmillan, 1989), p. 61.

23. Zoreh T. Sullivan, *Narratives of Empire: The Fictions of Rudyard Kipling* (Cambridge: CUP, 1993), p. 15. Mulvaney's sorrow is explored in 'The Courting of Dinah Shadd' collected in *Life's Handicap* which also includes 'On the Greenhow Hill' in which Learoyd loses the love of his life to consumption. Ortheris is driven to the brink of insanity by an awareness of the futility of his position in 'The Madness of Private Ortheris' in *Plain Tales from the Hills*.

24. The myth underpins the brotherly love ethic at the core of *Beau Geste* (1939), which opens with the invented Arabic proverb: 'The love between a man and woman waxes and wanes like the moon, but the love of brother for brother is constant like the stars and endures like the word of the Prophet'.

25. The marriage in 'The Man Who Would Be King' first published in *The Phantom Rickshaw* (Allahabad: A.H. Wheeler & Co., 1888), is doubly taboo as it is to a 'native' woman, but the 'contrack' prohibits all women 'white or black'.

26. His role is in keeping with that which Toni Morrison has identified as typically given to a parallel 'other' in US fiction, the Afro-American: see Toni Morrison, 'Unspeakable Things Unspoken', *Michigan Quarterly Review*, 28, 1 (Winter 1989), pp. 1-34.

27. Cutter's motives and assumptions about India are humorously exposed as he over-interprets Thug behaviour. During the climax to the film, he is pinned down by Thug snipers a few feet from the treasure for which he lusts. After several hours in this tantalizing position he complains: 'is there no limit to the torture that the oriental mind can devise'.

28. At one stage, to allow Gunga Din to escape, Cutter marches into the midst of a Thug ritual singing 'The Roast Beef of Old England' and tells the entire gathering that they are all under arrest.

29. *Kipling's Verse*, pp. 400-401, 479-81. These sentiments may also be identified in the battle scene of *The Light that Failed* as cited in Paffard, *Kipling's Indian Fiction*, pp. 56-57.

30. *Kipling's Verse*, pp. 406-409. There is no line in the film equivalent to: 'An' for all 'is dirty 'ide,/he was white, clear white, inside,/when he went to tend the wounded under fire!'

31. *Kipling's Verse*, pp. 406-409.

32. Although Kipling's narrator assumes that Din will be damned, the term 'Lazarushian' introduces a subtext of redemption. Of the two biblical Lazaruses, one is raised from the dead in John 11, 1-44 and the other, the principal character in the parable of Dives and Lazarus (Luke 16, 19-31) is saved while the rich man, who ignored his poverty in life, is damned. The parallels to the story of Gunga Din are clear, for the rich man calls for Lazarus to bring him water but is told that it is impossible for a saved soul to cross into hell to ease his suffering. Here, as in the short story 'Naboth' *(Life's Handicap)*, Kipling's narrator's unwitting use of a biblical allusion turns in the mind of the reader to offer a critique of the Imperial project. On 'Naboth' see Sullivan, *Narratives of*

Empire, p. 12.

33. Behlmer, *Behind the Scenes*, pp. 100-101. It was in this form that the film began its illustrious career in re-release, making back its $2,000,000 cost by 1941.

34. Richards, *The Age of the Dream Palace*, p. 137.

35. Beyond its pro-British content, the Guru is clearly Hitlerian. Of the key participants in the film Douglas Fairbanks Jr., Ben Hecht and Charles MacArthur all played prominent roles in the movement to bring the US into World War Two.

36. Clayton R. Koppes and Gregory D. Black, *Hollywood Goes to War: How Politics, Profits and Propaganda Shaped World War Two Movies* (New York: Free Press, 1987), pp. 224-25, also Richards, *Visions of Yesterday*, p. 5.

37. The genre revived in the wake of John Ford, dir., *Stagecoach* (Walter Wanger, 1939) and George Marshall, dir., *Destry Rides Again* (Universal, 1939).

38. Richards, 'The Boys Own Empire', p. 157; John Sturges, dir., *Sergeants Three* (UA/Essex-Claude, 1961).

39. Victor Saville, dir., *Kim* (MGM, 1950); Tay Garnett, dir., *Soldiers Three* (MGM, 1951) similar films included Allan Davis, dir., *Rogues March* (MGM, 1953); Henry King, dir., *King of the Khyber Rifles* (Twentieth Century Fox, 1954). Wolfgang Reitherman, dir., *Jungle Book* (Disney, 1964) stands apart from these films, saying more about US race-relations in its vocal casting.

40. The servant embraced the name. He wrote an allegorical story to entertain the British and American officers for whom he worked, which was published as Ali Mirdrekvandi Gunga Din, *No Heaven For Gunga Din* (London: Gollancz, 1965).

41. On 'Kim' Roosevelt and the overthrow of Mussadiq see James A. Bill, *The Eagle and the Lion: The Tragedy of American-Iranian Relations* (New Haven: Yale University Press, 1988), pp. 86-97.

42. On James Bond and Kennedy see David Burner, *John F. Kennedy and a New Generation* (Glenview, Ill.:Scott, Foresman and Co., 1988), p. 63.

43. Sam Peckinpah, dir., *The Wild Bunch* (Warner, 1969); George Roy Hill, dir., *Butch Cassidy and the Sundance Kid* (Twentieth Century Fox, 1969).

44. John Huston, dir., *The Man Who Would Be King* (Columbia et al., 1975). For the original story see Rudyard Kipling, *Wee Willie Winkie* (Harmondsworth: Penguin, 1988).

45. Stephen Spielberg, dir., *Indiana Jones and the Temple of Doom* (Paramount/Lucasfilm, 1984). Stephen Sommer, dir., *Rudyard Kipling's The Jungle Book* (Disney, 1994).

46. 'Recessional: 1897', *Kipling's Verse*, pp. 328-329.

47. *Kipling's Verse*, pp. 398-399. The 'rat meat' quotation is from Michael Herr's narration written for Francis Ford Coppola, prod./dir., *Apocalypse Now* (Omni Zoetrope, 1979). Abuse of Veterans has become a sub-genre of the Vietnam War film from the fictional Rambo of *First Blood* to the real-life of Ron Kovic in *Born on the Fourth of July*.

48. Coppola's protagonist meets an insane war photographer who spouts Kipling's 'If–'. A scene in which the protagonist is confronted by French colonists who had 'stayed on in Vietnam' was cut from the final version of the film, see Fax Bahr and George Hichenlooper, dirs., *Hearts of Darkness: A Film Maker's Apocalypse* (Zoetrope et al., 1991).

49. Originally from the heading to chapter 5 of *The Naulahka*, reprinted in *Kipling's Verse*, p. 537.

50. 'Common Form', *Kipling's Verse*, p. 390 cited on CBS Evening News, 18 April 1995.

GRAHAM DAWSON

A Lament for Imperial Adventure: *Lawrence of Arabia* in the Post-Colonial World

The Lawrence of Arabia legend has proved to be one of the enduring myths of military masculinity in twentieth-century Western culture.[1] The famous story of the British intelligence officer who lived among Bedouin Arabs, became a commander of their guerrilla army, and led them to freedom from Ottoman tyranny during the latter part of the First World War, has been told and retold in an abundance of forms since its original narration (as 'the Greatest Romance of Real Life') by Lowell Thomas over seventy-five years ago. Subsequent versions include T.E. Lawrence's own *Seven Pillars of Wisdom*, numerous biographies and – the most popular vehicle of all – the David Lean and Robert Bolt feature film, *Lawrence of Arabia*, first released in 1962 and re-issued (in a painstakingly restored version) in 1988, to 'extraordinary attention' and critical acclaim.[2] These retellings, far from being simple reproductions of essentially the 'same' story, offer widely discrepant representations of their hero and his exploits. Indeed, since the 1950s, Lawrence has become a fiercely contested cultural icon. In these conflicts over the Lawrence legend, it is possible to trace a history of imaginative investment in an ideal form of imperial masculinity and its increasing disturbance and eventual breakdown on entering the post-colonial world. Close reading of the shifts and transformations evident in these texts can provide insight into the process whereby the gendered narratives of imperialism have been reinterpreted and rewritten under pressure from anti-colonial resistance and critique.

Lowell Thomas's original 'Lawrence of Arabia', produced in his 1919 film show and subsequent biography, met a popular desire to see the virtues of heroic imperial masculinity reasserted (albeit in a suitably 'modern' form) in response to the Great War and its immediate aftermath. In narrating 'the strange story of Colonel Lawrence' as an adventure, Thomas clearly utilized the idealizing conventions of chivalric romance to incorporate Lawrence's evident differences from the soldier heroes of Victorian and Edwardian tradition. His Lawrence might be youthful where they were elderly; he might be a scruffy and irregular lover of native customs where they were impeccable, pukka White Men; he might suggest a troubling sexual ambivalence, even femininity, turned out as the 'blond Bedouin' in flowing robes and smooth-shaven face.[3] But he could whip the Turks, out-Arab the Arabs, and generally demonstrate that effortless, omnipotent superiority of 'the Englishman in foreign parts' which had long been the hallmark of the imperial adventure hero.

Despite his own deeply ambivalent relationship to Thomas's heroic fantasy and the proliferating public legend rooted in it, Lawrence remained England's 'most famous adventurer' into the 1930s.[4] At the time of his death in 1935, his 'mysterious power' had become the focus for right-wing nationalist and fascist fantasies of a British 'political saviour'; as witnessed, for example, in Basil Liddell Hart's biography of 1934 (which immediately ran to many printings):

> I am told that the young men are talking, the young poets writing, of him [Lawrence] in a Messianic strain – as the man who could, if he would, be a light to lead stumbling humanity out of its troubles – he seems to come nearer than any man to fitness for such power – in a state that I would care to live in ... He is the Spirit of Freedom come incarnate to a world in fetters.[5]

Constructed by Thomas as, in effect, a man who could do anything, T.E. Lawrence remained closely identified with these intensely idealized fantasies of imperial authority and omnipotent power during the rest of his own lifetime and beyond.

From the mid-1950s, a very different kind of biography emerged to challenge the Lawrence legend, in which idealization is replaced by its psychic opposite, denigration. Renewed interest in his 'perverse' psycho-sexual make-up – stimulated by Lawrence's own *Seven Pillars of Wisdom*, but flattening out its complexities and contradictions – is utilized in a full-scale debunking of the hero, in which sado-masochism and his alleged homosexuality are linked with charges of self-glorification and dishonesty. Richard Aldington, in his pioneering *Lawrence of Arabia: A Biographical Enquiry* (1955), interprets the key to Lawrence's personality as 'an abnormal vanity' and its 'identical opposite – abnormal self-depreciation'; finding the sources of these traits in his early life, especially his difficult relationship with a strict and domineering mother, his discovery of the family's guilty secret that his parents were not married, and his own consequent illegitimacy. In *Lawrence of Arabia: The Man and the Motive* (1961), Anthony Nutting's interpretation of the infamous Deraa incident (the pivotal episode in Lawrence's *Seven Pillars*, where he describes his sexual violation and brutal whipping at the hands of Turkish soldiers) imagines Lawrence learning that he was a 'rabid masochist, whose happy endurance of pain disclosed a perversion of the flesh rather than a triumph of the spirit. Thus exposed to himself and mocked by his tormentors he broke down and submitted to their pleasure'.[6]

Subsequently, even writers attracted or sympathetic to Lawrence have had to take seriously this psychological critique of the hero. The psychiatrist, John Mack, for example, argued in 1976 that:

> [Lawrence's] illegitimacy caused him problems of self-esteem; he created an idealized mediaeval self and suffered greatly when he failed to measure up to impossible standards. In *Seven Pillars*, he tried to create such an ideal self-image but could not sustain it and relapsed into frequent self-depreciation, sometimes exaggerating his deeds when his awareness of failure was greatest.[7]

Developing the project begun in *Seven Pillars* itself, the popular adventure story of Lawrence of Arabia is complicated in these biographies by modernist fragmentation and disturbance: a dark antithesis to the idealized adventure hero is exposed in order to be explained by psychological interpretation. Yet, in thus undercutting the heroic image, this kind of psychological biography also works to over-individualize the Lawrence legend, obscuring its conditions of existence as a product of the popular communications media sustained by continuing public interest; and thus robbing it of any wider cultural resonance and meaning. The 'impossible standards' and 'ideal self-image' identified by Mack were not wholly peculiar to the individual Lawrence, but were culturally available forms of British masculinity. Lawrence's perceived failure to 'measure up to' and 'sustain' these ideals can be read as a personal failure to assume a desired masculine identity, of the kind that Thomas imagined him as embodying. But these shifting assessments of Lawrence are also the product of wider cultural conflict over the very standards and ideals themselves.

The crucial context for this conflict, and for the debunking Lawrence biographies which are contemporaneous with it, is the collapse of British imperial power, and the consequent and far-reaching transformation of the national imaginary, after the Second World War. Heralded by the Boer War of 1899-1902, and well underway by 1918, the waning of imperial might had gained momentum throughout the 1920s and 1930s, under the impact of the Irish War of Independence, the strength of Indian nationalism, and new relationships with the Dominions. This twentieth-century 'story of decline' had been arrested temporarily by the establishment of that new empire in the Middle East to which Lawrence (with his conception of 'our first brown dominion') had contributed. But even there, the discovery of oil in Iraq in 1920 coincided with a full-scale, popular rebellion 'which cost Britain more than she had spent on all her wartime operations in the middle east to put down, and more than 400 soldiers' lives besides'. Although Britain emerged from the 1939-45 war with its empire intact, the dismantling of the Indian Raj in 1947, coupled with its weakened position in a world order now polarized between the American and Soviet superpowers, fundamentally undermined imperial authority. A plethora of anti-colonial movements of national liberation began to contest it with increasing confidence and, where they were resisted, with armed force. Riots in the Gold Coast produced a Black government under a British governor in 1950 and the independent state of Ghana by 1957. The Sudan and Malaya also won independence in the 1950s, the latter after a major colonial war (1948-58): a spectacle that was repeated in Kenya (1952-56) and Cyprus (1954-59), to the discomfiture of sections of the British public.[8]

Above all, it was the Suez crisis of 1956 that brought home the realities of Britain's new position. Gamal Abdel Nasser's revolutionary nationalist movement had seized power in Egypt in 1952, and within a few years had forced Britain to give up its military bases on Egyptian territory, sending anti-imperialist shock-waves through the Arab world and 'effectively ending British suzerainty in the Middle East'. When in 1956 Nasser seized control of the Suez Canal and nationalized the company which ran it, Britain joined with France and Israel to restore control by military invasion, only to withdraw the invasion force under the combined threats of Soviet missiles on London, the U.S. refusal to support the pound, and implacably hostile world opinion.[9] If the Suez debâcle exacerbated a prevalent sense of 'waste, unfairness and helplessness' among pro-imperialists at the demise of imperial power, it also exposed the hollowness of imperialist claims to moral purpose:

> The ethos of Empire, as of war, was acceptable to the British when it was backed by convictions of honour – by the belief, false or misguided, that the British were acting rightly, for the good of themselves and the world. Fair play! In most of their wars the British had been so convinced. ... Now, in Port Said, 1956, there was only pretence – a sham virility, a dubious cause, a nation divided.[10]

Besides generating intense conflict within the British imperial imaginary, Suez is linked in many accounts of the 1950s with a more pervasive cultural crisis of British values and identity. Robert Hewison has described how the work of the younger generation of artists and writers was characterized by 'a criticism of the cultural values that had been passed on to postwar society'; by 'the hostility of the new writers of the 1950s to both aesthetic and social attitudes of the 1930s'; by (as Doris Lessing put it) 'a confusion of standards and the uncertainty of values'. The decline of Empire contributed to this crisis, even among what Alan Sinfield calls 'the dissident middle class intelligentsia [who] were constituted in opposition to the empire-building middle class'.[11]

One of its effects was the calling-in-question of traditional masculine authority and identity. In an often-quoted speech from John Osborne's *Look Back in Anger* (1956), Jimmy Porter articulates a particularly masculine malaise:

I suppose people of our generation aren't able to die for good causes any longer. We had all that done for us, in the Thirties and Forties, when we were still kids. *(In his familiar, semi-serious mood).* There aren't any good, brave causes left. If the big bang does come, and we all get killed, it won't be in aid of the old-fashioned grand design. It'll just be for the Brave New-nothing-very-much-thank-you. About as pointless and inglorious as stepping in front of a bus.[12]

The 'people' referred to here, of course, are men, while the causes mentioned in the play include the imperial mission and the Second World War (itself complexly bound up with Empire). The crisis of the new generation of men is being registered here in terms of a widespread de-cathecting (or de-energizing) of heroic adventure as a public narrative inviting identification and active participation. By 1960 National Service had been abolished, marking a significant break in the transmission of masculine ideals and standards as forms to identify the self with (or against); and a range of rebellious masculine styles such as the teddy boy and the beatnik had emerged. The 'generation gap', that became such a marked feature of the later 1950s and 1960s, was lived out in cross-generational misrecognitions between traditionally dominant and newly oppositional forms of masculinity, the stake being the maintenance of a masculine authority that was once rooted in imperial imaginings. 'One cannot imagine Jimmy Porter', wrote Kenneth Tynan in a famous review of Osborne's play, 'listening with a straight face to speeches about our inalienable right to flog Cypriot schoolboys'.[13]

Lawrence became one of the figures registering the impact of the loss of Empire upon British masculinity. The debunking, Aldington-type biographies are symptomatic of a more generalized reckoning with the values, standards and ideals of a pre-1939 imperialism. Aldington's own re-assessment of Lawrence's heroic reputation struck at the heart of idealized Englishness. Sir Ronald Storrs, with whom Lawrence had first arrived in Arabia in 1916, and who had gone on to become Governor of Cyprus, denounced Aldington in a BBC broadcast for maligning a hero who was 'a touchstone and a standard of reality', demanding: 'To what purpose has this been done? ... What can be the gratification in attempting to destroy a famous name – an inspiration to youth all over the free world?'[14] Here as ever, the Lawrence heroic image proved contradictory. While Storrs claimed him as an establishment figure, Nutting, a Foreign Office minister outspokenly supportive of the Eden Government's hard-line stance on Suez who went on to resign over its capitulation, sought to dissociate Lawrence from imperialist values. Lawrence himself had always been uncomfortably resistant to any such alignment: as Aldington put it, 'he differed entirely from the pukka sahib or Blimp-type' in 'not [sharing] their Wog and Gippo attitudes to Arabs'. In this, Aldington might well have been aligning Lawrence's own ambivalent relationship to traditional authority with the questionings of the new, postwar generation. Instead, and in common with Nutting, he berates Lawrence for 'favouring Arab rather than British interests' (a claim that, in its linking of 'pathological' sexuality and treachery to the state, offers an imperialist variant on the contemporaneous Cold War association of homosexuality with 'evil'). For the Arab historian, Suleiman Mousa, on the other hand, Lawrence is 'a cold-blooded imperialist agent who cared nothing for the Arabs and sought only to advance British interests'.[15]

Clearly, by the early 1960s Thomas's fantasy of the powerful British hero leading the subject races to freedom was generally regarded with deep suspicion, its imagined integration of interests and identities fragmenting along a realigned and differently charged axis of power. Indeed, these conflicting representations of Lawrence are characterized by their extreme splitting of the hero into sharply polarized aspects, each charged with the projected psychic qualities of either idealization or denigration – from Thomas's omnipotent and virtuous 'blond Bedouin' to Nutting's 'almost demonic suicidal sado-masochist who uses the Arabs to fulfil his own lust for revenge'.[16] Always a locus of the unconscious phantasies of imperialist culture, after 1956 the Lawrence of Arabia story had become deeply embroiled in the psychic aftermath of Suez. This is the necessary context in which to place the 1962 feature film, directed by David Lean from a screenplay by Robert Bolt; titled, simply, *Lawrence of Arabia*.[17]

Unsurprisingly, *Lawrence of Arabia* proved to be 'an unusually controversial picture', being widely read on its release as an oppositional, anti-imperialist text. A bitter row about its politics and characterization developed, with the Estate of T.E. Lawrence refusing permission to call the film *Seven Pillars of Wisdom*, Lady Allenby objecting to its alleged slander of her husband (the Commander-in-Chief of the Egyptian expeditionary force against the Turks), and accusations that screen-writer Robert Bolt's CND sympathies had influenced his portrait of Lawrence. At its first press screening, one critic acclaimed it as British cinema's first 'queer epic', rhapsodizing over its treatment of Lawrence's young admirers, Farraj and Daud, and the relationship with his Arab friend and rival, Sharif Ali.[18]

The film's stance towards imperialism, however, might more accurately be described as ambivalent. Incorporating elements drawn from both the popular adventure story and modernist psycho-biography, *Lawrence of Arabia* refuses to take one side or another in the conflict over the Lawrence heroic image, but instead explores the relation between them. *Seven Pillars* is clearly a primary source, but the film includes material absent from Lawrence's account, as well as offering a filmic interpretation of some of its key episodes. It is informed by a detailed awareness both of Thomas and of subsequent, more critical biographies: Sir Anthony Nutting served as principal adviser to the producer, Sam Spiegel. If, as Spiegel declared, 'we did not set out to solve the legend of Lawrence of Arabia, we tried to perpetuate it', the film proved remarkably successful.[19] For Robert Bolt, on the other hand, the film had a more serious focus:

> Here was a man [Lawrence], physically insignificant, born a bastard, conscious of special powers. An awkward man, deliberately so. He finds acceptance not among his own but among an alien people, in borrowed robes, and not as one man among others, but as a god-sent Leader. He is alone. He can do what he wants. Is that a privilege or an intolerable burden?[20]

The film's dramatic energy derives from its use of this question as a springboard for an explicit investigation of the Lawrence legend and its contemporary relevance. Lowell Thomas's myth-making is subjected to ironic scrutiny, while at the same time the film retains something of the wonder and excitement of Thomas's legendary narrative. Imaginative investment and critical distance are held together in a powerful, dramatic tension. Most interestingly, the subjective dimensions of this dichotomy are explored by the juxtaposition of the adventure hero with its dark inverse, located as a psychic conflict within Lawrence himself.

Following Thomas and *Seven Pillars*, the narrative focuses on Lawrence's involvement in the Arab Revolt: from his leaving the Cairo Map Department en route for Arabia to the moment when he leaves Damascus, his quest at an end, following its capture by the Allied and Arab armies. In the first part of the film Lawrence undergoes a Thomas-like transformation, in the course of two epic journeys that take him from Cairo to the Arab leader, Feisal, and on to the capture of Akaba. Initially establishing Lawrence as a clumsy clown, dismissed as worthless by his C.O. in Cairo, the film transports him (and the viewer) into an epic desert landscape in which he makes himself anew. Unlike Thomas's romantic Arabia, Lean's strange and unknown landscape is dangerous.[21] The long camel-rides are monotonous and arduous. The heat kills: on one occasion Lawrence and the Bedouin have to cross overnight a waterless expanse of desert, known as 'the sun's anvil', before sunrise the following day, or perish. In adopting Bedouin customs and enduring the desert's hardships and dangers, Lawrence discovers a new dignity and courage. His growth in stature is dramatized by the foregrounding of a minor episode in *Seven Pillars*, where Lawrence returns alone to rescue a man lost in the desert during the night. The Arab leader, Sharif Ali, rewards Lawrence's courage by burning his shabby British Army clothes and dressing him in white Sharifian robes, as an Arab.[22]

Lawrence's triumphal return and recognition as a Bedouin hero marks the onset of phantasies of omnipotence, first explored in a debate with Ali, whose interpretation of the episode as an expression of the will of God is countered by Lawrence's insistence that success is dependent only on human will-power. This refusal to accept the limits set by divine law causes the Bedouin to salute Lawrence as a saviour of life and a man uniquely in command of his own destiny. Lawrence comes to imagine himself as a contemporary prophet imbued with quasi-divine powers, who seeks inspiration under a thorn tree and claims to be able to 'work miracles' – to lead the Arab people to their freedom. All this is shown to stand in explicit contrast to the humility and faith of his Muslim allies, like Ali, who pray for God's help in braving the dangers of the desert. When Ali objects to Lawrence's intention to cross Sinai en route for Cairo, protesting the difficulty, Lawrence retorts: 'Why not? Moses did it'. The omnipotent, wish-fulfilling hero is shown to be one of Lawrence's own identifications, as he himself comes to believe in the reality of his own fantastic power.

The film understands this assertion of unlimited human will to be a deeply transgressive, Faustian act that puts the self at risk. Lawrence's imaginative investment in heroism undergoes a sudden and dramatic reversal into its opposite – a man taken over by fear and self-hatred – under the impact of psychic disturbances which increasingly obtrude into the narrative. Chief among these is Lawrence's self-identification as a destroyer of life. Called upon to perform the ritual execution of a murderer, required by Arab law to avoid a blood feud, Lawrence is confronted with the implication that omnipotent power over life also involves omnipotent destructive power. The hero has met his demon; and on the film's third, gruelling journey across Sinai, accompanied by the two young admirers in his care, Farraj and Daud, the demon returns to haunt him. Lawrence's failure to save Daud from death by quicksand is a trauma that plunges him into a haunted abstractedness. Destructive phantasies of omnipotent responsibility here produce a depressive scenario of horror and guilt, in which Lawrence punishes himself by refusing to ride, and instead walks grim-faced and dirty beside Farraj on the sole remaining camel.[23]

Lawrence's ensuing crisis of identity is played out for the first time on his reappearance in Cairo, which completes a three-stage circular journey and brings to a close the first part of the film. If, in Thomas, this return is a moment of recognition for Lawrence as a hero, in *Lawrence of Arabia* it is the occasion of competing and incompatible (mis)recognitions that pull him apart. Religious transgression of desert law is replaced here by racial transgression of colonial apartheid. Marching up the imposing marble steps into Army HQ with the Arab boy, Lawrence is first misrecognized as 'a dirty little Arab' by the guards, who seek to prohibit them from entering this citadel of power; and then encounters the hostile silence of the officers' mess where he takes Farraj for refreshment. Visually, Lawrence (and the viewer) is at this moment identified with the Arabs and against the tight-buttoned military smartness of the racist British messroom. At the same time, the dirtying of Lawrence's white robes in the Sinai desert marks his psychic descent from god-like inspiration to demonic denigration and self-punishment: the icon sullied. These visual connotations of a morally 'fallen' Lawrence complicate identification with him, and function as a figure of the confused and divided self who appears before Allenby. Unlike the benevolent and authoritative father-figure of Thomas and *Seven Pillars*, Allenby is imagined here as a manipulative flatterer who plays upon Lawrence's messianic phantasies in order to ensure his return to Arabia and continuing usefulness.[24] Allenby's positive recognition of Lawrence rekindles a manic excitement ('I'll have Arabia in chaos'), helps him to (temporarily) overcome his trauma, and offers an authoritative (if also temporary) resolution to Lawrence's conflicting identifications in fostering the belief that Arab interests and British interests are at one. Lawrence's own mania is shown to be decisively underpinned and made 'realizable' by the imperial authority of British High Command.

In the second part of the film, Lawrence appears as a man torn by psychic conflict between two dichotomous identifications, that constitute a deeply and irrevocably split masculinity. His rapid oscillations between the depressive and the triumphal, the ordinary and the extraordinary, are connected to the unifying or splitting of his identifications with the British and the Arabs. The resolution offered by Allenby initiates a sequence of events in which Lawrence repeats the conflictual scenarios in an increasingly destructive spiral. Restored to his idealized self and clad again all in white, Lawrence is next seen revelling in an adventurous attack on a Turkish train, only for depressive deflation to return after he again has had to kill. His capture whilst spying in Deraa stems from courting danger by flaunting himself in the town, protected only by an omnipotent sense of magical invulnerability ('I'm invisible'). Misrecognized as a fair-skinned Circassian subject of the Ottoman Empire, and thus exchanging colonial omnipotence for the vulnerability of the colonized, Lawrence is forced by physical and sexual violation to confront his own ordinariness: he has 'a body like other men', whatever his will to the contrary.

Lawrence's abandoning of omnipotent phantasy is also equated here with the further forced recognition of his own racial identity: '"Look Ali, look". (*Pinching his skin*). "That's me. What colour is it? That's me. And there's nothing I can do about it. ... I'm not the Arab Revolt, Ali, I'm not even an Arab"'. Phantasies of omnipotence founder on the incommensurable difference of race. However, the inescapability of colonial relations, and the necessity of finding some place to occupy within them, makes this return to ordinariness yet another unrealizable fantasy. At his next appearance back in Cairo, Lawrence has resumed his Army uniform and reverted to the awkward clown trying to belong, amid talk of 'squash-courts' and 'wogs'. By contrast, Allenby's unscrupulous desire to have Lawrence back in the field at the head of an Arab army, and his ability to bring this about by the deployment of British imperial resources, makes the only alternative fantasy seem the more realizable.

'I'm going to give them Damascus!': for the last time, Lawrence attempts to square the circle by returning to Arabia, only to re-enact in its most damaging form in the film his psychic oscillation from omnipotent triumphalism to depressive anxiety. At the village of Tafas, the Arab army discovers a Turkish massacre of men, women and children. Instead of internalizing his horror at yet another spectacle of death in an experience of psychic conflict and self-punishment, on this occasion Lawrence identifies fully with the exhilaration of violent release as he takes up the Arab call for 'No prisoners' and leads their charge on the retreating Turkish column. The result is an orgy of killing and destruction: the film's most powerful invocation of the horrors of war, both as a literal statement and as a metaphor for the hell of a psyche overcome by phantasies of its own omnipotent destructiveness. Discovered in shock after the attack, his white robes stained bright red, Lawrence has assumed the most feared shape of his imagined other, more 'cruel and barbarous' than the Arabs he had earlier condemned as such.

The Tafas massacre is the decisive episode in *Lawrence of Arabia* because it is here that Lawrence's messianic dream of nobly leading a people to freedom is finally destroyed, and his quest brought to an end. As in *Seven Pillars*, the narrative closes hollowly after the capture of Damascus, where Lawrence's efforts to place control of the city under the authority of the Arab Council fail due to the Arabs' lack of 'modern' experience and know-how. Allenby waits patiently until chaos breaks out, and then steps in to restore order. In *Seven Pillars* the depressive image of Lawrence leaving Damascus in exhausted sadness – a man 'so stained in estimation that afterward nothing in the world would make him feel clean' – is to some extent held in check by the image of a benevolent Allenby assuming control and setting Lawrence free from his burden of responsibility.[25] In *Lawrence of Arabia* there is no such countervailing image. Allenby is presented in a wholly cynical light as the chief representative of a realpolitik which is shown to have defeated Lawrence, destroying him and his dream. Lawrence is driven away from Damascus in a car past Arabs on camel-back who no longer recognize him, to whom he can no longer speak, with whom he will never again ride. 'Well Sir, going home?', asks the driver (the film's final words); but 'home' no longer exists for Lawrence. The film ends fascinated with failure, evoking an intense yearning for what is being left behind.

The powerful elegiac quality of this ending can be explained in terms of *Lawrence of Arabia's* contradictory positioning of the viewer in relation to the romance of Lawrence's adventure. The film certainly subjects this narrative to critique, in terms of the messianic excess of Lawrence's motivating fantasy. It also highlights the paradox in his own relation to the Arabs: his fascination with the otherness of the 'traditional' and authentic Arab way of life, and his frustration at their lack of modern qualities and understanding. His third epic camel ride across Sinai, for example, is in one sense made necessary and in another enabled by the destruction of the telephone by Arab looters. The film suggests that Lawrence needs the Arabs to remain 'traditional' in order to sustain his own investments in them and to guarantee his own epic opportunities; even though the outcome of his political ambitions – 'Arabia for the Arabs now' – depends on Arab ability to create a free and independent modern state. Modernization is precisely what the Arab leaders themselves are shown to desire: Feisal's own wish is to acquire the technology of a modern, mechanized army to fight the Turks, while Sharif Ali desires an education in the working of modern, democratic institutions. Furthermore, Feisal explicitly identifies as a projective investment 'the great hunger for desolate places' of the 'desert-loving English'; and he accuses Lawrence of being 'a Gordon of Khartoum', exposing the acquisitive romanticism of Western Orientalist fantasies and their risk to the romantic imaginer. These scenes introduce moments of possible self-consciousness for Western audiences about their own relation to this filmic Arabia.

On the other hand, the viewer is also invited in the earlier sequences to make powerful, imaginative investments in Lawrence, in 'Arabia' and in the film as such. The chief vehicle for this is the cinematography of the desert. This is breath-takingly beautiful. Shot on seventy-millimeter film that provides added depth of focus and sharpness of detail for the wider screen of cinemascope, it captures the vastness of space, the richness of colour, the subtlety and clarity of light that gives way to a mesmeric shimmering of heat haze. From the first sunrise shot, the camera dwells lovingly and at length on these visual properties of a landscape wherein human beings are reduced to the tiniest of dots moving beneath the massive grandeur of towering rock formations and the perfect curves of the big dunes. This cinematography constructs 'the Arabian desert' of the film (actually shot in Jordan and Morocco) as a visual feast, a veritable landscape of the imagination. Supported by Jarré's score, this visual dimension intensifies the emotional pitch of the film to epic heights, implicitly endorsing Lawrence's sense of growth into new and superior modes of being. By these means the film actively organizes the viewer's investment in the Lawrence legend and they are never fully displaced or undermined by the narrative's subsequent dramatization of conflict, nor by its ironic scrutiny of the very myth-making process that makes such investments possible in the first place. They remain residual but active, and determine the intense sadness and sense of loss with which the film ends.

For *Lawrence of Arabia* is ultimately a lament for the lost romance of Empire, overturned by a wholly modern power-politics represented by both Feisal and Allenby, who are shown to have cynically manipulated Lawrence for their own ends throughout. Lawrence, it appears, was never 'in control', and his failure was always inevitable. But the film narrative endorses Lawrence in this moment of failure through the exhilaration with which it tells of his attempt to make a new world. What is most memorable about *Lawrence of Arabia* is the epic uplift and expansiveness in its treatment of those first journeys in the desert and Lawrence's heroic mastery of this environment. The film suggests that the forces which destroy Lawrence as a romantic adventure hero destroy, too, the very possibility of such a hero as an energizing myth. In its ending, it laments the loss of Empire as a possible location where adventure romance could continue to be imagined. It laments the loss of the romantic periphery itself, with its 'traditional' way of life, under the pressure to modernize, and to contest imperial power not with swords and camels, but with artillery, aeroplanes and engineers. And it laments the relinquishing of the imperial adventure hero as a particular form of masculine transcendence and imagined release from the pressures of difference, psychic conflict and contradiction.

This loss was registered in 1962, at a precise moment of reckoning with the emerging features of a post-colonial world. Since 1962, Western audiences have watched on their television screens the working-out of the mischief sown by British and French imperialists through their settlement in the Middle East after 1918. The Six-Day War and Israeli annexation of the Occupied Territories, the emergence of the Palestinian Liberation Organization, the invasion of Lebanon and the shattering of Beirut, the Palestinian Intifada, the Iraqi invasion of Kuwait, the war to force Iraqi withdrawal, and the brutal Baathist reprisals against Shi-ite and Kurdish rebellions: all of these events can trace their origins back to the imperialist carve-up of the southern Ottoman Empire.[26] A film like *Lawrence of Arabia* could not be newly made today, and its re-issue in 1988 was a profoundly nostalgic moment, for a world in which it was still possible to feel sad about the failure of the imperial mission.

The re-issue was a great success, with Eighties' film reviewers generally waxing lyrical about its aesthetic qualities. Yet their political evaluations reproduced the ambiguities (and ignorances) that are evident throughout the story of the Lawrence legend. One review, noting that '*Lawrence* has sometimes been condemned as a piece of jingoism', reflected that 'it is hard to imagine many Western films treating an Islamic War of Independence [which the Arab Revolt decidedly was not] with quite such sympathy today, and the British characters are on the whole treated far more sardonically than the Arabs'. An American critic, on the other hand, suggested that 'Lawrence offers the kick of empire – it is a profoundly conservative movie that will doubtless be upvalued in the current cultural climate'.[27] These contradictions, and the uncertainties that underpin them, are well summed up by a review in The Guardian: 'Lawrence of Arabia was always one of the cinema's greatest adventure films. Now, with these scenes and bits of scenes restored, it emerges as one of the greatest and most disillusioned studies of British colonialism ever made'.[28] Since the adventure tradition has worked precisely to energize British colonialism, this assessment is a contradiction in terms: the film's adventure narrative is qualified and then undermined by the colonial disillusionment, which is in turn limited in impact by the adventure. As a definition of the narrative's ambivalence, however, it is perfect.

The reappearance of Lawrence as a political reference point, at public meetings and in television histories during the Persian Gulf War of 1991, suggests that his story nevertheless retains its centrality within the British imaginary of Arabia and the Middle East. To this day, it remains among the most likely sources of popular knowledge about the region and its people, thus helping to reproduce Anglocentric assumptions and perspectives, and to transmit into the present the imagined relations of power from a bygone colonial era that are inscribed in them. This continuing potential of the Lawrence story, to organize British imaginings of who 'we' are and how we are related to others, is an exemplary lesson that it is not simply the historical form of adventure that matters, but the active psychic investments made in it; which bring it alive, and to which it gives a cultural form. Forms of identification and recognition are at stake in current conflicts as in earlier ones, and at heightened moments of tension and anxiety such as the war against Saddam Hussein's Iraq, the traditional defensive repertoire derived from colonial imaginaries remain available for reactivation.[29] If, by contrast to the turmoil of the contemporary Middle East, the Lawrence legend as recounted in the Lean/Bolt film bears the hallmark of nostalgia for simpler, more innocent days, it is important to insist that the British imperial adventure in the Middle East was, from its inception, a far from innocent story. Nor, as Lawrence himself knew only too well, was the masculine adventure hero at its centre entirely free of guilt.

NOTES

1. This article is derived from a longer analysis of the Lawrence legend in Part Three of my book, G. Dawson, *Soldier Heroes: British Adventure, Empire and the Imagining of Masculinities* (London: Routledge, 1994), pp. 165-230 (especially Chapter 8).
2. *Guardian*, 9 February 1989; L. Thomas, '"The Uncrowned King of Arabia", Colonel T.E. Lawrence, The Most Romantic Career of Modern Times', *Strand Magazine*, 59 (January-June 1920), later expanded into *With Lawrence in Arabia* (London: Hutchinson, 1925); T.E. Lawrence, *Seven Pillars of Wisdom: A Triumph* (Harmondsworth: Penguin, 1962); David Lean, dir., *Lawrence of Arabia* (Horizon, 1962).
3. Thomas, 'Uncrowned King', pp. 41-2.
4. M. Green, *Dreams of Adventure, Deeds of Empire* (London: Routledge and Kegan Paul, 1980), pp. 325-6.
5. J. Meyers, *The Wounded Spirit: A Study of 'Seven Pillars of Wisdom'* (London: Martin Brian and O'Keefe, 1973), p. 138; D. Stewart, *T.E. Lawrence* (London: Paladin Grafton, 1979), pp. 293-9; B. Liddell Hart, *T.E. Lawrence: In Arabia and After*, cited in S.E. Tabachnick and C. Matheson, *Images of Lawrence* (London: Jonathan Cape, 1988), (hereafter referred to as *Images*), p. 46.
6. Aldington cited in *Images*, pp. 52-5; Nutting ibid., p. 61.
7. J. Mack, *A Prince of Our Disorder: The Life of T.E. Lawrence*, cited in *Images*, p. 75.
8. J. Morris, *Farewell the Trumpets: an Imperial Retreat* (Harmondsworth: Penguin, 1979), p. 255; B. Porter, *The Lion's Share. A Short History of British Imperialism 1859-1970* (London: Longman, 1975), pp. 252-54, 322-30.
9. Morris, pp. 522-29; P. Mansfield, *The Arabs* (Harmondsworth: Penguin, 1978), pp. 298-303.
10. Morris, pp. 523, 528.
11. R. Hewison, *In Anger: Culture In the Cold War 1945-60* (London: Weidenfeld and Nicolson, 1981), p. 136; A. Sinfield, *Literature, Politics and Culture in Postwar Britain* (Oxford: Blackwell, 1989), p. 116.
12. J. Osborne, *Look Back in Anger* (London: Faber and Faber, 1960), pp. 84-85.
13. Cited in Hewison, p. 134.
14. Cited in E. Kedourie, 'Colonel Lawrence and his Biographers', *Islam in the Modern World* (London: Mansell, 1980), pp. 263-4 (no reference given).
15. Aldington, cited in *Images*, p. 55; S. Mousa, *T.E. Lawrence: An Arab View* (1966), cited in ibid., p. 73; 'Queers and treachery' in Sinfield, pp. 60-85.
16. *Images*, p. 61. For 'splitting' and 'projection', see Dawson, pp. 31-48.
17. See note 2. The quotations below are transcribed from a video recording of the film.
18. Kedourie, p. 262; A. Turner, 'Slash It Again, Sam', *Guardian*, 25 May 1989, p.23; P. French, *Observer*, 28 May 1989, p. 44.
19. Cited in Turner.
20. *Journal of the Society of Film and Television Arts*, 10 (Winter 1962-3), special issue on Lawrence of Arabia, p. 4.
21. For Thomas's romance, see Dawson, pp. 175-80.
22. See *Seven Pillars*, pp. 260-3, p. 129, for these two separate episodes.
23. For the Kleinian 'depressive position', see Dawson, pp. 35-43.
24. *Seven Pillars*, pp. 682-83; for Thomas, see Dawson, pp. 182-83.
25. *Seven Pillars*, p. 682.
26. P. Mansfield, *A History of the Middle East* (London: Viking, 1991).

27. K. Jackson, *Independent*, 25 May 1989, p. 17; J. Hoberman, 'Radical Sheikh', *Village Voice*, 14 February 1989, pp. 59-60. See also I. Johnstone, *Sunday Times*, 28 May 1989, p. C11; D. Denby, *Premiere*, February 1989, cited in 'National Film Theatre Programme Notes'.
28. Turner, p. 23.
29. *The Gulf War: the Arab View*, Channel Four, 1991; E.W. Said, *Covering Islam* (London: Routledge and Kegan Paul, 1981); E.W. Said, 'Empire of Sand', *Guardian Weekend Supplement*, 12-3 January 1991, pp. 4-7.

SUSAN HAYWARD

Reading Masculinities in Claire Denis' *Chocolat* (1988)

This paper comes in three parts. First a framing and focusing of Claire Denis' film *Chocolat*, including a brief synopsis of the film. Second, a summary of Denis' stated purpose in making the film and what we can read from that in relation to the film itself and the construction of subjectivity. Third and finally, an investigation of the construction of 'masculinity' as it concerns the main male protagonist, Protée – the black man-servant also referred to in the film as *'le boy'*.

At first, when I came to write this paper, I was not convinced that I had the right title – i.e., *Reading Masculinities in* Chocolat – and in fact I don't, because as it turns out I am going to discuss constructing masculinities rather than reading them. But this is perhaps merely following good academic practices of splitting hairs and changing the title of one's essay in mid-stream since it could be argued that, in order to see masculinities constructed, one first has to read them as being there. But that was not the point I was struggling with when first embarking on this paper. It was the plural of 'masculinities' that worried me because I could only see/read a binary opposition in the representation and construction of Protée as 'either/or' 'masculine/feminine'.[1] However, upon reflection and further analysis I think it is possible to talk about the construction of (plural) masculinities in relation to Protée and this is where this paper is going to lead to.

I. *Framing and focusing* Chocolat

Chocolat was directed by Claire Denis, a French woman filmmaker, who as a child was brought up in French colonial Africa – specifically the North Cameroun. The film is set in late colonial times, the 1950s, so the notion of decay and lack of control prevails as does the notion of patriarchy, western patriarchy, being under threat.[2]

'*Chocolat*' as a term in French means several things. It is used in relation to colour, as part of an idiom, and refers to the product itself. All three meanings are reproduced within the film. In that it refers to skin colour, *'chocolat'* points to the body and to racial difference: the body as site/sight of racial difference – Protée's body in the context of this film. As an idiom ('t'es chocolat') it means to be had, to be cheated, robbed – so within the film the question becomes who cheats/robs whom? Finally, of course, it also refers to the product itself and moreover to its properties as an exotic enhancer of coffee (mention of this is made in the film by the openly racist coffee-planter, Delpich). It so happens that coffee was, during this period, the main cash crop of the North Cameroun and was controlled by the French colonialists – thus the chocolat reference here refers (however indirectly) to the economic exigencies of colonialism.

The film's narration is related almost exclusively through the form of a flashback. The flashback is that of the older France, the central female character, who has returned to the Cameroun to meet up with her past. As I shall go on to explain in the next section the filmmaker, Denis, makes it clear that although it is France's flashback, the film is not narrated in its entirety from her subjectivity. We are presented, Denis tells us, with two subjectivities: France's and Protée's. The narrative is as follows. France, now an adult, returns to the outpost in North Cameroun where she was brought up. She is given a lift by an Afro-American ex-patriot. During this ride she flashes back to her childhood days (as a 6-8 year old). France's father – a colonial officer called Marc – is often away on tours of duty or expeditions (or widening roads!). The first part of this film concerns just such a time when he goes away. He leaves Protée, the black house-servant (epithetised in French as 'le boy'), in charge of his wife, Aimée, and his daughter. In this first part of the film which covers the absence of the father/husband we witness the nurturing relationship Protée has with France as well as a mounting tension between Aimée and Protée that is focused around the unspeakable notion of desire. We also witness France becoming progressively like her mother in her ambivalence towards Protée. In the second half of the film, still in flashback, a plane crash brings a motley crew of colonialists into France's home (including the coffee-planter, Delpich) and they bring in their wake a lapsed seminarian/priest, Luc, who – as a fallen-angel-cum-harbinger of truth[3] – exposes the attraction between Aimée and Protée, forcing a sexual confrontation. Shortly after this unmasking, Protée literally throws Luc out of the house and Aimée (who may or may not have witnessed that eviction) attempts to seduce Protée by touching his leg. He refuses her advances and she has him removed as house 'boy' by her husband and set to work in the garage where the generator is housed. For this betrayal ('chocolat') by Aimée (who in attempting to seduce Protée has already done a 'chocolat' on her husband), Protée punishes/betrays France's trust by letting her burn her hand on the generator's furnace pipe. He turns away from her and disappears into the dark. This emblematic shot refers to the colonialist 'chocolat' on the colonized – robbed of resources and power as colonized, this darkness suggests also that even once independence is reached the plundering of the colonialists will be impossible to redress. We return to the present where both the ex-colonialist, France, and the American ex-patriot, 'Mungo' Park, recognise that neither of them belong in this country.

II *Denis in interview – re-garding the texts*

In the numerous interviews conducted upon the release of *Chocolat,* Denis provides some revealing and intriguing comments that help us into a first reading of the film text. Denis says she felt a moral obligation to talk about colonization, but how? As far as the archetypes of colonization (i.e., the whites) were concerned, this represented no problem for her to represent. But what about the blacks? How could she, she asked herself, show the blacks ('montrer les noirs' are her precise terms)? As a white she obviously could not adopt a black subjectivity, so what procedure to follow? Denis came up with the idea of using a little (white) girl, France, whose memories of that time in the 1950s – in the form of a flashback – would constitute *a* point of view. Denis justified this decision by stating that a bonding/rapport does occur between white children and black servants. Because of this she felt she could use the little girl to talk about the blacks and, through her look, be able *to see* the blacks in the person of Protée. This was the only way she felt she could legitimately represent them, since that was all she knew. As she says: 'I used this privileged relationship to show, without seeking to explain them (the blacks), without practising an offensive *'psychologism'*, the real inhabitants of this African country'.[4] Denis also insists that Protée is the pivotal character – the link between the Europeans and Africans, the centre of everything, the mediator at the same time as he polarises 'all the feelings of humiliation, hate, love and regret'.[5] As a last point of relevance to this particular study, Denis says that, starting from the principle that all the scenes are seen either by France or Protée (the little girl or *'le boy'*), 'if neither are there to see or hear them, then, the scene does not exist'.[6]

When Denis says she is going to talk about colonization, is going to show *('montrer')* the blacks by using the little girl, when she says that she will use the little girl to talk about *'le boy'* and through that discursive method make it possible to see *'le boy'* (to see blacks in the person of Protée), I think a number of very interesting issues around reading masculinities and constructions of masculinities are raised – to say nothing about issues of colonization. Denis tells us she is talking about colonization through the girl's eyes (it is her point of view). But France as a 6 year old is of all the characters in the film the one *most* on the margins. In terms of age, sex and sexuality she is a pre-pubescent little girl. She is, therefore, not sexualized and she is without power. Protée, however, is a grown man. But, though a man, he is referred to as 'le boy'. The potent male (black male) is returned to pre-pubescence through his title, 'le boy'. He too is on the margins and without power (as colonized and black 'other'). And, because he is agenced through France (it is her look that permits seeing 'le boy') he again becomes, metaphorically speaking, de-sexualized. He is de-sexualized because he is rendered visible through France's eyes. He is not perceived as or through his sex but through his racial otherness: she is the *look* that allows Denis to show the blacks. Speaking of 'otherness' from the margins and without reference to sexual difference is a radical shift from traditional film discourses around colonialism (i.e., 'the potent black male as threat to the whites, especially the white female', 'fetishisation of/and fascination with the black male phallus'). Representing colonialism from the position of powerlessness evacuates stereotypes and makes it possible to see differently what is there. This is an issue to which I shall return because it serves to explain why Protée gets multi-positioned in France's eyes. Denis argues too that Protée also has a point of view (what he or France do not see does not exist, she says). So now colonization is being talked about through that which has been made visible: race, blackness *and* also, it seems to me, through the body – as is exemplified by Protée's naked body in the shower which France *sees* (a point that will be elaborated upon in the next section).

Now, in telling 'it' (colonization) through the body one would immediately expect the narrative to become sexualized, that is, that 'it' would be told through a gendered subjectivity. But that is not quite what happens. Something more complex occurs. And this happens, first, because Protée is also talking from the margins as colonized – which places him ambiguously in relation to gender identity: those with a point of view in this film (France and Protée) are those without power and those who are positioned as feminine. Second, this complexity in the narrating and subjectivity occurs because there are at least two points of view: Protée and France's. The question becomes how to read this doubling-up? In order to address this issue of point of view it seems useful to examine it through reference to Laura Mulvey's discussion of the three looks in mainstream narrative cinema.[7] The three looks are that of the camera, the look within the film, and the spectator's. In mainstream cinema all these three looks are traditionally perceived as male. The filmmaker/cameraman behind the camera's eye is traditionally male. The gaze within the film is agenced by the male protagonist who looks at the female. The female is positioned 'to be looked at' and this in turn constructs the spectator psychically as male looking at the female, thereby deriving pleasure and rendering the female fetish.

Clearly in *Chocolat* these looks get inverted, if not deconstructed (before our very eyes). First, the filmmaker is female – a first eye is, therefore, feminine. Second, the film is in flashback and we are told it is the little girl's look. Thus it is the older France's mind's eye, her memory and therefore her look. A look that is also outside the film looking in on her past. A second female eye as camera is, then, in place. Third, the look within the film is the little girl's look, we see what she sees – so a third look is female. The person being looked at in the film is Protée, a male, and not the traditional female. So the question becomes: is the black male fetishised? However we know that he also looks (what he and France do not see does not exist). It is precisely because he *also* looks that the 'danger' of being fetishised is undermined even though the potential for fetishisation is not dispensed with altogether insofar as Protée does occupy a female position, gets commodified as female (a point I shall go on to explain in the next section). Finally, where does all this leave the spectator? In Mulvey's analysis, the spectator in viewing (positioned as male) enjoys a narcissistic identification with his Ego-ideal (in the form of the male protagonist). In Denis' film the spectator is denied a narcissistic ideal by the very fact of it being feminised. The spectator adopts alternately two positions: France's, the young pre-pubescent girl, and Protée's, the black man-servant/ *'boy'.* So again it would seem that the traditional process of the look – this time of identification – is disrupted which means we are denied ultimately a fixed gendered position (because of the constant slippage between the two, because both positions are without power and because of Protée's feminised position).Thus all three of Mulvey's looking positions get doubled up and the exchanges of looks, therefore, weave an intricate pattern where no one ends up in a 'to be looked at' or fixed position. This relay of looks, where no one has power, functions to empty out the fetishistic effect of colonization (i.e., containing the threat of the black male phallus). This is Denis' way (her only way, if we recall her words) of talking about blacks without making them into abstractions. Let me now return to the question of telling 'it'/colonization through the body and see what this yields. In terms of colonization and the body – and colonization *of* the body – Protée's body is not fetishised. Difference is represented in racial not sexual terms and the generic slippage serves to underscore this. Denis is talking about gender and power, she is talking about blackness and whiteness but in that 'refusal' to show issues of colonization in sexual terms she has made it possible to represent colonization through the body without fetishising it. To do so would be to fail to address what colonialism is really about. She exposes the process whereby western patriarchy attempts to make safe what threatens *its* colonizing 'phallus' (thrust – widening roads). We know that fetishism is one of two ways in which the male contains the female body and makes it safe. Therefore, we must assume that by not enabling the fetishising of Protée's body to occur – thanks to the relay of looks – Denis is pointing to the fact that colonization, in its attempts to contain and make safe the indigenous 'other' is doomed in the end to fail. Western patriarchy's ability to survive has depended on its ability to suppress the female other. It is hardly surprising then that it exported that system of subjugation to other 'others', since it is to that system that patriarchy owes its existence and survival. However, colonization will never be a permanent state of affairs and this, Denis makes clear, is because to see the colonized 'other' as female/de-masculinised, contained and safe (as western patriarchy attempts to do) is to completely misunderstand, misrecognise even, the relations between oppressor and oppressed.

III *Constructions of masculinities/subjectivies and the protagonist Protée*

In this film which seeks to talk about colonization what dominates is the representation of the domestic female sphere – not the male sphere, the men, the *'colons'* (colonialists) at work. As spectators, we – like Aimée the wife and Protée the *'boy'* – see them go off to work. We get to see very little of the male sphere, or indeed the technical sphere (Marc's job includes going on expeditions, widening roads, etc.). We only get brief diegetic inserts of Marc on a journey and these flashes are France's – ones she has reconstructed, as older France, from her father's drawings and notes in his notebook which she now possesses. These flashes point to the fact that this narrative is coming from a female point of view and they make it clear that expeditions and technical exploits are (white) male affairs and exclude women (including the feminised, de-sexualized Protée). Women, white women, are in the colonies only to reproduce France (hence the significance of the little girl's name).

However, in the domestic sphere boundaries are much less exclusive. Protée is within the domestic, female sphere (as house-*'boy'*) and, by being in it, it could be argued that his body/sexuality has been colonized, emasculated and that as such he assumes a double-gendered identity. This is exemplified by the fact that it is he who nurtures France. He gives her to eat, feeds her. He teaches her his language. He plays riddle games with her. And so on. He is, therefore, the parent, the mother and the father. France is virtually ignored by her mother, Aimée. What is significant where Protée is concerned is that both Aimée (the real mother) and France develop strong bonds with him. Protée becomes the substitute father for the missing one. Where is the father? Where is the Symbolic order, the law of the father, patriarchal law? This absence refers also to the idea of late colonial France as lacking control and of western patriarchy being under threat. Protée, not the absent father, is the one gifted with language (he speaks three languages to our knowledge: French, English and Cameroun). Like his namesake, Proteus, he is the protector, the man of many metamorphoses who can see into the future and who speaks the truth (the impending end of colonialism).

But Protée not only has a mother/daughter relationship with France (he feeds her), he also has a son/mother one with her. In one sequence we see her feeding him. This stands as an ironic comment about colonizing France and her new sons, '*la France civilisatrice*' as France the nation perceived itself to be with its colonized countries – here France is '*la mère civilisatrice*'. However this particular scene is given an odd twist at the end, pointing to a degree of ambiguity between the two, or in their relationship. In this sequence France obliges Protée to go down on his knees and she spoon-feeds him from her bowl of soup (which he had prepared for her and which she finds too spicy). At one point she drops some soup onto the open palm of her hand which she is holding under the soup spoon to prevent dripping onto the table-cloth. Protée takes her hand and licks off the soup. They exchange glances and her look is one of stunned amazement and not a little bemused. His expression is inscrutable – as if he understands perfectly what he has just done, again pointing to his mythic namesake as the one who 'speaks' the truth. Denis also appears to be talking about different types of power games here. France chooses to feed Protée, he chooses to lick her hand. He licks the hand that feeds – that of colonial France. But this is the 'same' hand that he will later lure France into burning – even though she chooses to handle the furnace pipe ('does it burn?' she enquires, Protée grasps the pipe without showing any reaction – he burns his hand of course – she follows suit). Through this mise-en-scène of power relations between the most without power, Denis demonstrates how there are certain choices that can be made and that do have a determining effect (like leaving the palm of both protagonists permanently scarred).

The bond between France and Protée, then, is not without its ambiguities and ambivalences. And as the film progresses we witness France behaving more and more like *her* mother. On the one hand, like her mother, she bosses Protée around – at one point in the film this takes the form of her showing no regard for his own private life (when he has gone to the local school to get a teacher to write a letter to his fiancée she interrupts his dictation and orders him to take her home). This of course shows how the dynamics of colonization of the oppressed/oppressor get carried forward from generation to generation. Yet, on the other hand, like his 'daughter' she comes to him for nurturance.

If Protée is mother/father, son/colonized to France then his relationship with Aimée is even more redolent with ambiguities. Early in the film, during one of Marc's absences, he is ordered into the position of protector by Aimée to guard over her in her bedroom at night against a predatory hyena. Instead of letting him go off and shoot the animal she beseeches him to stay with her: *'reste avec moi'*, she insists and she does not say *'nous'* even though France is also present in her bedroom and in her bed. So he is positioned here as husband/protector before father/protector. Later he is positioned as husband/lover. First, she orders him to tie up the back of her evening gown (Marc is still away!) and as he does so there follows an amazing relay of looks via the mirror which give very little room for doubt as to the mutual desire. A second positioning is far more explicit. Aimée is sitting out in the dark crouched down by the French windows. As Protée comes to shutter them up she touches his leg in an attempt to seduce him but he rejects her advances quite roughly. Finally, his vulnerability to a positioning as a passive sexual object to Aimée's gaze and, therefore, of being commodified as fetish is exposed in a scene (prior to the aforementioned seduction attempt) where he is seen by her and France showering in the *'boy's'* shower outside. The context of this scene makes the ambiguity of their relationship all the more evident. Prior to this scene, almost as if in a lovers' tiff, Aimée chucks Protée out of her bedroom (he is tidying away her lingerie!) and orders him to bring her water for her shower which she takes immediately as he is pouring the water into the overhead water vat. This gives him the 'teasing' possibility of seeing her naked which is why he walks away from the ladder in such anger. Almost immediately after that sequence comes the scene of his shower where he is outside and totally exposed. What prevents the view of his nudity from being fetishistic, however, is that although both Aimée and France look at Protée, we see them looking at him from his point of view. Fetishised he may not be, but his reaction, one of anguish and humiliation, makes it clear that he has suffered the ignominity of being seen in his difference (sex and race) without his consent which is of course the power of the oppressor over the oppressed.

Conclusion

Protée's subjectivity is, then, constructed in a number of way's. First, he is constructed as 'other' and thereby as feminine: he works within a domestic feminine sphere, he is mother/nurturer, he is also the potential or real object of the gaze – Aimée's or France's. Alternatively, he is constructed as 'same' as husband/protector/'lover'. It is instructive in this context that when Marc comes home from one of his expeditions (shortly after the exchange of gazes in the mirror between Aimée and Protée) he says of himself to Aimée *'il est là ton boy'* ('your boy is home', meaning himself) and sweeps her off to their bedroom – all in front of Protée's eyes of course. The point is that by referring to himself as *'boy'* he and Protée become one and the same. Third, Protée gets constructed as 'sexual other' by and to the white woman and thereby does become fetishised. At one point in the film some of Aimée's female friends remark to her as they watch him moving about: *'il est beau ton boy'*. This represents a role-reversal not only in terms of gender but also power relations. White women are using male colonialist discourses and positioning themselves as beholders of the male gaze.[8] Finally, he is constructed as a sexual desiring agent. In these last two constructions (as sexual other and sexual agent) Protée becomes constructed as subject *and* object masculine. As object masculine (fetish) he is unable to agence desire, much like women in mainstream cinema. As subject masculine (the exchange of gazes in the mirror) he still cannot agence or act on his desire – the oppressed cannot love the oppressor – which is why, later, he rejects Aimée's desire for him.

In terms of colonization and speaking about it, Denis has reflected it through race (white and black), gender and the constructions of masculinity (Protée's in particular). She has also shown it through the domestic sphere and, in so doing, it has appeared that all those caught in the domestic sphere seem to be without power and, therefore, passive and female. However, this is not quite the case. Aimée has the power (verbally and via her husband) to eject Protée from the female space after he rejects her sexual advances – she tells Marc that Protée must go and work in the garage, there is no negotiation. Protée has the power (physically) to eject the seminarian-priest, Luc, from the house that he protects. He also rejects the advances of colonizing France, first in the form of Aimée then, later, France (the daughter) when he lures her into burning her hand.

Thus, in terms of talking about colonization we can perceive an almost Foucauldian reading here: a *mise-en-scène* of power relations to reveal that power relations are not purely and simply hierarchical nor are they permanent. This reading asserts that change is possible, but not without its ambiguities. Indeed the closing shots of the film, of the Cameroun twenty years into its independence, makes this point clear. France has returned to the airport and observes porters loading indigenous cultural artefacts onto a plane. Alongside with coffee (a vestige of its colonized past), artefacts of a pre-colonized country are the contemporary export products. Although 'free', the memory of the effects of colonization (coffee) and what it virtually erased (artefacts) lives on either as a consumer commodity or in museums and antique collections. As a last statement in a series of *'chocolats'* Denis tells us that the traces of colonialism – in this instance exploitation and plundering – are never completely erased.

NOTES

1. I first started work on this film in conjunction with another ex-patriot filmmaker's film, *Outremer* by Brigitte Roüan (1990). At that time I was examining these films through the optic of voices from the margins (women's voices) 'speaking' about colonialism. A paper based on that research was given at the San Diego MLA Conference in December 1994 and I wish to acknowledge here my indebtedness to the British Academy and their generous Travel Grant which made my attendance at the conference possible.
2. North Cameroun became self-governing in 1957 and fully independent in 1960.
3. One of Denis' sources of inspiration is the filmmaker Wim Wenders with whom she worked as assistant director prior to making *Chocolat,* her first feature film. Luc has a Wenders' aura to him as the evil angel reminiscent of negative forces in *Wings of Desire* (1988), a film for which she acted as assistant director to Wenders.
4. These statements come from her interview in *Première,* 134 (1988), p. 124. This is the French publication and is not to be confused with the American one of the same name (translation is by the author).
5. This statement comes from *Première* (USA publication), 2, 7 (1989), p. 42.
6. From the above-cited interview in *Première* (French publication), op. cit., p.125.
7. See Mulvey's seminal essay on visual pleasure in *Visual and other Pleasures* (London: Macmillan Press, 1989). The debate around the gaze has evolved since the first printing (1974) of this very important essay in feminist film theory. However, the question of the three looks still holds true.
8. We must recall however that he is fetishised by those who are also on the margins and without the real power – since these are women who are merely there to reproduce France. This then is hardly a case of making Protée 'safe' since, within this context, his sexuality (though not without its attraction and potential for miscegenation) is tabou: the white men may sleep with their black women slaves/servants (as Delpich does) but the white woman may not sleep with her black *'boy'.* Nonetheless, this scene is about repeating the discourses of colonialism showing, thereby, how the relations between oppressor/ oppressed get reiterated.

GARGI BHATTACHARYYA

A daydream of alternative subject formation – The Exotic White Man[1] – companion story to The Fabulous Adventures of the Mahogany Princesses

Not my object, my thing, my fantasy. I'm looking – but I can't fix him in my sights.

More and less human than us, he reddens easily. The scuffs of living come up tender on his skin. Not a story of the past, but still some map of pain. His surface cracks under pressure, grabs destruction from heat, weeps mucous tears. No lubricant to ease this brittleness – being wet just means being more sore.

Even as he flakes away and falls apart, the white man can't see himself. The world's audience can't recognise another's glance. Unaware, he lets it all hang out. Flaunts his paunch, scratches his crotch, wipes body ooze on his surroundings, convinced the marks don't show. Settling down for the performance, sinking into smugness, slumping as if the body belongs to someone else. Certainly no picture. Who'd look at that?

This weakness is touching. A clumsy child, finger in nose. So vulnerably oblivious. My job is to soak up the mess without accusing the source. Endless care and no more tears. My charge is too innocent for accountability, too pre-responsible for blame. The piss-stains on the carpet are nobody's fault. People with no sense of self deserve protection. I meet the bargain and hold the trust. The fiction of the one-way look, a master lie to live by.

I'm laying out the pieces – one by one, side by side. I touch, sniff, lick each fragment, curating carefully. The contract has come back round and I'm paying what I owe, the care that I have received. Who knows you better than me, recorder of your delicate places, vessel of your wounds. I hold what your life could never be. In me your fears are carried back as trophies, what hurts belongs to someone else. Trust me because I remember what you have been.

Looming in out of vision, she felt that she had won. Impossible to focus at this range – no barriers until, too late, they were broken. She knew that in his mind's eye he held a picture-reminder of her, a prompt for the frightening moments when looking didn't work. She knew that he remembered those other spaces where she was his object – that it was this memory of mastery which got him hard, guided him across her warmth. To him touch meant colour, form, responses filtered back through the thing he knew. Sensation as picture.

This was his weakness. She held his expectation, stroked and petted. Touched carefully, knowing he thought in pictures and stories, that her special skills were lost in his translations.

> The artist is somewhat prone to see the foreigner as a comic creature. Our features were odd, our pinkish colour somewhat revolting, our kinder moments endearing. And this was how we were seen, odd creatures from far away who were sometimes quite charming, and sometimes hatefully cruel. In this book we shall have to take ourselves as others found us.[2]

Boy flesh – unfamiliar meat. Less pliant, less movement. The polite words flick by – wiry, gaunt, artistic, sensitive androgyne, gawky manchild. Of course, that wasn't it. Nothing like the thrill of the new. She wanted to remake him as an image of herself. Her mirror, her object – vessel to her dreams, mould to her body. In him she saw a slip, a twist, an inside-out version of the world she knew. The same, the same, the same. Same picture, same story. A confirmation of her hopes and fears screening out the possibility of anything different. What he lacked was proof of what she had. Against him she puffed up, splayed out, shone.

Sometimes he turned his head as if pulled by recollection. Some other place from before or to come. A home elsewhere. She dried up in the breeze from that movement, the thought that she didn't centre the world. The idea of a place beyond their two cracked her heart wide open, and out flew the safety of her name.

Crisis and Management

I've been thinking about stories and leaps of imagination. So far education has told me that some contracts are in place as a historical legacy – 'postcolonial' discussion in particular traces the most ugly shadows of the past as seemingly endless repetition. This kind of history traps us all in the same old binds. Learning can be no more than a ritual retelling of these familiar tales of evil. Transfixed by how bad things have been, it seems disrespectful to think of alternatives, to put that painful past behind us.

I recognise that colonial histories cast long shadows – and more importantly that plenty of brutal colonial relationships are not yet done with – but I also think that learning should be about new possibilities.

So this is an exercise in imaginative leaps, because we all need to believe that breaking colonial contracts is possible.

Something strange is going on with the white boys – a change, a crisis, a dissolution. I'm starting from this widespread recognition. Whatever we call it, what happens to them has implications for us all. How can we name ourselves without this normative reference point? Who are we going to be when the post of everyone's other isn't open any more? Whose crisis is this?

I'm also beginning to think that it is impossible to do the right thing in academic talk about 'race'. Nothing you can do will please an audience still in love with the romance of the avant-garde. Too eager to please and the sweetness annoys – too angry and the accusation embarrasses. I'm assuming that you want to be hurt just enough, in keeping with the discipline of 'race' talk in UK education, the contract where the Masochist says 'hurt me, hurt me' and the Sadist says, 'No'.

I want to tease in the spirit of this contract, but I also want to let this contract go. No point in framing more arguments about the evils of the world – we know it and don't want or need to hear it again. There is no point to replaying destructive cycles of accusation – it's too familiar and stuck in old bad habits, even if it is what the audience came for.

So instead – an informed prediction, a joke curse, a story that is almost true. I'm not trying to convince you of what I say – just stretch our ideas of what is feasible. I'm starting from two high-profile media-hype stories – one about protests against the export of veal calves in Britain and the other about white people not replacing their own population. I like to think that both stories are about white supremacy and its imminent demise – but, as I warned, it takes a stretch of imagination to see this.

Cows

The success of the European peoples has been closely tied to their biota – and cows figure heavily, milkily, big dewy eyedly in this picture.

I'm starting from two bits of family folklore – not for authenticity, but admittedly to tease a white audience just enough. Like most folklore these stories are attempts to make sense of the inexplicable – and like all interpretations drawn from empirical observation, they tell you as much about the cultural framework of the observer as anything else.

i) Whitefolk are raised on beefsteak and milk which makes them big, heavy, resilient to disease. They are clumsy but strong – we are better looking but sickly.

ii) Whitefolk love animals more than their own children, certainly far more than us, dark-skinned echoes of their own form. I'm trying to understand why.

The protests against the exports of veal calves bring together for the first time the respectable white population and policing designed for the less than human – black, striking, travelling. Even the police recognise that there is something strange about this. An article for a police publication by Detective Inspector John Woods is quoted in *The Times* in which the writer warns, in relation to animal rights protests and media coverage of policing,

'Nightly pictures prove a large proportion of the protesters are white, middle-class, middle-aged and female. They are from a section of society who could normally be expected to offer total support for the police'.[3]

In the winter of 1994/95, reading the papers would make you think that the spontaneous demonstrations against the poor conditions in which calves were transported to France for slaughter heralded the dawn of a new era of popular protest in Britain.[4] In the beginning at least, these were 'regular people' – not the assorted undesirables who normally encountered the British police force's increasingly tooled up methods of crowd control. These were ordinary folk - people for whom being apolitical was a virtue – and they had been forced into protest because of the strength of their feelings. And the issue which had fired them up was the treatment of animals.

I used to think that this was another unpleasant reminder of white perversion – incomprehensible priorities, designed to add insult to the bloodbath of black injuries. Now I think that some other logic is at work – a mutation which is just now creeping into view.[5]

The Demise of the White Race

White people are dying out – they know it and they are scared.

This story can take various forms, but the common theme is that the social relations of whiteness are not conducive to reproduction. The development of whiteness, as identity and way of life, suddenly reveals a built-in obsolescence, unable to sustain itself. I want to acknowledge here the contribution of some kind of 'gender shift' to this process – the whole range of disputed developments around reproductive technology, feminism, sexual practice, and assorted fallout – as a way of indicating that the people most in crisis are *white boys*. White girls are placed very differently in relation to scare stories about white obsolescence – after all, their wayward behaviour has also contributed to the demise of the white race.

The scare stories have been around for some time. Something like Peter Brimelow's book *Alien Nation* makes explicit the WASP anxieties which us Cultural Studies types have been whooping over for years.

Here we get *Falling Down* in statistical form – hard facts to fill in existing neuroses. All of those wishing prophecies fulfil themselves – shifts in domestic arrangements oust men from their lazy homes of privilege, the demise of the military-industrial complexes of the cold war makes much skilled white male labour obsolete, including a whole swathe of white-collar workers, wage-labour becomes more dispersed, part-time, casual, service based, female, black, the world turns and the white men seem to have no place any more. All of this becomes violently apparent in any attempt to map the mixed terrain of the contemporary US city.

The US story takes place in relation to a global story in which white people are ageing and not replacing their young, while everyone else splurges out too many people to maintain. However, despite losses, the odds are in favour of the dark-skinned. You have the machinery of the state, capital in old-style heavy and flighty flexible finance forms, the food, the comfort, everything we might recognise as power. We have only ephemeral cultural productions which you covet and immense fecundity which you have lost.

But none of the other assets can make up for losing the ability to make babies. Think of this as a moment of crisis – not gender dysfunction but a by-product of recognising gender as dysfunction, a revelation made possible by a very particular societal formation, type of economy, geo-historical moment. And the possibility offered is a chance to practice the belief that white supremacy is not inevitable. Sometimes white dominance can seem endless and inevitable, springing from nowhere, destined to last for eternity. Even reading books, or perhaps particularly reading books, can make you feel like this.

Biology and Imagination

Lately I've been reading a book which isn't like this. *Ecological Imperialism* by Alfred Crosby plots euro-ascendance, particularly in the Americas, as a by-product of ecological factors. 'The first maize could not support large urban populations; the first wheat could, and so Old World civilisation bounded a thousand years ahead of that in the New World'.[6]

This is luck – your main staple can yield more from early cultivation than those of other climates. To Crosby, this dietary bonus is increased by another bit of luck – the ability to digest milk into adulthood. It is this visionary and unpopular determinism which makes me love this book and want to follow through its suggestions – a way of thinking about the accident of white domination which looks for concrete advantages, the things which have made the difference. Crosby expands his suggestion, 'The metaphor of humans and domesticated animals as members of the same extended family is especially appropriate for Northwest Europeans'.[7]

This is the minority of the human species and of mammalia more generally who can maintain through to maturity the infantile ability to digest quantities of milk. Not everyone can do this – although again this is down to luck and climate, rather than to the survival skills of a master race. However, the dietary advantages of wheat, meat and milk allow population expansion when numbers are what really count. And that's not all ...

Old World domestication of a variety of animals also gave rise to ambiguous gains in other areas – disease and immunity.

'When humans domesticated animals and gathered them to the human bosom – sometimes literally, as human mothers wet-nursed motherless animals – they created maladies their hunter and gatherer ancestors had rarely or never known'.[8]

If you can extend your population through improved diet, the losses of new sicknesses can be absorbed and new immunities developed. People die, but the race prospers. The extended family of north european milk digesters and their sleep-in livestock grow so numerous and resilient that they want to spread out to other parts of the world. Other people recognised this interdependence and its threat, Crosby writes of Maori reaction to white settlers that 'jealous of the high birth rates of the missionary families, [they] accused the Christians of multiplying like the cattle'.[9]

I think that it is worth laying aside our learned-long-ago scepticism about the role of 'nature' in human society – the 'determination' which Crosby is describing involves a whole hodge-podge of chance interactions. This is not about in-built superiority, of whitefolk, cows or wheat – no one component makes sense alone, resilience springs from the whole interactive caboodle. Crosby explains this again and again from a number of angles, perhaps anticipating a widespread wariness of any argument which seems, however carefully, to trace european ascendance to 'nature' in any way.

'For a clearer example of the portmanteau biota as a mutual-aid society, let us consider the history of forage grasses, because these weeds (remember, a weed is not necessarily an obnoxious plant, only an opportunistic plant) were vital to the spread of European livestock and therefore to Europeans themselves'.[10]

We are not talking about the superior genepool of caucasian *ubermensch*. Crosby is at pains to distinguish his thesis from this kind of old-style racist argument. Whitefolk win coincidentally as part of a particular biota at a particular moment – in themselves they are nothing, their prosperity dependent on weedy little weeds and a host of other seemingly insignificant players in their immediate food/immunity system. It is important to remember this when portmanteau biota seem to take on racial names, feeding back into

another mythology of white ascendance and biological back-up. Crosby explains again,
'What does "Europeanized" mean in this context? It refers to a condition of continual disruption: of ploughed fields, razed forests, overgrazed pastures, and burned prairies, of deserted villages and expanding cities, of humans, animals, plants, and microlife that have evolved separately suddenly coming into intimate contact'.[11]
Whitefolk win at a certain moment because of accidents of diet and how foodstuffs are cultivated. Prosperity is measured in meat. Trollope explains the attractions of Australia for the working class of 1870s: 'the labouring man, let his labour be what it may, eats meat three times a day in the colonies, and very generally goes without it altogether at home'.[12]
There are few more tangible ways of measuring quality of life.
Now the cycle has come around.
These same 'accidental' features are wiping whitefolk out. The red-meat culture of high immunity and high production spawns cholesterol anxiety – new economic organisations demand new systems of body care. The sedentary living of the post-development world in the late twentieth century cannot thrive on meat three times a day. Yesterday's luxuries become today's addictions. In 1987 in the US, in a report by the Surgeon General, 1.5 million of the total 2.1 million deaths in the year were connected to dietary factors, including too much saturated fat and cholesterol. As we are reminded in untold magazine diets, red meat is a prime culprit. Now red meat three times a day will almost certainly kill you.[13]

White Dinosaurs and Extinction Hype

White obsolescence sells airport paperbacks (my favourite kind of book – the last kick of visionary metanarrative and the heroic autodidacticism of modernity).
Let's concentrate on two main takes – as indications of wider debates.

1) Take one is *Alien Nation* by Peter Brimelow – Mr White apocalypse and media darling, in a craggy Englishman-abroad kind of way. His concern is to halt the dark-skinned non-anglo immigration and to maintain the anglo way of life in the US. This is old-style racist paranoia – there are more and more of these bestial people and they are going to swallow us up, steal what we have and give nothing back in return. Nothing much new about this – except the hype and the future projection.
Brimelow goes for the gullet in his account of impending catastrophes, 'There is a sense in which current immigration policy is Adolf Hitler's posthumous revenge on America'.[14]

He explains that in the aftermath of the Second World War the 'US political elite' (his phrase to connote decision-makers in a wrapped up undemocratic power structure) responded to the horrors of fascism with a concern to abandon racism and xenophobia in the new world they hoped to build. To Brimelow it is this concern which culminates in the Immigration Act of 1965, technically the Immigration and Nationality Act Amendment.

> And this, quite accidentally, triggered a renewed mass immigration, so huge and so systematically different from anything that had gone before as to transform – and ultimately, perhaps, even to destroy – the one unquestioned victor of the Second World War: the American nation, as it had evolved by the middle of the 20th century.[15]

Those unquestioned good guys of the United States, in their open-hearted desire to be fair to everyone, have unwittingly opened the door to their own destruction. The Brimelow line is hardly original – it echoes a whole cacophony of white backlash sentiment from North America and other parts of the wealthy developed world. Like all good pundits, Brimelow plays off this existing popular understanding – that's his angle, saying out loud what everyone (supposedly) already knows and feels.

> Race and ethnicity are destiny in American politics. The racial and ethnic balance of America is being radically altered through public policy. This can only have the most profound effects. Is this what America wants? [16]

Brimelow articulates some kind of widely felt gut feeling among (white) Americans, it seems. Why else the hype? He makes that peculiar kind of racist sense which bills itself as both everyday commonsense and beyond reason, the unarguable populist strategy which says both that this is what everyone with any sense knows and that these sentiments stem from primal depths which cannot be articulated or disputed.

> essentially, a nation is a sort of extended family. It links individual and group, parent and child, past and future, in ways that reach beyond the rational to the most profound and elemental in the human experience.[17]

Brimelow describes the nation as a unit which functions through affective bonds – with an implication that these bonds are being broken apart in the United States. However, despite all the bluster about speaking unwelcome truths, Brimelow is hard pushed to say what exactly he (and the rest of long-suffering and sensible America) is frightened of. His explicit concern is that whites are becoming a minority – white people in the US are living longer and having fewer children, assorted dark-skinned groups (and particularly 'newcomers') are having plenty of children and have a much younger population to start with. 'So the true impact of immigration is the proportion of immigrants *and their descendants* in the American population'.[18]

Brimelow explains the significance of this trend, in case we do not recognise the enormity of this shift,

> So what impact will all this have on America? In one word: profound. ... The Government officially projects an ethnic revolution in America. Specifically, it expects that by 2050, American whites will be on the point of becoming a minority.
> My little son Alexander will be 59.[19]

However, what exactly this profound change means remains unclear. This, presumably, is a call to that set of relationships beyond reason which joins families, nations, societies and historical eras in a network of interdependency. The fear is that 'our' own nearest and dearest will live with the consequences of white minority status – yet what these consequences are is never said. The prospects are too horrific to contemplate, yet sensible people know what they are, despite fudging from official bodies. 'The Census Bureau is apparently afraid to estimate the fateful day when American whites actually cease to be a majority'.[20]

Clearly, Brimelow feels that the loss of white majority status is a big deal and that predicting just how close it is will cause public (ie. white) outcry. And given his talent for riding the hype machine, his hunch is probably right. White people are probably quite worried about the non-replacement reproduction levels of their population, and the expression of this worry can take a number of dangerous forms.

2) Take two is more liberal, and takes in a broader sweep. In *Preparing for the Twenty-First Century* Paul Kennedy describes a global population in which whitefolk get older and sparser, while the dark-skinned continue to multiply and die young. Kennedy is fearful for the 'environment' rather than any more explicit invocation of white privilege – but those fecund black masses still give him the 'willies'.

Kennedy begins with an analogy between the Europe of the late eighteenth century and more contemporary accounts of crisis in the West and beyond – the jumping off point is Malthus and a sense that the mismatch between population growth and technological development is a continuing dilemma and dynamic in the world.

> As the better-off families of the northern hemisphere individually decide that having only one or at the most two children is sufficient, they may not recognize that they are in a small way vacating future space (that is, jobs, parts of inner cities, shares of population, shares of market preferences) to faster-growing ethnic groups both inside and outside their national boundaries. But that, in fact, is what they are doing.[21]

Poorer, darker people have more children and are younger all round; older, paler people have a more technologised and comfortable lifestyle, but are running out of people. Kennedy reckons that the interplay between these sets of trends is what will determine the future of the human race. Whether we survive (for Kennedy this seems to mean everyone, not only or primarily whitefolk), how well we all live – these things depend on the management of the different population crises of the rich and poor worlds. Towards the twenty-first century, all our destinies are tied. 'The environmental issue, like the threat of mass migration, means that – perhaps for the first time – what the South does can hurt the North'.[22]

Kennedy is indicative of more recent eco-sensibilities in the West. No longer the preserve of the freaky margins of white life, green populism has meant that towards the new millennium doomsday is figured in terms of ecological disaster – a nightmare which has taken over from self-inflicted nuclear annihilation as number one topic for progressive primary school project work and popular paperback apocalypse. Kennedy echoes many of the same concerns raised by Brimelow – he is also worried about the impact of demographic changes. However, unlike Brimelow's explicit fear that anglo culture and dominance is coming to an end, Kennedy sees oncoming disasters as crises of sustainability. The problems he foresees are global – although he acknowledges that their horror is that events in the unlucky South of the world now are shown to have repercussions for the formerly complacent North.

I'm interested in the way that Kennedy presents white obsolescence as an ecological disaster – or at least as a by-product and/or contributory factor in these dangerous trends. He does let us know that ageing is not the only problem facing the peoples of the developed world,

> While life expectancy for older white men and women has increased (much of the rise in health-care spending has gone to those over seventy-five), that for black women and especially black men has fallen. Because of this widespread poverty, Oxfam America – famous for its aid to developing countries – announced in 1991 that it would also focus, for the first time ever, upon the United States itself.[23]

The much talked about 'greying' of America is heavily skewed towards the white population (this is Brimelow's point). Not only are poorer, darker sections of US society not keeping up with this mixed blessing of affluence, some communities are *dying younger* – in a sick reminder that poverty is often a key linking feature of diaspora identity, an unwanted affinity between scattered peoples and left long ago homelands. To Kennedy this is an echo of global trends which are destructive for everyone – such wide disparities in resource allocation are not so much unjust as unsustainable. And right now arguments about sustainability and globally felt ecological costs seem more effective than familiar calls for justice. Kennedy tries to put things in terms of everyone's interests, 'A population explosion on one part of the globe and a technology explosion on the other is not a good recipe for a stable international order'.[24]

But, as with Brimelow, it isn't clear what disaster he is describing here. After all, stability is an ambiguous concept – and many people wish that many things would *not* stay so insistently the same.

Despite the many thoughtful and thought-provoking ideas raised by Kennedy's book, in the end he too wishes that those dark-skinned people would not have so many babies, an argument which is hard to make without some echo of racist logic. He wishes that the dark women of the poor world would get 'feminism', learn the positive dysfunctions of gender.

> In general, women in developing countries with seven or more years of education (and presumably from the better-off classes?) marry approximately four years later than those without education, have higher rates of contraceptive use, *and* enjoy lower maternal and child mortality rates – so both they and their offspring have better chances in life. This clearly implies that a change in the status of women would significantly reduce population growth in the developing world. But how likely is that in those parts of South Asia, Africa, and the Muslim world where gender restrictions are so pronounced?[25]

Isn't this the kind of first-world white feminist line we all learnt better than in the eighties? The kind of thing which fuels so much postcolonial study? The twist in this rendition is that here the first world declares its own interest – the spread of this enlightenment is good for white survival.

Brimelow and Kennedy write from very disparate perspectives, yet in their different ways they are both voicing concern over changes in the complexion of the world population. Either way, these stories say that the demise of the white race is bad for the planet – we will never manage without them.

Looking on the Bright Side

In response to all this hysteria what I am suggesting is the need to practice perverse imagining, to try and see the possibilities hidden in scary events. The less powerful you are, the more important this is.

Also, how can we learn if we don't entertain other possibilities?

Admittedly, this is a hard one to repackage as victory. If it was just numbers we would have won long ago. But with a stretch of imagination, maybe we can see beyond the horror stories.

Here are some unlikely ideas about what might happen – perverse imaginings.

1) Forever everyone has been hoping for miraculous technological innovation – feed your numbers and lots of other stuff becomes possible.

2) The resource-rich people-short world will need care – the answer to who will nurse the formally strong signals a karmic victory. What goes around comes around.

3) As one world order collapses, exhausts its own logic, begins to eat its own, maybe population size will again become a significant advantage.

Kennedy, in fact, outlines this possibility, summarising a range of debate,

> while there may be short-term costs associated with looking after and educating lots of young children, over the longer term there will be a larger population of productive workers between fifteen and sixty-four years old. Given the ingenuity and inventiveness of human beings, the more of them there are, the better; if on average there are two or three really creative people in every hundred, better to have a population of 100 million than 1 million.[26]

More likely, there will be no victory, just a shift – a new collection of wounds. For the dark world the challenge is to imagine ourselves without the demeaning counterpoint of whiteness, to stop being transfixed by the ogres of the past.

White Meat

The European biota has built the baseline from which white power can stem – good diet, extended population, technological development, world domination. At certain times, numbers have been crucial – meat and milk make all the difference.

Of course, now that time has passed. Addiction to meat is killing white people. Yet breaking the meat contract can't work either. The era of this biota is over – that kind of expansion can't win in those locations any more. Whitefolk wish to safeguard their own standards of living, trade reproduction for technological enhancement, live longer themselves rather than squandering resources on needy dependants. Those choices come out of the historical prizes of meat. But the prizes of meat cannot be reaped today – the era of expansion they fuelled has gone.

The sentiment of desperate animal-loving (so prevalent in contemporary Britain, as already discussed) is a warped recognition of the caucasian-cattle interdependence – but not eating their eco-friends can't save the white race now. Belatedly white people recognise their close kinship with their domestic animals, and using the clumsy tools of western rationality/the enlightenment, can only recognise these others as versions of themselves. You respect cows by thinking of them as people – extending criteria of need which are still denied to most of the world's dark-skinned population.

Of course, this is a misrecognition of what is in decline – the problem is not the treatment of cows but that cows are no longer an eco-treasure towards the 21st century.

Michigan Militia

You don't have to look too far to find signs of white crisis these days. The bombing of the Federal Government building in Oklahoma on 20 April 1995 has been another event to shake the white psyche. *The Times* of 24/4/95 tells us that the 'Search For Alien Scapegoats Leads Americans to their own Backyard',

> On Thursday night, America went to sleep with the depressing assumption that the nation had been attacked by evil foreigners. On Friday it awoke to the terrifying news that the worst terrorist attack on US soil was probably the work of Americans.[27]

This is another take which doesn't fit my meat story. It seems that white obsolescence brings up these contradictory responses – both anxious care of the metaphorical family of domesticated animals and white-on-white violence. Although early media coverage stressed that the bombers were 'Americans' not 'foreigners', it soon became apparent that here 'American' was an easy code for a certain kind of US citizen, redneck patriot of the American heartland, the reliable white backbone of a violently divided nation, until then.

> The news that the suspects were almost archetypal products of America – an army veteran from upstate New York linked with a Michigan farmer and his brother – left the media, and America as a whole, temporarily stunned.[28]

The framework of us and them, the logically same and those dangerous others, can't explain the obsolescence of the white race. This is death from within, self-destruct not victim of attack.

Recent strains of white violence almost recognise this. The new white disaffection – the whole whingeing syndrome of WASP victimage – cannot be pinned on the trespasses of an alien enemy. Again, the logic of the same is hard to escape – the root of this pain cannot be 'us', it must be 'them', different, other, elsewhere. But the familiar argument twists to accommodate new fears and new situations – 'our representatives are our enemies'. The fictions of democratic representation obscure this important battle between 'people' and 'state', apparently. 'Anyone who talks about communism doesn't get it. The enemy is fascism in the White House'. So – bomb people like us – the bizarre spectacle of white self-destruction as a protest against white self-destruction.

I do think that something shifts with Oklahoma – the tearful declarations about America's loss of innocence with this event are, surely, indicative of something. Frightening as this bombing was, these levels of violence are not unknown in human history or, even, contemporary events. What freaks people in this instance is the relationship between perpetrators and victims. For white America, it seems, Oklahoma has become a symbol of a warped aggression, directed inwards, towards its own. In the dysfunctional family of whiteness, rogue sons are running riot. Far more than teenage high-jinx, these boys act like they have got nothing left to lose – a nihilistic anti-heroism more usually associated with dispossessed populations. Since when has the violence of the powerful been terrorism? When white America starts killing its own in acts of terrorism (as opposed to venting its righteous aggression in racial violence, sex crimes, domestic beatings, child abuse, profit-motivated crime, road rage and military occupation) something is cracking in the house of the powerful. For the rest of us this is a realisation of the truly irresponsible violences of a dying people. Old enemies stay dangerous and become more ruthless and unpredictable.

In response to these events, the question for us all, anglos and others, troubled whiteys and expectant dark-skins, is:

Will we survive white obsolescence?

I can only understand events around veal exports as an irrational politicization – what kind of recognition of common interests is this? Surely even whitefolk cannot believe that this is the most significant issue of injustice in contemporary Britain, the one worth risking life and limb, the struggle which will lead to universal freedom, or even the more modest goal of self-empowerment. So I can only read veal as a veil for some other unspeakable fear, a sense of coming catastrophe. And I think it makes sense to view Oklahoma as part of the same crisis, related death throws from an agitated people. The white world senses its loss of ascendancy, but can respond only with desperate actions which contribute to the demise.

In our interconnected world of eco-horrors and high-tech networks, more than ever the actions of the rich white world (still now holders of capital, sources of information, entertainment and arms, all-round big influences in many people's lives) have repercussions for us all. I'm not interested in reforming white subjectivity, families, populations - but I am interested in surviving the fallout from the death of the white race ... a challenge to all our imaginations.

NOTES

1. 'Worlds away' from Luce Irigaray, *Speculum of the Other Woman* (Ithaca, New York: Cornell University Press, 1985).
2. Cottie A.Burland, *The Exotic White Man* (London: Weidenfeld and Nicolson, 1969), p. 11.
3. 'Supporters alienated by macho policing', *The Times*, 27 January 1995, p. 5e.
4. For some examples see *The Times:* 'Protesters Turn Back Calves Cargo', 3 January 1995, p. 5d; 'Animal Rights Mob Attacks Lorries in Siege of Shoreham', 4 January 1995, p. 5a; 'Livestock Convoy Beats Protest to Board Ferry', 5 January 1995, p. 6a. For policing and security issues see *The Times:* 'This is a Tyrannical Penalty Against a Small Town', 20 January 1995, p. 5d; 'Supporters "Alienated by Macho Policing"', 27 January 1995, p. 5e; 'Woman is Killed in Veal Lorry Protest', 2 February 1995, p. 1c.
5. For opinion pieces in the right wing press about these events see Bernard Levin, 'Animal Liberation Affront', *The Times*, 10 January 1995, p. 16c; Margot Norman, 'When the Protesters Come Out of Their Crates', *The Times*, 16 January 1995, p. 17a. Both pieces express bewilderment at the strength of feeling over this particular issue and suggest that animal rights protests are a symptom of wider disaffection and feelings of powerlessness.
6. Alfred W.Crosby, *Ecological Imperialism, The Biological Expansion of Europe, 900-1900* (Cambridge: Canto, University of Cambridge Press, 1986), p. 18.
7. Crosby, p. 26.
8. Crosby, p. 31.
9. Crosby, p. 239.
10. Crosby, p. 288.
11. Crosby, p. 291.
12. Crosby, p. 300.
13. For more on this and other meat issues see Jeremy Rifkin, *Beyond Beef* (London: Thorsons, 1992).
14. *The Times*, 22 April 1995, p. 18a.
15. *The Times*, 22 April 1995, p. 18a.
16. *The Times*, 22 April 1995, p. 18d.
17. *The Times*, 22 April 1995, p. 18f.
18. *The Times*, 24 April 1995, p. 18d.
19. *The Times*, 24 April 1995, p. 18e.
20. *The Times*, 24 April 1995, p. 18e.
21. Paul Kennedy, *Preparing for the Twenty-First Century* (London: Fontana, 1994), p. 45.
22. Kennedy, p. 96.
23. Kennedy, p. 303.
24. Kennedy, p. 331.
25. Kennedy, p. 342.
26. Kennedy, p. 31. For more on this see 'Too Small A World?', *Independent on Sunday*, 28 August 1994, p. 15a, and 'Overpopulation is not Africa's Problem', the *Independent*, 5 September 1994, p. 13a.
27. *The Times*, 24 April 1995, p. 12a.
28. *The Times*, 24 April 1995, p. 12c.

JOSEPH BRISTOW

Passage to E.M. Forster: Race, Homosexuality, and the 'Unmanageable Streams' of Empire

They lay entwined, Nordic warrior and subtle supple boy ... There they lay caught, and did not know it, while the ship carried them inexorably towards Bombay.
E.M. Forster, 'The Other Boat'

I

In one of his many essays on the East that date from the early 1920s, E.M. Forster turns his attention to a geographical location that, for decades to come, would exert extraordinary emotional and political pressures upon him. Writing at a time when Egyptian resentment against the British occupation was starting to die down, Forster focuses on the large brooding figure whose imperialist shadow loomed over Port Said. 'Salute to the Orient!' he exclaims, in tones that quickly deepen in their mockery. 'Given at Port Said presumably, where the status of M. de Lesseps points to the Suez Canal with one hand and waves in the other a heavy bunch of stone sausages'.[1] As if this derisory description were not absurd enough (with the 'sausages' representing a dredging-rope), Forster proceeds to render even more ridiculous the self-aggrandizing attitude struck by a figure who for him ostensibly enshrined the worst aspects of empire. Continuing in this satirical vein, Forster imagines Ferdinand de Lesseps, the chief engineer of the passage between East and West, declaring 'Me voici' in an expansive gesture grandly sweeping out towards his handiwork, only to add 'Le voilà' as an 'afterthought'. 'It leads rather too far, that trough', remarks Forster, 'to the mouths of the Indus and the Ganges' – rivers which, as his sentence unravels, he disparagingly calls 'unmanageable streams'. But as the arch wording of this paragraph draws to its close, Forster's final clauses suggest that the 'unmanageable' condition of India reveals much more about his own anxieties than any 'afterthought' de Lesseps may have had. 'Nearer Port Said', he observes, 'lie trouble and interest enough, skies that are not quite tropic, religions that are just comprehensible, people who grade into the unknown steeply, yet who sometimes recall European friends'. The inferences to be drawn from these comments are plain to see. In the distant land of 'unmanageable streams', there is a much more intense mixture of 'interest' and 'trouble' – the true 'tropic' heat, incomprehensible religious beliefs, and men and women who in their 'unknown' reaches perhaps prefer *not* to recall their 'European friends'.

I have dwelt on this paragraph at length because it accentuates the main tensions that can be readily detected in Forster's diverse writings on Egypt and on India. This is an extensive corpus of work. It begins with his 'Indian Journal' of 1912-13, and gathers pace with the large number of letters he wrote from Alexandria while stationed there during the First World War. His knowledge of Egypt came to public attention in 1922 with *Alexandria: A History and a Guide,* and with several of the essays contained in *Pharos and Pharillon,* published the following year. His reflections on Egyptian and on Indian politics – especially the rising forms of nationalist agitation – appeared in a series of notable unsigned contributions to the broad Liberal periodical, the *Nation and Athenaeum,* during 1922 and 1923. His engagement with the shortcomings of British imperialism in the period after the Armistice in 1918 culminates, of course, in what most critics would agree is his greatest – if most contentious – work of fiction, *A Passage to India* (1924). Much later, Forster brought together some of the correspondence he had mailed to England while working in 1921-22 as the Secretary to the Maharajah of the native Indian state of Dewas Senior; furnished with an editorial commentary that connects the episodes detailed in these letters, *The Hill of Devi* was issued in 1953.

These writings often disclose Forster's distaste for the racial bigotry and arrogant behaviour of the British imperialists, whether he is alluding to the supremacist attitudes of the Milner Mission to Egypt in 1919-20 or to the enduring narrowmindedness of the Anglo-Indian community, who were understandably appalled by his representation of them in his novel of 1924. Time and again, Forster publicly scorns the triumphs of empire. 'May I never resemble M. de Lesseps', he insists in 'Salute to the Orient!'; 'may no achievement upon no imposing scale be mine, no statistics, philanthropy, coordination or uplift'. Yet even here the force of his denunciation is not quite as complete as one might think. Rather than disown any such claims to posterity – all of them emanating from Victorian ideals of progress – Forster adds how he would like to bequeath his own, albeit modest, legacy. His preference is to be remembered, not for any kind of moral 'uplift', but for 'scattered deeds', ones that would last for a 'few years only' before being promptly consigned to a 'wayside tomb'. Such sentiments suggest that Forster is not exactly resisting the imperial prowess represented by the statue of de Lesseps. For all his vigorous mockery, he in many respects shares the angle of the engineer's gaze.

In repudiating the injuries of empire, Forster paradoxically reinscribes them, if in a less clearly discernible form.

This clash of interests becomes most prominent, I believe, in those writings that mediate Forster's sexual experiences with Egyptian and with Indian men. The present essay seeks to show how the contours of his inter-racial homoeroticism bring almost to breaking-point the persistent antagonism one often finds in Forster's anti-imperial efforts to imagine 'friendship' between colonial rulers and subaltern peoples; the desire for connection between both parties is for him indissociatable from fantasies of dominative violence. Although rarely concentrating on the homoerotic dimension to this conflict, countless recent discussions of *A Passage to India* have drawn attention to Forster's ambivalent attitude towards empire. If, in that novel, his narratorial jibes at the members of the Club at Chandrapore find perhaps greatest amusement in recalling the Anglo-Indians' performance of *Cousin Kate*, then the native Indian population is hardly spared the narrator's scorn. 'Suspicion in the Oriental is a sort of malignant tumour' – this is perhaps the most infamous moment of narrative condescension.[2] But rather than recapitulate the observations made by those critics – such as Benita Parry and Edward W. Said – who have most clearly identified the imperial mentality that shapes much of Forster's purportedly liberal thought[3] (a liberalism, one needs to recall, that preoccupied an earlier generation of critics),[4] I wish to turn instead to the larger political contexts that framed Forster's erotic encounters with racially subordinated men during his periods of residence in Egypt and in India between 1912 and 1922. His private memoirs, journal entries, and correspondence with close friends bring into focus the sources of a conflict between his political and sexual preferences that lurks beneath the surface of his highly acclaimed novel. These works make for compelling reading, since they reveal how he was uncomprehendingly drawn to the location where he felt obliged to deride the grandiosity of de Lesseps' salute to the Orient.

II

Let me, then, begin with Forster's first voyage East in 1912, since it holds certain clues to the painful tension between homoerotic experience and imperial domination that aggravates many areas of his later work. Travelling with his Cambridge mentor, Goldsworthy Lowes Dickinson, Forster came into contact with Captain Kenneth Searight, a dashing young officer who kept a detailed record of his 'minorite' liaisons.[5] The comprehensive account of Searight's sexual adventuring, which amounted by his own calculations to the seduction of 129 boys between 1897 and 1917, was still being compiled when parts of it were shown to Dickinson and Forster during their voyage East. Ronald

Hyam claims that the manuscript Searight completed in 1917 – which takes the form of a long autobiographical poem entitled 'The Furnace' – counts as one of only two surviving sexual 'confessions' by Indian army officers from this period.[6] In the extant manuscript, Searight devised some thirty-three different symbols to identify the specific sexual acts he had conducted with each boy, along with information about their names, age, height, and the date and place where the different forms of intercourse occurred. It scarcely needs stating that Searight's tireless attention to taxonomic devices such as these reveals both a military and a missionary desire to produce a certifiable knowledge of the native 'other' that is very much of its time. Such systems of classification had a precedent in Richard Burton's writings on the 'Sotadic Zone': a wide-ranging area tending towards the equator that, on his view, joined together cultures where pederasty was endemic. (His notorious essay was written in 1885, the year in which the Labouchere Amendment put a legal ban on acts of 'gross indecency' between males, even in private.) Although it would appear that Forster's sexual encounters in Egypt and in India did not match Searight's either in frequency or in their capacity for experimentation, it is reasonable to infer that this meeting at Port Said opened Forster's eyes to sexual possibilities in the East.

By March 1917, while working as Head Searcher for the British Red Cross in Alexandria (a post that involved doing the rounds of hospitals, and questioning wounded soldiers for news of their missing comrades), Forster had grown intimate with Mohammed el Adl, an Egyptian tram conductor. This relationship was to remain, for the rest of his days, one of the two main loves of his life. The memory of el Adl would haunt Forster for decades after this lover had died of consumption in 1922. In 1963, for example, when writing to William Plomer, Forster makes what is a quite typical comment on the ways in which various threads of his creative imagination are curiously intertwined. Having been asked to respond to an enquiry about whether Oniton Grange in *Howards End* (1910) is based on a real house or not, he declares that this imaginary home is associated for him with the Clun Forest celebrated in A.E. Housman's covertly homophile collection of poems, *A Shropshire Lad* (1896). The movement from Oniton Grange to Housman's 'Clun' is significant, not least because it shifts perspective from a residence built on the profits of an imperialist stockholder (the money-grabbing Henry Wilcox) to a man whose lyrics bore a strong resemblance to the writings of the 'Uranian' poets whose paeans to boy-love at times courted controversy in the late-nineteenth century.[7] No sooner has this transition been made from the imperial stronghold of Oniton Grange to Housman's homophile pastoral than Forster is prompted to write that this 'little matter has set me to thinking of the past which is sometimes evoked by its smallness'. And he adds: 'A big matter – Mohammed el

Adl – has occurred to me'. He reveals how he has been consigning to a
box various 'scraps' and 'memories' of his lover. 'With one exception',
writes Forster, 'he has been the greatest thing in my life'.[8] What, then,
was it about el Adl that forty years later spoke so powerfully to
Forster's desires?

Forster's fond thoughts about el Adl are most explicitly detailed in
two sets of documents: the series of letters he wrote to Florence Barger,
who knew as much as any of Forster's intimates about his sexual needs
and wants throughout his middle age; and the still unpublished
memoir of his lover that he started writing in 1922, and drew to a close
in 1929. By 13 September 1917, he responds to Barger's question about
what he and el Adl 'do'. 'Talk mostly', he replies.[9] Stating that he and
el Adl can enjoy only two hours a week together, Forster notes the
difficulties he has in bringing his lover back to his apartment. Not the
least of his worries is being put under suspicion by the authorities. It
needs to be remembered that it was not just that homosexual relations
were legally prohibited (Egypt at this time was a British Protectorate,
with courts that could lay down sentences against acts of gross
indecency), but also that the country – given its strategic military
position – was under strict military surveillance: throughout 1914-18
severe forms of censorship were imposed on communications of all
kinds. 'We have laid down certain rules', he remarks. 'We meet and
part *at* certain places – both in civilian costume – and never travel
together on trams'. If his lover is dressed in what Forster describes as 'a
long and rather unpleasing nightgown over which you button a frock
coat', the two may walk together only in the 'neighbourhood' of el
Adl's room. But if these impediments were not enough, there is for him
a much more pressing problem that activates the pronounced
antagonism in the ways that Forster negotiates both his sexual
affiliation with an Egyptian man, and his racial difference from his
lover:

> His is unfortunately ~~rather~~ black – not as black as a child's face or ink, but
> blacker than [the doctor and poet, Ernest] Altounyan or [the man whom Forster
> had long adored after first tutoring him in Latin, in 1906, Syed Ross] Masood –
> so that our juxtaposition is noticeable. It was thoughtless of him to have been
> born that colour, and only the will of ~~God~~ Allah prevented his mother from
> tattooing little blue birds at the corners of his eyes. Blobs on his wrist have
> sufficed her.

Even though, at first glance, these sentences suggest that the fact of
blackness is in itself a complete misfortune (a point compounded by the
erasure of the adverb 'rather'), the other hesitancy in the script is
revealing. For it indicates that this all too evident chromatism is
attached to an acknowledgement of the inappropriate language Forster
finds himself imposing on el Adl's body. Not by the 'will of God' but

by the 'will of Allah' – this momentary correction might encourage us to look again at the fear of the contrastive 'juxtaposition' where an emphatic difference of colour threatens to jeopardize their love-affair because it is doubly illegitimate – inter-racial and homosexual – under imperial rule. That said, the subtext is clear: Forster's romance would surely be easier if only el Adl was white. But, there again, given the attention paid to the tattoos on el Adl's wrists, one cannot help but think that the chromatic 'juxtaposition' between them is a source of erotic fascination. If endangering them both, at least for him their differing complexions draw attention to the possibility of their intimacy. On this view, racial difference has the capacity to make publicly perceptible their sexual 'juxtaposition'.

But this 'juxtaposition', as Forster knew, was in many respects more than a little one-sided. Sexually, he felt the relationship gave greater pleasure to him than his partner. On several occasions, the unpublished memoir of el Adl shows that Forster's desires – most pressingly, his wish to be penetrated – were not reciprocated. There appears to have been some confusion about the nature of their erotic encounters. 'Perhaps for this reason', Forster regretfully wrote, 'my carnal ecstacies [*sic*] with you have never been supreme'.[10] Several pages later, he notes: 'It appears to me, looking back, that you were not deeply attached to me, excited and flattered at first, grateful afterwards – that's all'.[11] Whether such emotions were ever recognized at the time of their love-making can only remain a matter of speculation.

Politically, too, the course of their relationship did not run smooth, but if for rather different reasons. Forster's decision to influence the path of el Adl's career makes one wonder about the extent to which he wished to improve or to corrupt the object of his affections. In the same month as his previous letter, he asked Barger: 'Do you really think it beastly to have made him a spy?'[12] Given that he ranked high in the Red Cross, Forster had exploited his connections to find el Adl employment as an intelligence-gatherer in the Canal Zone. Such work was altogether more 'lucrative', he informed Barger, than working on a tram. Since Forster claims to have lost his 'high moral values' on this score, the loss, he claims, can be compensated for in el Adl's new-found earnings. Rarely might one encounter a more paradigmatic instance of imperial philanthropy covering its bad conscience.

By finding el Adl this kind of work, Forster knew he had pressed his lover into the service of an empire that was anxious about the commercial and political security of an occupied territory whose value in the war against Germany and Turkey could not be underestimated. In the pamphlet on the government of Egypt that Forster produced for the Research Department of the Labour Party in 1920, he shows how appalled he was by the imperial exploitation of the Egyptian animals, food, and fodder that occurred during the war; he pointed out that the inadequate and tardy payment for such resources contributed greatly to the rise of anti-British feeling by the time of the Armistice. As he himself observes, one million Egyptians (a thirteenth of the whole population) had been commandeered into a Labour Corps serving the needs of the British rulers. 'Up to 1919', before the rioting against the British had well and truly begun, 'the Egyptians were allowed such plebeian virtues as industry and good temper, but they were regarded as an inferior race, incapable of taking the initiative or of suffering for an ideal'[13] – such as empire itself. No wonder Forster's decision to find el Adl 'lucrative' work grieved him. 'I am ashamed, ashamed', he admitted in February 1918, 'to have to ask him to behave as I do'. This sense of shame, however, is accompanied by the assertion that his love for el Adl is 'the most wonderful thing' that has 'ever happened' to him.[14] The greatest sexual rewards, it would seem, have their basis in not a little guilt.

Forster's love thrived in a country where, as subsequent writings show, he felt forced to question how much his erotic desires were influenced by an imperial mentality, one that was highly conscious of the background that gave rise to the Egyptians' militant demands for freedom. Whatever the sexual setbacks, it was in this vexed political context that his relationship with el Adl continued to flourish during 1918 until early the following year. By that time, it was clear to Forster that he would have to leave his position at the Red Cross, now that the Great War had ended. But he was keen not to depart, particularly as el Adl had shown early signs of consumption. During this acutely difficult period, Forster began writing his rather unconventional 'guide' to the city in which he had first met el Adl.

It is worth pausing for a moment on this quite comprehensive work – one that is rarely discussed in studies of Forster's canon – because it helps to open up ever further his conflicted perspective on the country in which 'the most wonderful thing ever happened' to him. Discussing Forster's critique of 'tourist discourse' – notably in the Edwardian novels – James Buzard claims that in *Alexandria: A History and a Guide* 'Forster again lays stress on the distant past's indicting connection with an early twentieth-century present'. This observation makes greatest sense when one realizes that '[o]f nearly all the city's chief "attractions", not a trace remains: Lighthouse, Ptolemaic Palaces, Library, Temple of Serapis'. Such is the nature of Forster's 'anti-guide', which refuses the '"synthesis" or "harmony"' sought by tourists and imperialists'.[15] Buzard's account, however, should not necessarily urge anyone to believe that Forster's idiosyncratic 'history' and 'guide' is wholly subversive in intent. It does, after all, represent the city as eerily dead and unpeopled, as if it had no contemporary cultural life of its own. Covered in ruins, bearing the impressions of many historical epochs, and having witnessed the encounter between East and West through both commerce and warfare, 'Alexandria', announces Forster, 'though so cosmopolitan, lies on the verge of civilization'.[16] Once one leaves the city, there is nothing but desert, leading further and further away from this last outpost of culture. Travel away from it leads only to 'unmanageable streams'. Not surprisingly, then, when Forster followed the 'trough' eastward from this location, the more troubled and dissatisfied he became, both politically and sexually – to the point of wanting to inflict pain upon the body of a native Indian.

III

In the private memoir entitled 'Kanaya', probably drafted in 1922, Forster records his sexual experiences with a servant of the court of the Maharajah at Dewas Senior, where he worked as Secretary between March and September that year. Having reached the land of 'unmanageable streams', Forster discovered that he had even greater access than in Egypt to willing sexual partners, even though their apparent compliance with his wishes made him despise them. The 'unmanageable' nature of India, wrote Forster, lay in the heat. 'The climate', he remarks, 'soon impaired my will'. 'I did not suffer from the heat in other ways', he adds, 'but it provoked me sexually'. Once he had discovered that masturbation brought no relief to his passions, he made advances towards a Hindu coolie, a boyish figure who he felt was altogether preferable to the 'Mohammedans in those parts', given their 'general air of dirt and degradation'.[17] But when he grew anxious about being discovered by the Maharajah, he confessed his activities, only to find that his employer was convinced that Forster's desire for boys must have been a bad habit picked up from Egypt. Keen to protest otherwise, Forster was never the less relieved to know that he would not lose his job. And what was more, a suitable boy would be supplied for him. But when Kanaya arrived, Forster was hardly excited: 'in too yellow a coat and too blue a turban, he rather suggested the part and his body was thin and effeminate and smelt of cheap scent'.[18] Faced with this young man, he found that for some time their sexual encounters 'went well'. But he still could not 'get from Kanaya the emotional response of an Egyptian, because he had the body and soul of a slave'.[19] That is presumably why he eventually received pleasure from boxing Kanaya about the ears. 'He hadn't even the initiative to cut my throat'.[20]

By the time Forster wrote these words, Egypt had been granted a limited amount of independence, if on terms that ensured – as a result of the Milner Mission – that Britain could keep using the country as a military base. London believed that the nationalist discontent led by Sa'd Zaghlul had once and for all been contained. But India, of course, had over a quarter of a century to wait for independence, and then on entirely different terms. 1922-23 is generally recognized by historians as marking the second of the main phases of Indian nationalist agitation, in which Mahatma Gandhi's non-cooperation movement largely helped to set the political agenda. But Forster's liberalism hardly stretched to the support of such insurrection. 'If the menace of British India subsides', he remarks in an essay published in 1922, the Princes of the native states – such as Dewas Senior – 'will return to their old ways'. And these 'old ways', as he sees them, involve far too many different traditions, systems of belief, and political tendencies. Even though Forster admires those native states that are shifting power from autocracy to democratic constitutionality, he finds himself unable to write a 'eulogy' to the 'new spirit that has entered India'.[21] So in spite of Forster's attack on the 'menace' of empire (his derisory account of the Prince of Wales's ill-timed visit to Indian in 1922 is tart to say the least),[22] his essays from this period adopt a comic-ironic tone towards Indian life and customs that is assuredly co-extensive with the Raj discourse that he abominated. Take, for example, how he regards the ceremony of serving pan in the broader context of Indian culture. 'The serving of Pan is in itself a little art – and the arts of littleness are tragically lacking in India; there is scarcely anything in that tormented land which fills up the gulf between the illimitable and the inane, and society suffers in consequence'. Confronted by this chasm between the sublime and the ridiculous, he claims that only the humble chewing of pan can restore our sense of 'humanity'. No one, he argues, should be led to believe that chewing pan is in any respect connected with the 'Mystery of the East'. 'The East is mysterious enough', he insists, 'mysterious to boring point'.[23] Such words may well leave one querying what 'humanity' is left in a writer who feels he can flatly condemn – regardless of his mordant tone – a subordinated culture in which he feels distinctly uncomfortable.

Forster's growing fascination, developing perplexity, and final revulsion with the 'Mystery of the East' comes into even sharper focus when one traces his remarks on India and the Orient in his voluminous correspondence with Syed Ross Masood. In many ways, Masood was Forster's first contact with Indian life; he was also Forster's first great passion. Although Masood could not requite the love that Forster declared for him in 1910, the two men maintained a long and lasting friendship, mostly through their frequent and intimate letters. In 1912, Forster enthusiastically announced: 'You have made me half an Oriental, and my soul is in the East long before my body reaches it'. But typically this comment is matched with incomprehension: 'I don't *understand* the East or expect to understand it, but I've learned to love it for several years now'.[24] Later, in September 1917, one suspects that Forster sees himself in danger of disclosing that his Egyptian experience may have made him into 'half an Oriental' in ways that Masood never could:

> One is as far from the East here as in London. All is so colourless and banal. – But I oughtn't to grumble too much, for I have good friends here, and have lately got to know an Egyptian whom I greatly like and who sometimes reminds me of you. (On the whole I dislike the Egyptians.)[25]

His divided attitude is intriguing. At first, it appears that Egypt – being equidistant from England and India – cannot match either place, since it is 'colourless and banal'. Yet Forster has none the less managed, in this seemingly depressing environment, to get 'to know an Egyptian' who would appear to substitute for the erotic intimacy that he desired, but was denied, with Ross himself. Hereafter, if Forster is going to become 'half an Oriental', it will occur on Egyptian, not Indian, soil.

Five years afterwards, when Forster was in the midst of drafting *A Passage to India*, he made the disillusionment with India that one finds in his essays of this period perfectly clear to Masood: '[W]hen I began the book, I thought of it as a little bridge of sympathy between East and West: but this conception has had to go, my sense of truth forbids anything so comfortable'. And just to drive the point home, he adds: 'I think that most Indians, like most English people, are shits and I'm not interested whether they sympathize with one another or not'.[26] This could well be taken as the most decisive declaration to support the prevailing critical view that by the early 1920s Forster had lost faith in his liberal idealism that he had worked through his earlier fictions, up to and including *Howards End*, where the imperative 'only connect' serves as an epigraph. Even though the essays of 1922, the letters to Masood, and the memoir of Kanaya have a different standing as variously public and private documents (they necessarily have a range of addressees, and their tone and texture alter accordingly), one can none the less see how each illuminates one of the major sources of friction in *A Passage to India*: the enduring contradiction between the thematics of 'friendship' in the novel and the sexual violence that we find at its centre, a form of violence that does everything it can to sever East from West.

Only one sustained critical intervention has so far been made into this vexed topic and its impact on Forster's *magnum opus*. Sara Suleri's powerful – but far from unproblematic – post-colonial analysis of the novel has already been critiqued by myself elsewhere, and there is no need to recount my concerns about her reading at any greater length here.[27] For my present purposes, I would simply say that Suleri's thought-provoking observations about the conflicted 'imperial erotic' that arises in the novel shows how easy it is to lay the blame for Forster's recoil from India upon a misapprehension of male homosexuality. The shortcomings of Suleri's reading are instructive, since they prove how difficult it remains for feminist, for post-colonial, and for queer critics to articulate the novel's persistent ambivalence towards patterns of imperial and sexual violence without duplicating the kinds of damage that Forster's narrative complexly subverts and supports. Recognizing that *A Passage to India* stands as 'one of English India's most troubling engagements in the fiction of cultural self-examination', she points out how the narrative adjusts the traditional masculinist gaze of empire upon the feminized native territory by revising the well-worn and discredited trope of 'friendship' that features largely in many earlier fictions of English India.

To Suleri, it is those passages in the novel that linger on the sexual fascination of the Indian male body – such as 'the man who pulled the punkah' in the courtroom scene[28] – that reveal 'a hidden tradition of imperial looking in which the disempowerment of the homoerotic gaze is as damaging to the colonizing psyche as to that of the colonized', thereby questioning 'the cultural dichotomies through which both are realized'.[29] But once Suleri has made this remark, she turns her attention to a number of sentences in the memoir of el Adl that Forster started in 1922, the year in which he also began work on the novel itself. The excerpts in question – which are selectively quoted in P.N. Furbank's distinguished biography – record how Forster, not long after he had received news of his lover's death, found himself calling his lover's name while strolling on the downs in the Isle of Wight. And he imagined himself being called in return by his 'friend': 'you calling me and I felt we belonged to each other now, you had made me an Egyptian'.[30] Such wishfulfilments, as Suleri sees them, achieve nothing less than 'an illusion of cultural transference' that is only possible now that el Adl is dead.[31]

Undoubtedly, Forster's desire to have been 'made an Egyptian' echoes the letter written ten years earlier to Masood, whom at that time he believed had made him 'half an Oriental'. But it is important to note that in the full text of Forster's memoir, dated 5 August 1922, this 'cultural transference' remains knowingly incomplete; in fact, the longing for connection is accompanied by heartfelt loss, as he writes out his grief with these words: 'I cannot make you alive, nor can I belong to you because you own nothing. I shall not belong to you when I die – only be like you'. Throughout, this intensely conflicted document comes up against emotions that it seeks to disavow. The fantasy of separation is shot through with a longing for consummation. Even though Forster claims to think 'more about himself and less of' his Egyptian lover with 'every word', the call of 'Margan, Margan' at 'Beebit el Hagar Station' preys on his mind. No matter how much he seeks to put Egypt behind him, he finds himself haunted by a cross-cultural yearning that cannot be repudiated.

The larger context of the memoir helps explain the internal divisions to the 'hidden tradition of imperial looking' that Suleri rightly identifies in Forster's novel, and it is certainly a more appropriate source to employ for this purpose than the diary entry on which she subsequently draws to strengthen her main point. Although it is not uncommon when reading Forster's mostly unpublished locked journal – along with his commonplace book – to come across statements that would, at first glance, suggest a sustained sense of physical self-loathing, these highly personal writings need to be used with some caution, especially when confused understandings of male homosexual desire – ones that persist to this day – can baffle readers. 'Famous, wealthy, miserable, ugly', writes Forster in 1925, '[I] am surprised I don't repel more generally: I can still get to know any one I want and have the illusion that I am charming, and beautiful ... Stomach increases, but not yet visible under waistcoat. The anus is clotted with hairs, and there is a great loss of sexual power – it was very violent in 1921-22'.[32] Undeniably, these sentences divulge a striking mixture of pride and disgust. But one fears that Suleri absorbs this passage into her discussion because it might confirm that Forster's uneasy outlook on empire was predicated on sexual impulses that congregated around the stereotypical site of sodomitical abjection: the anus. The negative strain of Suleri's reading becomes even more pronounced when one discovers her suggestion that the Marabar Caves – that location of inexplicable violence in *A Passage to India* – might be called the 'anus of imperialism'.[33] If, in Suleri's words, Aziz has become 'an emblematic casualty' of Forster's 'colonial homoerotic'[34] (with which it is more than possible to agree), then one could equally argue that she has subjected his homosexuality to a not so dissimilar form of treatment.

Rather than view Adela Quested's entry into the Marabar Caves as a violent displacement of Forster's aggressive sodomitical imagination (which is one unfortunate consequence of Suleri's analysis), it is, I think, more useful to pursue why aspects of his fiction and his essays from 1922 onwards kept returning to Egypt when it was clear that India – 'mysterious to boring point' – had failed him. One could hardly claim – particularly on the basis of 'Salute to the Orient!' – that Egypt gave Forster comfort in his experiences of empire. In fact, Port Said provides the setting for one of the most intensely murderous stories he ever wrote. But the closer his imagination returned to Port Said the more Forster felt urged to activate the conflict between empire and homosexuality that had frustrated and disappointed him while living further East.

IV

Only on two occasions in *A Passage to India* do we see a contrast between Egypt and India, and both are revealing in their recoil from the intolerable mystifications of the sub-continent. No one can help noticing how much of this complicated novel thematizes its Indian geography in terms of 'muddle' or obscuration, and the trajectory of the narrative leads its English protagonists away from what the narrator calls 'the strangest experience of all' – which is India itself.[35] When Fielding sails back to the Mediterranean, we learn how he settles into a world that he knows is his own: 'The buildings of Venice, like the mountains of Crete and the fields of Egypt, stood in the right place, whereas everything in poor India was placed wrong'.[36] But when Adela Quested sets sail for England, the narrative is noticeably less decided when pausing over Egypt as the first port of call with western civilization. 'With Egypt the atmosphere altered'; the 'clean sands ... seemed to wipe off everything that was difficult and equivocal'.[37] Her dreadful time in India – how she fled the Caves, only to tumble into cactus-bushes; the wrongful charge of rape against Aziz, which is eventually dropped; her bitter excommunication by the Anglo-Indian community at Chandrapore – can be duly forgotten, now that almost every aspect of India has been cast in a despondent light. Yet no sooner does she feel that she can 'wipe off' her troubles than her brief stay at Port Said involves the following puzzling exchange:

> She went on shore with an American missionary, they walked out to the Lesseps statue, they drank the air of the Levant. 'To what duties, Miss Quested, are you returning in your own country after your taste of the tropics?' the missionary asked. 'Observe, I don't say to what do you turn, but to what do you re-turn. Every life ought to contain both a turn and a re-turn. This celebrated pioneer' (he pointed to the statue) 'will make my question clear. He turns to the East, he re-turns to the West. You can see it from the cute position of his hands, one of which holds a string of sausages'. The missionary looked at her humorously. He had no idea what he meant by 'turn' and 'return', but he often used words in pairs, for the sake of moral brightness.[38]

On the face of it, the missionary's idle musings have barely any significance. But that, of course, denotes the novel's outward political thrust: for the narrator is deriding both American ideals of the 'pioneer' and de Lesseps' overbearing spirit of empire, in words whose satirical edge we have already encountered in 'Salute to the Orient!' This fun-poking juxtaposition of the empty-headed American next to de Lesseps' high-handed imperialism, however, indicates the aesthetic leanings of the novel as well. To begin with, this excerpt surely characterizes what had by 1924 become a fairly standard modernist dissatisfaction with industry and empire: violent ideologies driven by the apparent 'moral brightness' of the Enlightenment. But whatever amusement one might derive from this episode, the statue – with its absurd 'sausages' – has a mesmerizing pull upon the narrative, since it acts as a focal point for the 'turn' and 're-turn' that enchants the missionary, who for some reason finds the statue (which towered above him) 'cute'.

How might one account for this bizarre epithet? The only observation

I would make is that this word occurs at a moment when a great many alternating currents converge upon Port Said, locating it as a site of fearful attraction – politically repellent and physically 'cute' at once. This distinctly American adjective may well be invoked here because it quietly alludes to the epic celebrating the global democratic vision enshrined in Walt Whitman's epic, from which the title of Forster's novel is taken. The Suez Canal was the 'Passage to India' that Whitman annexed to *Leaves of Grass* in 1871. Even more to the point perhaps is the status that Whitman's poem had long enjoyed in British culture, for it was read from its earliest appearance there in the late 1860s as a sexually subversive work, with its implcit homoerotic promotion of comradeship between men. Forster's choice of a Whitmanian title for his novel alone would have signalled to some of his more literary readers the pattern of same-sex desire he was seeking to explore, as publicly as permissible, within its pages. De Lesseps' statue, therefore, served as an icon that condensed many dreams and dissatisfactions, about which one can only speculate when confronted with the missionary's lingering interest in the 'turn' and '*re*-turn' between East and West.

The 'turn' and '*re*-turn' to Port Said would oscillate wildly in contemporaneous writings by Forster, who seemed only too conscious of how this location marked a profound antagonism between Occident and Orient. His letters of 1921 and 1922 strike contrasting attitudes towards the place that would never cease to haunt him. Forster's rendezvous with el Adl, which occurred when he was travelling East to take up his post in India, is recorded in almost gothic terms: 'we walked down the Mole and saw the toes of the de Lesseps statue, the upper regions being invisible darkness'.[39] This eerie image certainly suggests that the figure making his repellent salute was powerfully associated for Forster with the love he bore. But this gothic representation could not be more distinct from his description of Suez to his mother in January 1922, on his return from India: 'The atmosphere, temperature and colours have been so exquisite and fresh; compared to India, where all is aged and complex, it is like a world in its morning'.[40] His high expectations of Egypt, however, would be dashed when he discovered that he would not be met by el Adl at this time, since his lover was extremely ill at Mansourah, being tended by his spouse. Port Said, therefore, was a place of love and death, of the world in its 'morning' as well as its loss, just as it was a location where his contradictory responses to imperial power – both de Lesseps' and his own – assuredly came to a head.

The work in which these conflicts explode – in an alarming frenzy of orgiastic violence – is 'The Other Boat', one of the homosexual stories that Forster suppressed during his lifetime, and which appeared posthumously in *The Life to Come and Other Stories* (1972). Forster's editor, Oliver Stallybrass, claims that it proved difficult to establish a copy-text for this story, since several passages appear in various forms on five different sets of autograph sheets.[41] Forster's persistent rewriting of this narrative, which probably began in 1915 and was drawn to a close in the late 1950s, suggests an ongoing struggle with intractable material. Telling a tale of deathly desire, 'The Other Boat' introduces all the dramatic irony it can to presage the tragic murder of a 'half-caste' man by his white lover. But despite its adroitness in exploiting the well-known technical devices of the tragic genre, the narrative finds it hard indeed to manage the ambivalent responses that shift rapidly between desire and death, and which intensify as the protagonists move closer and closer towards Port Said.

'The Other Boat' maps two journeys, set ten years apart, between East and West. The first section is taken up with Mrs March's return voyage to England from her unbearable time in India. Although the context for her return is at first unclear, we soon learn that she and her children had deserted her husband because he had 'gone native somewhere out East and got cashiered'.[42] While sailing home, her children meet the boy whom they name Cocoanut ('because of his peculiar shaped head'), and whose 'touch of the tar-brush' causes her great offence,[43] not least when Cocoanut terrorizes her by claiming she has intruded on the '[m]en's quarters' of the ship.[44] The second phase of the story charts the passage of her eldest child, Lionel, now a grown man, from Tilbury to India. He has obtained his berth through Cocoanut, whom he met by accident in England. Lionel is travelling East to become engaged to a woman named Isabel. But when he finds that he must share the same cabin as Cocoanut (the boat is overcrowded), a rather different destiny awaits him. Even though he initially experiences guilt from having turned his cabin-mate's advances (attempting, but failing, 'to report an offence against decency'[45]), the two of them soon settle into a sexual rhythm, which increases the further they drift away from England: 'More happened off the coast of Sicily, more, much more at Port Said, and here in the Red Sea they slept together as a matter of course'.[46]

Although we are told that Lionel's 'colour-prejudices were tribal rather than personal'[47] (which means that he publicly condemns Cocoanut while adoring his clandestine intimacy with the 'subtle supple boy'[48]), the imperial demand to subjugate his sexual partner deepens with their love-making. But so too does Cocoanut seek to undermine the man who feels obliged to shun him outside their cabin. What we find in 'The Other Boat' is a complicated negotiation of power relations between the military urges of the 'Nordic warrior',[49] as the narrator names him, and the sexual manipulativeness of the man 'who belonged to no race and always got what he wanted.'[50] Under these conditions, Lionel grows uneasy with his privileges as a white imperialist who is indulging illegal sexual desires, while Cocoanut is quickly associated with corruption of all kinds. Since Cocoanut holds two passports, Lionel cannot tell whether his lover is Portuguese, Danish, 'Asiatic' or 'Negro'.[51] That is why Lionel declares 'you're no better than a monkey'. To which Cocoanut replies: 'Lion, he don't know nothing at all'.[52] These nicknames, with their roots in legend and fable, indicate that from now on the law of the jungle will rule, as each partner tries to outwit the other, in a homoerotic allegory where intimacy across the colour line proves exciting since it is driven by a dynamic that endangers their lives. Not only lovers, the Lion and the Monkey are enemies, and they shall fight their orgasms to the death.

Hereafter, as more and more emphasis is placed upon wanting to 'know' the nature of this treacherous eroticism, the story becomes increasingly interrogative in tone. 'Have you ever shed blood?' asks Cocoanut, teasingly. Even though he promptly replies 'No', Lionel cannot forget his time during a 'little war' that resulted in an assegai being lodged in his groin. The strategically placed scar – close to the genitals – clearly conveys the tortured feelings of sexual power and sexual vulnerability, imperial pride and imperial guilt, that rack Lionel's conscience. Forced to tell the truth about having 'shed blood', he instantly experiences a flickering phantasmagoria of images where '[v]ividly and unexpectedly the desert surged up, and he saw it as a cameo from the outside'.[53] With all the hydraulic insistence of the unconscious with its unrepressible drives, Lionel is the protagonist in the scene that appears before him: 'The central figure – a grotesque one – was himself going beserk, and close to him was a dying savage who had managed to wound him and was trying to speak'.[54]

In his brilliant reading of both 'The Other Boat' and Forster's equally violent account of inter-racial desire between men, 'The Life to Come' (which is set in sub-Saharan Africa), Christopher Lane remarks that these two colonial fantasies whose circulation Forster restricted among his closest friends lay bare the antagonistic subtext to *Maurice* and *A Passage to India*, novels in which one can detect that cross-class and cross-cultural desire has a heightened eroticism because it is split between empowerment and guilt.[55] Lane implies that by the time Forster was writing out both these thematically related works, he had absorbed some of the popularized forms of psychoanalytic thought that may account for many of his more turbulent and hallucinatory passages. Especially important in this respect is Forster's essay 'What I Believe', the earliest version of which appeared in 1938. There he notes: 'Psychology has split and shattered the idea of a "Person", and has shown that there is something incalculable in each of us, which may at any moment rise to the surface and destroy the normal balance'.[56] Sexuality, to be sure, was recognized as the main force that would surge forth and wreak havoc upon the formerly sacrosanct belief that the 'personality' was 'solid', and the 'self' a discrete 'entity'.[57] No longer, then, is it at all possible to 'know what other people are like'.[58]

It is into this void of nescience that the 'The Other Boat' ultimately descends when Lionel finds he cannot return his lover's solicitations: 'Kiss me ... Kiss me'.[59] By this point, Lionel knows that he must face up his better conscience, 'for Isabel's sake, as for his profession's', as well as for his mother who 'understood nothing and controlled everything'.[60] Sensing that he must comply with the rule of his mother's monstrous power ('blind-eyed in the midst of the enormous web she had spun'[61]), he snubs his lover only to feel Cocoanut biting him on the forearm. Once blood has been drawn, Lionel is thrown psychologically 'back in a desert fighting savages'.[62] Having strangled his lover, he ejaculates, and 'with the seeds of love on him'[63] he takes his own life by plunging naked into the waves. And where does this happen? In the Red Sea. For these lovers, there is no escape from this location, since it is the place to which Forster's most urgent sexual journeys would return. This is the site where the closest of bonds between East and West are made and broken, where imperial violence and homoerotic desire find themselves most palpably entwined. No wonder Lionel's body is left to the sharks, while the corpse of Cocoanut is removed from the ship. Never could their love have been allowed to travel, as the boat eventually does, to Bombay.

NOTES

It would not have been possible to complete this essay without consulting many of Forster's papers held at the Modern Archive at King's College, Cambridge; the archivist, Jacqueline Cox, helpfully guided me towards the relevant materials. My thanks to The Provost and Scholars of King's College, Cambridge, for kindly allowing me to quote from previously unpublished material. I am grateful to Hilda D. Spear of the University of Dundee for sending me copies of her research into Forster's Egyptian writings. Finally, I should like to acknowledge the Stanford Humanities Center for providing the space and time in which to finish this piece of work.

1. E.M. Forster, 'Salute to the Orient!', in Forster, *Abinger Harvest* (London: Edward Arnold, 1936), p. 247. All further quotations are to this edition and are included in the text. This essay first appeared in the *London Mercury*, 4 (1921), pp. 271-81.
2. Forster, *A Passage to India*, Abinger Edition, ed., Oliver Stallybrass (London: Edward Arnold, 1978), p. 267.
3. Benita Parry, 'The Politics of Representation in *A Passage to India*', in A Passage to India: *Essays in Interpretation*, ed., John Beer (Basingstoke: Macmillan, 1985), pp. 27-43; and Edward W. Said, *Culture and Imperialism* (London: Chatto and Windus, 1993), pp. 246-47.
4. The most influential critic from the first generation of Forster scholars is Lionel Trilling; he was quick to note the writer's unease with the liberal ideology

supposedly enshrined in the fiction: '[A]ll his novels are politically and morally tendentious and always in the liberal direction. Yet he is deeply at odds with the liberal mind, and while liberal readers can go a long way with Forster, they can seldom go all the way ... [because] sooner or later ... [t]hey suspect Forster is not quite playing their game; they feel that he is challenging *them* as well as what they dislike'. See *E.M. Forster* ([1943]; New York: Harcourt Brace Jovanovich, 1971).

5. 'Minorite' is the word Forster uses in his 'Indian Journal, 1912-13' to describe the sexual episodes recorded in Searight's diary. See Forster, *The Hill of Devi and Other Indian Writings*, Abinger Edition, ed., Elizabeth Heine (London: Edward Arnold, 1983), p. 122.

6. Ronald Hyam, *Empire and Sexuality: The British Experience* (Manchester: Manchester University Press, 1990), p. 128.

7. On the the work of the 'Uranian' poets, see Timothy d'Arch Smith, *Love in Earnest: Some Notes on the Lives and Writings of English 'Uranian' Poets from 1889 to 1930* (London: Routledge and Kegan Paul, 1970).

8. Forster, 'To William Plomer', 20 November 1963, in *Selected Letters of E.M. Forster*, ed., P.N. Furbank and Mary Lago, 2 vols (Cambridge, MA: The Belknap Press of Harvard University Press, 1983-85), II, p. 287.

9. Forster, 'To Florence Barger', in *Selected Letters of E.M. Forster*, I, p. 270. Further quotations from this letter are taken from this and the following page. Robert K. Martin has suggested to me that the passage from this letter quoted below may be read in a light altogether more favourable than the one I cast upon it, by virtue of an implicitly ironic tone. This raises for me the question of where irony figures in Forster's racial thinking.

10. Forster, unpublished memoir of Mohammed el Adl, King's College, Cambridge, f.16.

11. Forster, unpublished memoir of Mohammed el Adl, King's College, Cambridge, f.19.

12. Forster, 'To Florence Barger', in *Selected Letters of E.M. Forster*, I, p. 275. Further quotations from this letter are taken from this page.

13. Forster, *The Government of Egypt: Recommendations by a Committee of the International Section of the Labour Research Department, with Notes on Egypt* (London: Labour Research Department, 1920), p. 11.

14. Forster, 'To Florence Barger', 18 February 1918, *Selected Letters of E.M. Forster*, I, p. 287.

15. James Buzard, *The Beaten Track: European Tourism, Literature, and the Ways to Culture, 1800-1918* (Oxford: Clarendon Press, 1993), pp. 327-38.

16. Forster, *Alexandria: A History and a Guide* (Garden City, NY: Doubleday, 1961), p. 204.

17. Forster, 'Kanaya', in *The Hill of Devi and Other Indian Writings*, p. 311.

18. Forster, 'Kanaya', p. 318.

19. Forster, 'Kanaya', p. 319.

20. Forster, 'Kanaya', p. 323.

21. Forster, 'The Mind of the Indian Native State', in *Abinger Harvest*, pp. 328, 331. This essay first appeared unsigned in two parts in the *Nation and Athenaeum*, 31: 5, 7 (1922), pp. 146-47, pp. 216-27.

22. [Forster,] 'Relections on India. II. The Prince's Progress', *Nation and Athenaeum*, 31: 2 (1922), p. 645.

23. Forster, 'Adrift in India, 5: Pan', in *Abinger Harvest*, pp. 313-14. This essay was first published as 'Pan' in the *Criterion*, 1 (1923), pp. 402-08.

24. Forster, unpublished letter, 'To Syed Ross Masood', 19 August 1912, King's College, Cambridge.

25. Forster, 'To Syed Ross Masood', 8 September 1917, *Selected Letters of E.M. Forster*, I, p. 269. (My transcription of this letter differs slightly from the published version.)

26. Forster, 'To Syed Ross Masood', 27 September 1922, in Furbank, *E.M. Forster: A Life*, II, p. 106.

27. See Joseph Bristow, *Effeminate England: Homoerotic Writing after 1885* (Buckingham: Open University Press; New York: Columbia University Press, 1995), pp. 85-87.

28. Forster, *A Passage to India*, p. 207.

29. Suleri, *The Rhetoric of English India* (Chicago: Chicago University Press, 1992), p. 136.

30. Forster, memoir of Mohammed el Adl, 5 August 1922, King's College Cambridge, f.10. This sentence is quoted by Furbank, *E.M. Forster: A Life*, II, p. 115. Further quotations are taken from the unpublished manuscript.

31. Suleri, *The Rhetoric of English India*, p. 137.

32. Forster, entry for 2 January 1925, Locked Journal, King's College Cambridge, f.64, quoted by Furbank, *E.M. Forster: A Life*, II, p. 135.

33. Suleri, *The Rhetoric of English India*, p. 132.

34. Suleri, *The Rhetoric of English India*, p. 134.

35. Forster, *A Passage to India*, p. 271.

36. Forster, *A Passage to India*, p. 270.

37. Forster, *A Passage to India*, p. 253.

38. Forster, *A Passage to India*, p. 253-54.

39. Forster, 'To Florence Barger', 20 May 1921, *Selected Letters of E.M. Forster*, II, p. 7.

40. Forster, 'To Alice Clara Forster', 19 January 1922, *Selected Letters of E.M. Forster*, II, p. 19.

41. Forster, *The Life to Come and Other Stories*, Abinger Edition, ed., Oliver Stallybrass (London: Edward Arnold, 1972), p. xix.

42. Forster, 'The Other Boat', in Forster, *The Life to Come*, p. 183.

43. Forster, 'The Other Boat', p. 171.

44. Forster, 'The Other Boat', p. 170.

45. Forster, 'The Other Boat', p. 174.

46. Forster, 'The Other Boat', p. 177.

47. Forster, 'The Other Boat', p. 174.

48. Forster, 'The Other Boat', p. 174.

49. Forster, 'The Other Boat', p. 174.

50. Forster, 'The Other Boat', p. 174.

51. Forster, 'The Other Boat', p. 181.

52. Forster, 'The Other Boat', p. 181.

53. Forster, 'The Other Boat', p. 186.

54. Forster, 'The Other Boat', p. 186.

55. Christopher Lane, 'Volatile Desire: Ambivalence and Distress in Forster's Colonial Narratives', in *Writing India, 1757-1990*, ed., Bart Moore-Gilbert (Manchester: Manchester University Press, 1996).

56. Forster, 'What I Believe', in Forster, *Two Cheers for Democracy*, Abinger Edition, ed., Oliver Stallybrass (London: Edward Arnold, 1972), p. 65. The first version of this essay appeared as 'Credo', *London Mercury*, 38 (1938), pp. 397-404. It was revised for publication as 'What I Believe', in the first edition of *Two*

Cheers for Democracy (London: Edward Arnold, 1951).
57. Forster, 'What I Believe', p. 66.
58. Forster, 'What I Believe', p. 65.
59. Forster, 'The Other Boat', p. 195.
60. Forster, 'The Other Boat', p. 193.
61. Forster, 'The Other Boat', p. 193. Narratorial interventions such as these form part of a much larger vein of misogyny that runs throughout Forster's fictions, frequently signalling that maternal authority is a constraining force on male-male desire. I raise this point at some length in *Effeminate England*, pp. 55-99.
62. Forster, 'The Other Boat', p. 195.
63. Forster, 'The Other Boat', p. 196.

ANDREW MICHAEL ROBERTS

Economies of Empire and Masculinity in Conrad's *Victory* [1]

Victory: An Island Tale (1915), by Joseph Conrad, begins with a heavily ironic passage which implicates the male body with the economy of empire. The climax of the novel is a tableau of the male gaze, in which two men 'mournfully' contemplate the white breast of a dying young woman. And the novel ends with absence or nothingness: the very last word of the text is 'Nothing!'. The reading of the novel which I am going to offer centres on these three passages and the outline of my argument is as follows. The psychological drama within the novel is structured around the form of homosocial exchange analysed by Eve Sedgwick, in which male power is confirmed and relations between men negotiated by the use of a woman (or women) as object of desire, competition and exchange.[2] This process has also been studied by Gayle Rubin and Luce Irigaray, who stress the relevance of an economic model, of what Irigaray terms a 'traffic' in women.[3] But the novel is also concerned with the economy of empire as such – the exploitation of resources, trade and modernisation – and with various forms of monetary exchange: lending, buying, stealing, gambling. These two economies, which I will term the economy of masculinity and the economy of empire respectively, are interwoven in Conrad's plot and in his rhetoric. However, each is destabilized by the other, in a simultaneous failure of the projects of empire and of normative masculinity.

Conrad's *Victory*, although a late work, returns to the imperial setting of his early novels, in the Malay archipelago. The protagonist, Axel Heyst, comes to the area as a wanderer, aiming to avoid human commitments as a result of the teaching of his father, a Schopenhauerian philosopher. But Heyst is drawn despite himself into two successive involvements. First he lends money to Morrison, a trading sea-captain in trouble, who in gratitude insists on Heyst going into business with him, so that Heyst becomes local manager of a coal mine on a remote island called Samburan. After the collapse of this enterprise, Heyst remains on the island, alone apart from a Chinese servant, Wang. But on a visit to the port of Sourabaya (on Java) he rescues a young woman called Lena from an all-female orchestra: she is being mistreated by the managers (Mr and Mrs Zangiacomo) and sexually harassed by a hotel-keeper called Schomberg. Heyst takes Lena back to his island. But they are followed by three villainous desperadoes (Jones, Ricardo and Pedro), who have been egged on by the jealous hotel-keeper's talk of hidden treasure. A complex struggle of wills ensues, ending in the death of Lena (who is shot protecting Heyst), of Heyst (who then commits suicide) and of all three villains (who have fallen out).

In the penultimate chapter the reader is offered a tableau of the male gaze, bringing together sexuality, death and the female body. Lena lies dying from a bullet wound which Heyst has just discovered by tearing open the top of her dress. Heyst's friend, Davidson, has arrived on the island just too late to avert the tragedy, and stands by him:

> They stood side by side, looking mournfully at the little black hole made by Mr Jones's bullet under the swelling breast of a dazzling and as it were sacred whiteness. It rose and fell slightly – so slightly that only the eyes of the lover could detect the faint stir of life. Heyst, calm and utterly unlike himself in the face, moving about noiselessly, prepared a wet cloth, and laid it on the insignificant wound, round which there was hardly a trace of blood to mar the charm, the fascination, of that mortal flesh. (p. 405) [4]

This is only the culmination of a number of scenes in which Lena is presented as an aestheticized and sexualized object of contemplation. Throughout the novel looking has been crucial: desiring looks, threatening looks, blank and indecipherable looks, offering the reader a range of possible viewpoints and identifications. Earlier, in the developing relationship between Heyst and Lena, there have been looks of male mastery and possession, but also suggestions of a developing mutuality:

> He looked fixedly at her, and with such grave eyes that she felt obliged to smile faintly at him, since she did not understand what he meant. Her smile was reflected, still fainter, on his lips. (p. 197)

Frequently, though, the woman's gaze is constructed or interpreted, not as an expression of her desire or need, but as a mark of her incomprehensibility and the occasion for the stimulation of male desire:

> in the intimacy of their life her grey, unabashed gaze forced upon him the sensation of something inexplicable reposing within her; stupidity or inspiration, weakness or force – or simply an abysmal emptiness, reserving itself even in the moments of complete surrender. (p. 192)

Why should the Conradian rhetoric of the incomprehensible be brought into play, merely because a woman looks at a man without being 'abashed'? The incomprehension here seems to be Conrad's as much as Heyst's, judging by a certain stylistic awkwardness and incoherence: 'stupidity or inspiration' and 'weakness or force' are opposed qualities, but it is unclear why they should be termed 'inexplicable'. Heyst's sense

of an abyss within Lena would seem to express his need for her
dependence; his need for her to remain the object of his desiring gaze,
rather than the subject of her own desire. And the narrative of the novel
might seem to endorse Heyst's desire by setting Lena up as an iconic
sexual object and by ending in her death and the effacement of her
subjectivity. In the death-bed scene Heyst and Davidson orient the look
of narrator and reader towards her body. Even Lena, at the moment of
her death, imagines herself as seen by a male Other: 'Exulting, she saw
herself extended on the bed, in a black dress ... while ... he was ready to
lift her up in his firm arms and take her into the sanctuary of her
innermost heart' (p. 407). We are offered the possibility of identifying
with Heyst's look, or of identifying with either Davidson or Lena, both of
whom are themselves, in different ways, identifying with Heyst's look.
Furthermore, we are invited to notice the faint movement of her breast,
even while we are told that only 'the eyes of the lover' could detect it.
Thus the reader, whether male or female, is offered a place in the
normative homosocial economy.[5] The story of the relationship between
Heyst and Lena might seem, then, to reinforce a homosocial structure. It
is within an economy of masculinity that Lena's role is worked out: the
plot is fuelled by male relationships and desires: Schomberg's lust and
jealousy; Ricardo's relationship with Jones; Heyst's maverick position in
the society of European males. The tableau of her death is presented, not
just to Heyst, but to Davidson and to the reader.

At this point I want to return to the opening passage of the novel, to
show how the economy of empire parallels but also unsettles this
normative heterosexual masculinity. The novel begins with materiality,
commerce, sameness and difference: 'There is, as every schoolboy
knows in this scientific age, a very close chemical relation between coal
and diamonds' (p. 3). The fact that coal and diamonds are the same
element was famously used by D.H. Lawrence as a metaphor for the
transformation of the self, for the absence of the 'old stable ego' in his
fiction.[6] Might Conrad's opening bear on human as well as chemical
relations? On the second page Heyst is assessed in terms of likeness
and difference: 'He was not mad. Queer chap – yes, that may have
been said, and in fact was said; but there is a tremendous difference
between the two, you will allow' (p. 4). Later we are told again that
Heyst was 'generally considered a "queer chap"' (p. 91) and in the final
pages of the novel Davidson says that Heyst 'was a queer chap. I doubt
if he himself knew how queer he was' (p. 408). Wayne Koestenbaum
has noted the marked use of the word 'queer', with sexual
connotations, in Conrad's collaborative novel with Ford Madox Ford,
Romance.[7] One should be cautious about reading in later usage: queer
would not have *meant* homosexual to Conrad. On the other hand,
within a regime of masculinity which combined widespread same-sex
sexual activity with widespread denial and homophobia, homosexuality

was a likely form which being 'queer' might take, especially since we are told that Heyst 'never talked of women, he never seemed to think of them, or to remember that they existed' (p.42). The outward contrast and inner connection of coal and diamond might suggest that being a 'queer chap' and being an ordinary one are covertly connected. The opening passage, after alluding to the fascination and value of coal, or 'black diamonds', as possible reasons for Heyst's attachment to his island, continues in a vein of ponderous Conradian irony:

> The Tropical Belt Coal Company went into liquidation. The world of finance is a mysterious world in which, incredible as the fact may appear, evaporation precedes liquidation. First the capital evaporates, and then the company goes into liquidation. These are very unnatural physics, but they account for the persistent inertia of Heyst, at which we 'out there' used to laugh among ourselves – but not inimically. An inert body can do no harm to any one. (p. 3)

Heyst's involvement with commerce had temporarily made him seem less different from the other European men 'out there', but after the death of Morrison and the collapse of the Company, an 'unnatural' process transforms him back into a passive 'inert body'. As manager Heyst had been engaged in active, productive activity, working the material body of the earth, but 'unnatural physics' reduce him to a body himself. A subtext of gender and sexuality seems present in these ironic manoeuvres around the nature of a man who is seen as a queer, passive body, rather than an active will and mind.[8] Irigaray describes the ideological formation that represents men as active and women as passive:

> man is the procreator ... sexual production-reproduction is referable to his 'activity' alone, to his 'pro-ject' alone. Woman is nothing but the receptacle that passively receives his product, even if sometimes, by the display of her passively aimed instincts, she has pleaded, facilitated, even demanded that it be placed within her. Matrix – womb, earth, factory, bank – to which the seed capital is entrusted so that it may germinate, produce, grow fruitful, without woman being able to lay claim to either capital or interest since she has only submittted 'passively' to reproduction.[9]

The financial and cultural relationship embodied in Heyst's work as manager of a mine parallels the gender relation described by Irigaray, since the European financial interests exploit the resources of the Malay Archipelago while retaining capital and profit for themselves. The transformation of Heyst, from observer to manager and back again is, however, only a shift between different forms of speculation, like different forms of the same element. The influence of his father's philosophical ideas has given Heyst 'a special insight' (p. 196) and made him a spectator of life: 'I could not take my soul down into the street to fight there. I started off to wander about, an independent spectator – if that is possible' (p. 196). Rejecting 'the street', Heyst nevertheless becomes a sort of *flâneur* of the world in general. He sees his involvement with Lena as 'his latest departure from the part of an unconcerned spectator' (p. 185) but 'at the same time he could not help being temperamentally, from long habit and from set purpose, a spectator still' (p. 185). Furthermore, he intensively observes Lena. Thus while Heyst's previous detachment from the world had been a matter of philosophical observation and speculation, his involvements, with the mine and then with Lena, are matters of financial speculation and sexual observation. When the mining company collapses, Heyst tries to reconvert the commercial into the philosophical, staying on Samburan no longer as manager but as a hermit philosopher lounging on his lonely veranda. However, the two forms of speculation are re-enmeshed by the presence of a woman. Heyst's lone presence on the island was the subject only of idle speculation among the European community; not exactly philosophical speculation but without a profit-motive. However, once Lena is with him, the pair become the subject of malevolent and interested speculation. Schomberg invests his jealousy in the greed of Jones and Ricardo, inciting them to undertake a speculative journey to rob Heyst of his supposed wealth and of Lena. So the plot manifests the homology between a psychic economy of homosocial masculinity (with woman as the object of exchange) and the financial economy of imperial capitalism (in which money and commodities are exchanged). Lena figures as a treasure, competed for, but also as a coin, circulated; her identity hovers between that of the 'essence' of 'Woman', evoked in images of idealized femininity, and that of token of exchange in a contest of male desire, jealousy, revulsion and repression, involving Schomberg, Zangiacomo, Heyst, Ricardo, Jones and Davidson. And perhaps the (male) reader. Yet Heyst's ambiguous and problematic role within each economy reveals instabilities in their parallel structures.

Furthermore, Heyst's queer inertness and the failure of his business project are not the only threats to normative heterosexual masculinity in the novel. While homosocial exchanges structure many of Conrad's fictions, *Victory* is unusual in making relatively overt reference to homosexuality. The relationship between the novel's principal villains, 'Mr Jones' and Martin Ricardo, is a combination of criminal partnership, feudal master-servant bond and barely-denied sexual attachment. Jones's hatred and fear of women and his murderous jealousy when Ricardo pursues Lena are fairly obvious indicators of his homosexuality, though the portrait is much distorted by a homophobia which can represent same-sex desire among men only as misogyny and a male couple only as a criminal partnership. The word 'unnatural', as in the 'unnatural physics' of the Coal Company, is also applied to Jones's pathological hatred of women (p. 266). Jones and Heyst are linked in various ways: Jones's affected malevolent indifference functions as a sort of dark parody of Heyst's assumed philosophic detachment and, as R.W.B. Lewis has noted, they are both 'gentlemen'.[10] The conventional connotations of the word 'gentleman' are undermined by its repeated application to Jones, just as the word 'manly' is unsettled by its repeated ironic application to the malevolent gossip of a hotel-keeper, Schomberg.[11] Questions of same-sex desire appear with greater subtlety in the relationship of Heyst and Morrison, which attracts a sense of uncertainty: 'Heyst became associated with Morrison on terms about which people were in doubt. Some said he was a partner, others said he was a sort of paying guest, but the real truth of the matter was more complex' (p. 10). We learn that the relationship originated in Heyst's financial rescue of Morrison and continued because of Heyst's delicacy of feeling but we may suspect that this delicacy masked an unacknowledged need for company on the part of the isolated Heyst. This pattern is repeated with Heyst and Lena and the parallel creates a certain sexual ambiguity. Heyst's concern for Morrison draws him into a potentially enriching though finally disastrous financial project – the coal mine. Heyst's concern for Lena draws him into a sexual relationship which greatly enriches his life but is similarly short-lived, ending in the death of both him and Lena. Heyst's father has not destroyed his son's human needs, but has repressed his ability to acknowledge them; only the needs of others enable him to seek company, active employment, or emotional and sexual fulfilment. So while Heyst's role of gallant rescuer in respect of Morrison and Lena is superficially in accord with conventional masculinity – indeed, in the latter case Heyst's 'long horizontal moustaches' and injunction 'Pray command me' (p. 73) suggest a parodic chivalry – its underlying psychology is more akin to a conventional femininity as Irigaray describes it: to a 'display of ... passively aimed instincts' and a role as a seeming receptacle for the needs of others.

The connection between the two relationships is prefigured when Heyst and Lena first meet. On first seeing Lena, Heyst looks at her 'as no man ever looks at another man' (p. 71). Yet in the next paragraph, when he gets up to speak to her, we are told that: 'It was the same sort of impulse which years ago had made him ... accost Morrison, practically a stranger to him then ... It was the same impulse. But he did not recognize it' (pp. 71-72). Shortly afterwards the narrator adds:

> It is very clear that Heyst was not indifferent. I won't say to the girl, but to the girl's fate. He was the same man who had plunged after the submerged Morrison ... But this was another sort of plunge altogether, and likely to lead to a very different kind of partnership. (p. 77)

The look is different, the 'plunge' is different, yet the impulse is of the same sort. This pattern, of similarity and difference, is repeated in Heyst's account to Lena of his friendship with Morrison. Lena describes her horror of Schomberg's sexual harassment, and says that she was 'cornered'. This is as much a literal as a metaphorical term, since we have earlier been told that Schomberg has 'assailed her in quiet corners' (p. 79). Heyst is quite clear what she is talking about, yet picks up her term in describing his relations with Morrison: 'One day I met a cornered man. I use the word because it expresses the man's situation exactly, and because you just used it yourself. You know what that means?' (p. 197). Lena is startled by the idea Heyst has conjured up, of a sexually harassed sea-captain, and when Heyst explains that 'I mean in his own way', she responds 'I knew very well it couldn't be anything like that' (p. 197). Heyst also refers to his friendship with Morrison, based on the fact that 'one gets attached in a way to people one has done something for' (p.199), as constituting 'a germ of corruption' (p. 200). Lena is understandably upset, since this might equally apply to her relationship with Heyst.

Twice, then, the idea of a sexual element in Heyst's relationship with Morrison is evoked and then put aside. Wayne Koestenbaum shows how Conrad and Ford present their collaboration on *Romance* as an illicit male activity.[12] Heyst and Morrison are similarly described as sharing a secret intimacy, 'like conspirators in a comic opera' (p. 19) which issues in what the text identifies as a 'romantic' business project (p. 24). It might be argued that these are all unsurprising effects in a fiction about a social context where men lived and worked closely together, often without women, but where open homosexuality was taboo. However, Eve Sedgwick has shown that the ways in which homophobia has distorted and informed literary discourses is revealing both of the nature of those discourses and of the nature of their social context.[13] Taking a lead from her I would suggest that the traces of homosexuality in Conrad's work are important in part because of the pressure they exert on the homosocial structures which are of primary importance, both in terms of plot and in terms of structures of narration and interpretation. As Sedgwick points out, patriarchal homosocial structures are often homophobic as well: in her terms, 'the potential unbrokenness of a continuum between homosocial and homosexual' is repressed or obscured within structures of power involving the exchange of women among men.[14] The hints of homosexual feeling in Heyst's relationship with Morrison disturb the homosocial structures present in plot and narrative, as do the suggestions of a feminisation of Heyst and the presence at certain moments between Heyst and Lena of a gaze of mutuality rather than of power. While the interaction of Heyst and Davidson in the penultimate chapter fits a pattern of homosocial exchange, notably in their contemplation of the dying Lena, the Morrison-Heyst-Lena triangle is not one in which the men exchange the woman or her image, but one in which a man (Heyst) relates in comparable ways to another man and to a woman. At certain stages of the novel Lena is more a substitute for Morrison (or vice versa) than a token of exchange.

The doubling of characters for which Conrad, Henry James and R.L. Stevenson are particularly noted can render problematic not only individual identities but also collective forms of identity such as gender, 'race' and sexual orientation. As well as the doubling of Heyst and Jones, and of Morrison and Heyst, there is a doubling of Heyst and Wang, the Chinese 'coolie' who remains on the island, notionally as Heyst's 'boy'. Notionally because, from the moment when he accepts the job with an 'unexpectedly ... deprecatory expression' (p. 178) Wang seems to get the upper hand, appropriating the keys to the storeroom and the revolver and outmanoeuvring both Heyst and the villains to survive, almost alone, the novel's bloody climax. In the representation of both Heyst and Wang there is a play between the idea of Adamic or archetypal man, beginning afresh, and the role of entrepreneur and instrument of global modernity (a common linking in the discourse of colonialism, *Robinson Crusoe* being the classic instance). Heyst's Coal Company is seen by the European traders as a threatening encroachment of what Chris Bongie has termed the 'New Imperialism' (modern, technological global capitalism) on their world of Old Imperialist individual adventure (*Victory*, p. 24).[15] Wang initially appears as just a tool of this New Imperialist venture, one of the 'imported Chinese labourers' (p. 178). Yet it later occurs to Heyst to see him as a competitor for possession of the island (p. 257). Like Heyst, Wang acquires a woman (one of the indigenous Alfuro people) and begins to exploit the natural resources, taking seeds from the storeroom to grow vegetables, for which Heyst 'in his own person represented the market' (p. 181). He thus outdoes Heyst in what Irigaray calls the 'pro-ject' of masculinity: in a form of parody of colonial dispossession, Wang appropriates the property of the defunct Coal Company to produce commodities which he sells back to its ex-manager. Resembling Heyst in his taciturnity (p. 180) and his initial lack of human ties (p. 307), Wang seems the more successful of the two in fulfilling the masculine roles of making money, fighting and protecting his woman. Yet Wang's actions, even as their effectiveness and rationality are acknowledged (p.307), are treated in racist terms as the result of 'instinct', 'impulse' and 'a Chinaman's ruling passion' (p.181). Essentialized in racial terms yet also frequently seen as incomprehensible (pp. 268, 322-23), Wang is thus represented analogously to Lena: as Karl Miller observes, 'women and foreigners were alike – unknown ground which might or might not bear fruit'.[16] Yet Wang, who at one point appears 'engaged in the young-ladyish occupation of picking flowers' (p. 283), refuses to be the ground for European exploitation, and becomes himself a tiller of the ground of the island. At the same time the Alfuro, the indigenous people who retreat to the other half of the island and with whom only

Wang has contact, are at once the dispossesed Other of the colonial economy and the object of exoticist fantasy, firmly hidden behind their barrier in the novel's 'political unconscious'.[17]

Thus Heyst, the white male European subject of modernity and the New Imperialism, who in mining days mouths its typical slogan of a 'great stride forward' (p. 6), is shadowed by Others of gender, 'race' and sexual orientation, his identity shifting in a series of role reversals and doublings. This unsettling of European masculine identity is reflected in the novel's conclusion, to which I now turn. 'There was nothing to be done there ... Nothing!' (p. 412). Heyst has become an 'inert body' for real and there is no more scope for masculine commercial activity to reinsert him into the homosocial order. In one sense this nothingness is the legacy of Heyst's father, who 'considered the universal nothingness' (p. 219). Heyst carries that abyss within him and when Lena is brought into his world she briefly rescues him from that nothingness by making him love her, though at the cost of her own life. R. W. B. Lewis writes of Jones that 'what becomes full and finally visible about him is a kind of absence, a nothingness'.[18] Problems of masculinity expressed in terms of absence, loss and of 'nothing to see' fit readily, and perhaps too readily, an interpretation in terms of Freudian castration anxiety or Lacanian theories of lack and Symbolic castration. While acknowledging the productivity of such interpretations, I share the reservation expressed by Stephen Heath, Teresa de Lauretis and others, that Lacanian theory tends to perpetuate phallocentrism by ensuring that issues of desire, including a supposedly non gender-specific lack, continue to be discussed in terms of the presence or absence of a structure metaphorically named after the male organ.[19]

The overt tone of Conrad's novel is elegiac, presenting the failure of masculine and financial speculation as existential tragedy. But, on the basis of the conflicts within the text, I want to read the ending in a more utopian spirit, by attending to the novel's explicit comments on masculinity. One of the most intense moments of Heyst's desiring look at Lena prompts an observation about the masculinity that accompanies and props up his pleasure in possessing and seeing her:

> He was still under the fresh sortilege of their common life, the surprise of novelty, the flattered vanity of his possession of this woman; for a man must feel that, unless he has ceased to be masculine. (p. 201)

Here the abyss opens under the logic of the same: a woman serves to constitute and confirm a man's masculinity, but through a transparently tautologous logic: Heyst feels vanity because he is masculine and he is masculine because he feels vanity. Elsewhere in the novel even as masculine and feminine qualities are essentialized, they seem to seep into each other:

> there was born in her a woman's innate mistrust of masculinity, of that
> seductive strength allied to an absurd, delicate shrinking from the recognition
> of the naked necessity of facts, which never yet frightened a woman worthy of
> the name ... Before this eminently masculine fussing she felt the woman's need
> to give way, the sweetness of surrender. (p. 308)

This passage, while drawing on familiar clichés of feminine pliancy,
presents masculinity as delicate, shrinking, fussy and blind to facts.

Margaret Whitford defends Irigaray's utopianism on the grounds that
'imagining how things could be different is part of the process of
transforming the present in the direction of a different future'.[20] She
quotes Irigaray's answer to someone who claimed not to understand
the meaning of 'masculine discourse': 'Of course not, since there is no
other. The problem is that of a possible alterity in masculine discourse –
or in relation to masculine discourse'. Whitford comments:

> Irigaray is trying to 'imagine the unimaginable' and it is in this light that we
> should understand her view that to aim for a state 'beyond sexual difference'
> without rearticulating our present organization of male and female would only
> maintain the deceptive universality of the male.[21]

This combines the aspiration towards a presently unimaginable future
with an imperative to rearticulate the social institutions of the present.
Such a rearticulation must rest on an understanding of the history and
development of those institutions. A re-examination of the work of
Conrad in terms of how it represents and is shaped by the institution of
masculinity, may contribute to that understanding and thus to the
imagining of a different future. Perhaps we cannot at present imagine the
absence of masculinity without evoking ideas of lack or loss, a formation
which seems to lead only back to the phallus. I am writing a masculine
discourse, in Irigaray's sense. When the male critic's act of seeing,
examining, representing is so firmly trapped within the sexualization of
the aesthetic, how can he claim to see, or try to reveal, an alterity in
masculine discourse? At the risk, then, of what may seem a gesture of
transcendence, I would like to offer an imagining of the Conradian abyss
or nothingness, not as negation, death or loss, but as an alterity of the
masculine, even if that alterity was for Conrad, and remains for many
men today, unspeakable.[22]

NOTES

1. This article is based on material to be published in my forthcoming book,
   Conrad and Masculinity (Basingstoke: Macmillan).
2. Eve Kosofsky Sedgwick, *Between Men: Literature and Male Homosocial Desire*
   (New York: Columbia University Press, 1985).

3. Luce Irigaray, *This Sex Which Is Not One*, trans., Catherine Porter with Carolyn Burke (New York: Cornell University Press, 1985): see especially 'Women on the Market' and 'Commodities Among Themselves' pp. 170-91, 192-97. Gayle Rubin, 'The Traffic in Women: Notes on the "Political Economy" of Sex', in *Toward an Anthropology of Women*, ed., Rayna R. Reiter (New York and London: Monthly Review Press, 1975), pp. 157-210 (pp. 191-92).

4. Joseph Conrad, *Victory* ([1915]; London: J.M. Dent & Sons, 1923). All further references are to this edition and are included in the text.

5. My account of the narrowing of a range of possible identifications / looks into a single one is based, by analogy, on Steve Neale's analysis of configurations of gender, power and looking in the cinema, involving the spectator's look at the screen, the look of the camera and the look of the protagonist. See Steve Neale, 'Masculinity As Spectacle', in *The Sexual Subject: A Screen Reader in Sexuality*, ed., Screen (London and New York: Routledge, 1992), pp. 277-87.

6. 'You mustn't look in my novel for the old stable ego of the character. There is another ego, according to whose action the individual is unrecognisable, and passes through, as it were, allotropic states which it needs a deeper sense than any we've been used to exercise, to discover are states of the same single radically unchanged element. (Like as diamond and coal are the same pure single element of carbon ...)'. D.H. Lawrence, letter to Edward Garnett, 5th June 1914, in *D.H. Lawrence: Selected Literary Criticism*, ed., Anthony Beal ([1956]; London: Mercury Books, 1961), p. 18.

7. Wayne Koestenbaum, *Double Talk: the Erotics of Male Literary Collaboration* (New York and London: Routledge, 1989), pp. 168-70. Koestenbaum comments that Conrad 'used the word "queer" to demarcate a region of feeling he could not explain' (p. 168).

8. Leslie Heywood makes a related   point when she writes that 'in Heyst's "elusive" evasion of definition, he has placed himself in the position of Woman, the unreadable text'. Leslie Heywood, 'The Unreadable Text: Conrad and "The Enigma of Woman" in *Victory'*, *Conradiana*, 26,1 (Spring 1994), pp. 3-19.

9. Luce Irigaray, *Speculum of the Other Woman*, trans., Gillian C. Gill (Ithaca, New York: Cornell University Press, 1985), p. 18.

10. R.W.B. Lewis, 'The Current of Conrad's *Victory*' in   *Joseph Conrad*, ed., Harold Bloom (New York and Philadelphia: Chelsea House, 1986), pp. 63-81 (p. 78).

11. On the ironic use of the word 'gentleman' and on the resemblances between Jones and Heyst, see Tony Tanner, Introduction to the World's Classics Edition of *Victory*, ed., John Batchelor (Oxford: Oxford University Press, 1986), pp. ix-xii, xv-xviii.

12. Koestenbaum, p.168.

13. Eve Sedgwick, *Between Men*   and *The Epistemology of the Closet* ([1990]; Hemel Hempstead: Harvester Wheatsheaf, 1991).

14. Sedgwick, *Between Men*, p.1.

15. Chris Bongie, *Exotic Memories: Literature, Colonialism and the Fin de Siècle* (Stanford, CA: Stanford University Press, 1991).

16. Karl Miller, *Doubles* (Oxford: Oxford University Press, 1987), p. 254.

17. The term is borrowed from Fredric Jameson's *The Political Unconscious: Narrative as a Socially Symbolic Act* ([Methuen 1981]; London: Routledge, 1989). The marginalized Alfuro, who play a significant but negative role in the plot of the novel, exemplify the repressed presence of certain of the conditions of the colonial economy.

18. Lewis, p.71.
19. Stephen Heath, 'Difference', in *The Sexual Subject*, pp. 47-106 (pp. 49-50, 60). De Lauretis quotes Lacan as follows: 'the interdiction against autoerotism bearing on a particular organ, which for that reason acquires the value of an ultimate (or first) symbol of lack (manque), has the impact of pivotal experience'. She comments that 'desire and signification are defined ultimately as a process inscribed in the male body, since they are dependent on the initial – and pivotal – experiencing of one's penis'. Teresa de Lauretis, *Alice Doesn't: Feminism, Semiotics, Cinema* (London: Macmillan, 1984), p. 23.
20. Margaret Whitford, *Luce Irigaray: Philosophy in the Feminine* (London and New York: Routledge, 1991), p. 19.
21. Whitford, p. 22.
22. In its conclusion, my argument converges with that of Leslie Heywood's accmplished deconstruction of gender difference in *Victory*. She concludes: 'In *Victory* ... there is the tendency for each opposition to become so extreme ... that the opposition itself collapses. It becomes its opposite, clearing a space (perhaps Nietzsche's "empty space"?) or instituting a blank within which some other logic than absolute difference begins to work itself out' (Heywood, p. 16).

CHRISTOPHER LANE

Passion's 'Cumulative Poison': Colonial Desire and Friendship in Kipling's Early Fiction

I *Impurity and Expropriation: The Colonial Impulse to Power*

Now, this is the road that the White Men tread
When they go to clean a land ...
Oh, well for the world when the White Men tread
Their highway side by side! – Kipling[1]

A stone's throw out on either hand
From that well-ordered road we tread
And all the world is wild and strange. – Kipling[2]

It's curious the fascination that white men feel drilling queer material into shape. – Kipling[3]

In their speeches and writings, many British Victorian colonials raise concerns about the successful implementation of law and authority. Their anxiety resonates beyond imperial governments and legislative structures; it also questions the internal coherence of colonial rule.[4] In interpreting this anxiety, I suggest in this paper that a conflict between desire and mastery prevailed on what I shall term Britain's 'colonial impulse to power'.

This oscillation between desire and mastery clarifies an uncertainty that surfaced in many colonial texts about how to inhabit and symbolize colonialism's political and psychic registers; it also foregrounds the drives and fantasies that propelled Britain's ongoing bid for global sovereignty. Kipling often referred to the 'breaking strain' that stymied his protagonists, for instance, when their national loyalty created intolerable fatigue and confusion over the precise meaning of their labour.[5] Although this 'breaking strain' implies that acts of personal sacrifice glorified Britain's empire, many historians tell us that Britain's drive to secure political and economic sovereignty also intensified and sexualized relations between men, projecting antagonism and hostility onto those outside its franchise.[6] Since Britain's colonial mastery generated profound ambivalence toward its subjects, British women may have represented supports and vanishing mediators whose partial absence allowed forms of colonial mastery to prevail.

This account, however, is only one side of an uncertain and contested story. If Britain's colonial power was as absolute and secure as its politicians maintained, how should we explain so many colonials' suspicions that this power was not only vulnerable but also, on another level, already lost? This anxiety between colonizer and colonized, and between men and women, at the turn of the last century differed greatly from the full weight of Britain's administrative power. It produces a paradox over the way that prominent colonials understood political instability at the level of ontological, group, and national fantasy, and the reason Britain's authority turned on a nebulous and quite precarious hinge between external security and internal control.

Before we consider Kipling's engagement with these psychic and rhetorical dilemmas, let us first turn to several prominent exemplars of colonial doubt: in his military speeches, for instance, Lord Horatio Kitchener – friend to Kipling, administrator in South Africa, political rival to the Viceroy of India, and discreet homosexual – considered this psychic rigidity a precondition for military success: 'No soldier who is unable to exercise due restraint in these matters can expect to be entrusted with command over his comrades ... Every man can, by self-control, restrain the indulgence of these imprudent and reckless impulses that so often lead men astray'.[7] Kitchener urged the soldier to examine and manage his 'reckless impulses' to prevent him from being 'led astray'. When this policy failed, as it often did, Kitchener proposed genocide and brutal subjugation as the corrective for a paucity of domestic and internal control. Calls for askesis and sexual chastity influenced not only this ferocious and unappeasable command, but also the premise that the native would not submit to outside rule without evidence of the colonial's self-restraint.[8] Adopting this paradox of controlled violence, Kitchener considered the vigilant internal discipline of passions as a valuable quality for export.

Recent critics have documented the colonial perception of indigenous peoples as lawless, seditious, and sexually promiscuous; this work provides an impetus for my study here. However, critics have paid less attention to the dynamic that was integral to Britain's 'Empire of the Selfsame',[9] and have often framed this dynamic by appealing to historical events. Contrary to this single emphasis on historical materialism, I suggest that an unremitting dread of external defiance *and* internal unmaking propelled Britain's drive for global mastery; that the unappeasable quality of this drive created a fervent ambition that many colonialists tried unsuccessfully to temper and vindicate by ethical appeals.

Let us consider more examples to support this claim: Robert

Needham Cust, a civilian who served in the Punjab in the 1850s and
'60s, acknowledged that 'the first sweet taste of unbounded power for
good over others, the joy of working out one's own design, the
contagious pleasure of influencing hundreds, the new dignity of
independence, the novelty of Rule and swift obedience, this and the
worship of nature in the solemnity of its grandeur and the simplicity of
its children, were the fascinations which had enchanted me'.[10] Henry
Lawrence, who directed many of Britain's contemporaneous policies in
the Punjab, elaborated on this point without appearing to jeopardize
his command's authority: 'It is all nonsense, sticking to rules and
formalities, and reporting on foolscap paper, when you ought to be on
the heels of a body of marauders, far within their own fastness, or
riding into the villages and glens consoling, coaxing, or bullying as it
may be, the wild inhabitants'.[11] Finally, consider the words of James
Fitzjames Stephen, an influential imperialist of the time (and Virginia
Woolf's paternal uncle), for his sentiment influenced Kipling's later
demands for colonial appropriation: 'The sum and substance of what
we have to teach them [amount to] the gospel of the English ... It is a
compulsory gospel which admits of no dissent and no disobedience ...
If it should lose its essential unity of purpose, and fall into hands either
weak or unfaithful, chaos would come again like a flood'.[12]

Despite the confidence of these statements, each appears haunted by
anxiety that a counterforce can unmake and usurp their authority from
within. We could describe this force as colonial *jouissance* since it
underpins each declaration and dissipates labour and power.[13]
Considering the full influence of this counterforce, we also might argue
that it obliged the colonial to compete with a corresponding impulse to
self-dispossession whenever he bid for a country's possession. Thus the
anxiety fueling the colonial's ambition to possess a country may have
precipitated a significant number of internal crises for the colonial and
his administration.

Since masculine rigour seemed amenable to channeling discipline into
an incitement to power, many colonialists deemed it a suitable force to
check these destructive impulses. For instance, Fitzjames Stephen
gendered force as the expression of resolute masculinity: 'Strength in all
its forms is life and manhood. To be less strong is to be less of a man,
whatever else you may be'.[14] However, Stephen never clarified the
referents to this 'whatever else'; they conflict with central axioms of
colonial masculinity.

These examples demonstrate that by the time Kipling came to
theorize imperialism, inexorable laws of progress, hierarchy, and
evolution appeared to determine the foundational logic of Britain's
empire, presenting 'mankind' as the governor of Nature's ordinance:
'Nothing is gained by coddling weak and primitive men. The law of
survival applies to races as well as to the species of animals. It is pure

sentimental bosh to say that Africa belongs to a lot of naked blacks. It belongs to the race that can make the best use of it. I am for the white man and the English race'.[15] This appeal to natural law generated a frame of categories and roles able to prescribe acceptable behaviour by condemning their infraction. The law seemingly resolved the problem of antagonistic and self-destructive drives by fostering an ideal by which to measure the subject's deficient relation to each political mandate. Kipling's imperial law established a 'transcendental signifier' against which to defend the Empire from the manifest dissent and chaos of its unruly impulses.[16]

Kipling often connected this anxiety with the process of writing and the general production and dissemination of colonial meaning; his fiction relies on an analogous injunction to expel all of its detrimental elements. Kipling termed this radical excision 'Higher Editing'; he sought to leave only a text's essential elements: 'A tale from which pieces have been raked out is like a fire that has been poked'.[17] However, Kipling's attempt to reduce the proliferation of meaning in his narratives inadvertently produced an elliptical and 'modernist' style that stressed allusion, inference, and interpretation as a means to withstand 'the pressure of the absent'.[18] Additionally, the excised is never absent in Kipling's writing; the pressure of a 'burden incommunicable' amplifies the precise limits of his narrative control.[19] In the opening sentence of a description of his 'Working-Tools', for instance, Kipling argues that 'Every man must be his own law in his own work'.[20] The narrator of 'False Dawn' later demonstrates the practical impossibility of this ideal: 'No man will ever know the exact truth of this story ... so the tale must be told from the outside – in the dark – all wrong' (p. 67).

With its appeal to law over desire's vicissitudes, Kipling's writing mirrors a defensive structure that tries to expel sexual intimacy and miscegenation from the text; this attempt repeatedly surfaces and fails in the following reading of *The Light That Failed* (1891). Benita Parry foregrounds Kipling's reliance on *parataxis,* for instance, arguing that the trope 'organizes incommensurable discourses in ways that obscure and conceal the antagonism of their ideas'.[21] The brevity of Kipling's fictional endings indicates the urgency with which he tried to disband the shattering chaos of desire; this brevity also foregrounds anxious moments of colonial authority by displaying his tenuous control over the text's periphery. Kipling's 'nostalgia for a center'[22] often manifests as an extensive fraternal diaspora, for instance, that relieves the uncertainty of 'race' by promising a reprieve from horrific formlessness: solidarity among white men provides at least imaginary defense against 'impure' elements of racial difference and sexual desire. Yet Kipling's fiction is never stable in this regard because the displacement of 'impurities' compels them to haunt their original structure. Let us therefore examine this difficulty of desire, and its uncertain resolution, in one of Kipling's most interesting narrative failures.

II *The Aim of Desire and The Passion That Fails*

> He must be a man of decent height,
>   He must be a man of weight,
> He must come home on a Saturday night
>   In a thoroughly sober state;
> He must know how to love me,
>   And he must know how to kiss;
> And if he's enough to keep us both
>   I can't refuse him bliss – Kipling[23]

> He was beginning to learn, not for the first time in his experience, that kissing is a cumulative poison. The more you get of it, the more you want. – p.182

> There are many lies in the world, and not a few liars, but there are no liars like our bodies, except it be the sensations of our bodies. – Kipling[24]

Critics generally condemn Kipling's first novel, *The Light That Failed* (1891), as a lamentable failure. While enigma and thematic irresolution riddle the work, the narrative splits between two remarkable and dissimilar endings. In the first, the protagonist Dick Heldar dies in the arms of his closest male friend, Torpenhow; in the second, amended version, Heldar forms a precipitous marriage to Maisie, a woman who has from the novel's outset expressed almost unmitigated hostility toward him. The narrator previously emphasized her uninterest in Heldar because their artistic rivalry disrupts the ensuing romantic attachment, creating an agony of unrequited love. Although neither version is successful in realist terms, Kipling preferred the first but proffered the second as a hasty revision to renew the interest of his disaffected readers.

This revision is incongruous because Maisie's abrupt change of heart and spontaneous repentance contradict the narrator's emphasis on her and Heldar's incommensurate demands. On the one hand, the narrator censures Maisie's preoccupation with painting as a selfish disregard for her 'suitor's' plight. On the other, her resistance is central to the narrative because it upholds the novel's basic concerns: the relentless unpleasure of Heldar's creativity, the extent to which he succeeds in convincing himself (if not the reader) of his passion for an 'unworthy' woman, and the self-destructive impulses that represent all heterosexual interest in the novel.[25] Maisie embodies all of these themes because the novel projects her as the reprehensible cause of Heldar's misery.

In this respect, the novel's split between two endings is not an exception to, but rather an emblem of, a wider narrative difficulty: the split documents the novel's resistance to sexual desire. *The Light That Failed* represents a crisis of object choice for which the classic scenario of the unavailable woman – and her conventional indictment – seems inadequate to explain its failure.[26] Maisie and other women in the text are recipients of an embittered misogyny, but the antagonism of desire that beleaguers Heldar not only precedes his involvement with Maisie, but also transforms her lack of interest into a conflict to which she has no obvious connection.

Thus, the text follows a split in Heldar between his desire's aim and the object that receives it – the object which he considers its *cause* – although his desire's character falls elsewhere, within the purview of masculine relations, and particularly the arms of one man whose attraction prevails throughout. We can attribute many critics' complaints about this text's flaccidity to a conflict between aim, desire, and object because the text exists irrespective of Kipling's metaphysical explanation for Heldar's despondency and the author's misogynist rejection of women as the principal cause of Heldar's misery. The phrase 'spoilt my aim' for instance,recurs in this text (pp. 10, 11-12, 14, 206), as an example and symptom of Heldar's psychic impotence and a precursor to his eventual blindness – an illness that stages his need for Torpenhow's specular assistance for him to focus on what he otherwise cannot see about his desire.

We can further illustrate Heldar's dilemma by the significance he attaches to kissing.[27] His obsession with Maisie begins – like Philip Carey's similarly hopeless 'demand' for Mildred Rogers in W. Somerset Maugham's *Of Human Bondage* (1915) – from an apparent lack of intimacy. Their first kiss occurs after his gun has misfired, its aim spoilt: 'Considered as a kiss, that was a failure, but ... it was the first' (p. 13). By granting Heldar only one kiss, Maisie makes each request exorbitant, leaving Heldar furious and later incapacitated by its 'cumulative poison' (p. 182); the demand always exceeds her response – and, one might suggest, his need. While Maisie constrains oral gratification in *The Light That Failed,* several bizarre and equivalent incidents represent this pleasure between men and between women. For instance, Heldar and Torpenhow hear the refrain from the musical – cited as an epigraph to this section – during their reuniting walk. Although the narrative curiously disembodies this stanza, it is not, as Kipling claims, a 'music-hall refrain' (p. 141), but rather an example of his own verse whose inclusion gives this scene particular significance: it encourages Heldar to sign up for military service, though the narrator never explains why a regiment of men would sing their desire for a man who 'must know how to love me,/ And he must know how to kiss;/ And if he's enough to keep us both/ I can't refuse him bliss' (p. 141). Later, Heldar receives an unsolicited kiss from a female acquaintance and comments, as if to reiterate this refrain: '"The amount of kissing lately has been simply scandalous. I shall expect Torp to kiss me next"' (p. 196). In fact, this homosexual possibility recurs throughout Kipling's work as the most feasible limit – or *point ad absurdum* – to same-gender contact. To put this issue another way, we could say that it recurs as the jocular expression of a wish that expands one man's affectionate interest for another, from the specific concerns of object choice to the generic field of homophilia. Thus Mulvaney, in 'With the Main Guard', reports a soldier's comment to his officer as follows: 'The Staff Orf'cer wint blue, an' Toomey makes him pink by changing to the voice ov a minowderin' woman an' sayin': '"Come an' kiss me, Major dear, for me husband's at the wars an' I'm all alone at the Depot"'.[28] Similar and unaccountable homoerotic rejoinders punctuate Kipling's short story 'Love-o'-Women': 'He might as well have said that he was dancing naked', comments Mulvaney to Ortheris incongruously to explain his sergeant's behaviour.[29] Mackenzie later declares of another soldier: 'I knew there was no callin' a man to account for his tempers. He might as well ha' kissed me' (p. 184).

Heldar's remarks about the scandal of kissing therefore are not exceptional to Kipling's economy of masculine desire; they are arguably that desire's most logical epiphany. Heterosexual desire characteristically disrupts the intimacy that men foster for each other, compelling same-sex friendship (or homophilia) bitterly to engage with the 'disloyalty' that cross-gender interest precipitates.[30] When Heldar's obsession with Maisie seems most chaotic and self-destructive, for instance, his relationships with men begin to fracture; in turn, they insist that he remain faithful to their group – masculine loyalty ensures his salvation. Fraternal bonding is thus a redemptive camaraderie against the debilitating influence of women: '"But a woman can be-" began Dick unguardedly. "A piece of one's life", continued Torpenhow. "No, she can't"' (p. 103).

The idea that intimacy with women can destroy Heldar's creative talent is consistent with this paradigm; such intimacy creates an instability that threatens all of his male friendships. Heldar's relationship with Torpenhow is contrary to this impulse, however, because it fosters creative talent and psychic stability, generating a productive cohesion between 'sublimation', group loyalty, and self-discipline. As the narrator remarks of this split between male and female objects:

> Torpenhow came into the studio at dusk, and looked at Dick with eyes full of the austere love that springs up between men who have tugged at the same oar together and are yoked by custom and use and the intimacies of toil. This is a good love and, since it allows, and even encourages strife, recrimination, and the most brutal sincerity, does not die, but increases, and is proof against any absence and evil conduct. (p. 58)

If love between men is 'good' when it is 'austere', shaped by 'the intimacies of toil', and able to ward off women's 'evil conduct', heterosexual love tortures Heldar because it frustrates his pursuit of 'higher' goals. Homophilia is thus regenerate, pure, and sublime, while heterosexuality is degenerate, impure, and abject. The narrator corrects any assumption that women's 'evil conduct' is merely an external threat; woman's repression also prevents fraternal bonding from corrupting *philia* into *eros*. As an appropriate analogy here, Freud argued that the 'Primal Horde' of brothers had to maintain a similarly vigilant 'esprit de corps' against the legacy of their presocial and homosexual barbarism.[31]

Heldar's defense cannot properly excise evil conduct or comply with the colonial demand for askesis, however; neither painting nor the regiment can draw off the remainder to this novel's desire. Instead, the desire tips first toward a 'bad' love for Maisie and then, with less compulsion and self-destruction, toward a 'love' – that is, approval, respect, and unshakable loyalty – for Torpenhow. Even this figure of salvation cannot foreclose a demand for physical contact; he represents this demand with additional intensity:

> 'Steady, Dickie, steady!' said the deep voice in his ear, and the grip tightened. 'Bite on the bullet, old man, and don't let them think you're afraid.' The grip could draw no closer. Both men were breathing heavily. Dick threw his head from side to side and groaned.
> 'Let me go', he panted. 'You're cracking my ribs. We – we mustn't let them think we're afraid, must we – all the powers of darkness and that lot?'
> 'Lie down. It's all over now.'
> 'Yes', said Dick obediently. 'But would you mind letting me hold your hand? I feel as if I wanted something to hold on to. One drops through the dark so'.
> Torpenhow thrust out a large and hairy paw from the long chair. Dick clutched it tightly, and in half an hour had fallen asleep. Torpenhow withdrew his hand, and, stooping over Dick, kissed him lightly on the forehead, as men do sometimes kiss a wounded comrade in the hour of death, to ease his departure. (pp. 137-38)[32]

The first version of the novel seems to be this passage's logical epiphany because the aim of Heldar's desire finally reaches its object – another man – when Heldar collapses and dies in Torpenhow's arms. In this ending's revised version, however, Kipling recasts intimacy between the two men as a passionate friendship, while an alternative path – love between women – seems to replace this unwritable fantasy. The substitution of lesbianism for male homosexuality was a frequent trope of the Art Deco movement two decades later; as I have argued elsewhere, Ronald Firbank adopted this trope throughout his fiction for similar reasons.[33] In *The Light That Failed,* 'the love which dare not speak its name'[34] also emerges from another sexual scene as desire for Maisie from the unnamed 'red-haired girl'. Here, we see a similar displacement of heterosexuality by homophilia because the 'red-haired girl' previously was a sexual rival with Maisie for Dick. It appears, then, that the second ending was the narrative solution to what Heldar and Maisie heterosexually resist, and what Heldar and Torpenhow find homosexually impossible: 'The red-haired girl drew her [Maisie] into the studio for a moment and kissed her hurriedly. Maisie's eyebrows climbed to the top of her forehead; she was altogether unused to these demonstrations. "Mind my hat," she said, hurrying away, and ran down the steps to Dick waiting by the hansom' (p. 68).

As with the earlier question about the musical sung by the passing regiment, the narrator does not comment on this incident, though it fulfills an important function in this novel. The narrator does not name or develop the 'red-haired girl' as a character, though she models for Maisie's painting, so her presence encourages a mild form of sexual rivalry between Heldar and Maisie for the same woman, and between Maisie and she for the same man (Dick). The 'red-haired girl' also voices an agony of homosexual longing, as if representing the displaced expression of an impossible love between Heldar and Torpenhow. Having kissed Maisie, for instance, she erupts at her cleaner with unaccountable rage: 'The woman fled, and the red-haired girl looked at her own reflection in the glass for an instant and covered her face with her hands. It was as though she had shouted some shameless secret aloud' (p. 72). Although we last hear the 'red-haired girl' urging, 'Maisie, come to bed' (p. 150) – Maisie's inability to sleep results from her insoluble relation to Heldar – the persistent cultural disavowal of women's sexual desire in late-Victorian friendships suggests that this incident does not intentionally signify lesbianism.[35] However, it does indicate a link between an impulse and the desired object at the close of The Light That Failed that is equivalent to the two men's final embrace and consistent with homophilia's exchange for marriage's conventional resolution in its revised ending.

This secondary 'lesbian' relationship displaces erotic interest between Heldar and Torpenhow by representing their intimacy as a defense against women's 'cumulative poison' (p. 182).[36] For instance, Heldar's life improves when he relinquishes his obsession for Maisie, and it coheres entirely when he returns to the brotherly fold. Having pursued Torpenhow to the Sudan for military service, Heldar also finds the inspiration to paint scenes of war, while the company of men re-solders his life's disparate aims, leaving him 'wild with delight at the sounds and the smells [of war]' (p. 201). The narrative implies that his regiment is reparative in psychic terms because it gives him purpose instead of abjection and reassurance after hopeless instability: 'The clank of bayonets being unfixed made Dick's nostrils quiver ... "Oh, my men! – my beautiful men!"' (p. 141). Since this reintegration takes place abroad, in military conflict and by the death of 'Fuzzies' (Sudanese soldiers), it also indicates what is at stake in each narrative and psychic pattern of expurgation: war allows Heldar to feel 'master of himself ' (p. 196) and 'good to be alive again!' (p. 192). Since one of this text's most distressing and inexplicable scenes is the recollection of an incident in which Heldar and Torpenhow happily ridicule the death of a Sudanese soldier, Heldar's epiphany and ritualized purification are also the grotesque effect of colonial subjection and racial slaughter:

> Then came to his mind the memory of a quaint scene in the Sudan. A soldier had been nearly hacked in two by a broad-bladed Arab spear. For one instant the man felt no pain. Looking down, he saw that his life-blood was going from him. The stupid bewilderment on his face was so intensely comic that both Dick and Torpenhow, still panting and unstrung from a fight for life, had roared with laughter, in which the man seemed as if he would join, but, as his lips parted in a sheepish grin, the agony of death came upon him, and he pitched grunting at their feet. Dick laughed again, remembering the horror. It seemed so exactly like his own case. (pp. 126-27)

With the exception of Kipling's most recent biographer, Martin Seymour-Smith, who claims that this scene 'has power as a true metaphor of how Kipling felt',[37] critics have thoroughly condemned Kipling's passage. Notwithstanding the problem of 'true metaphor', it is imperative to ask why Kipling's metaphor took this form in establishing an analogy between his depression and his fantasies of racial violence. For other critics, Heldar's memory indicts British barbarity by enlisting the death of a Sudanese man as a source of pleasure and contemptuous laughter for white men. The idea that 'stupid bewilderment' could be 'intensely comic', that being 'hacked in two' would produce a 'sheepish grin', and that 'the agony of death' could bolster the memory of a 'quaint scene' is itself so obscene that it has impeded further inquiry. However, the argument that this scene illustrates only Kipling's callous indifference seems inadequate in this context; the link between humiliation and mirth – and that the respondents are virilized and sexualized by their laughter – demonstrates the *jouissance* maintaining their intimacy as it fuels their fascistic bid for power.[38]

A less extreme, if no less racist, example of projection arises before Heldar returns to the army, when he considers the inspiration for one of his paintings – the portrait of a woman he began during a sea voyage from Lima to Auckland; her image configures every conceivable fantasy and prejudice: 'She was a sort of Negroid-Jewess-Cuban; with morals to match ... who served as the model for the devils and the angels both – sea-devils and sea-angels, and the soul drowned between them' (p. 98).

Following the topography of E. M. Forster's short story 'The Other Boat' (1915-16), which I have interpreted elsewhere,[39] Heldar produces the painting 'on the lower deck' (p. 98) to signify difficult and inaccessible fantasies, and to allow the woman to figure desires that seem unwritable elsewhere. Since femininity and race condense a threat that Heldar flees, I suggest that this 'Negroid-Jewess-Cuban' also embodies *The Light That Failed*'s narrative logic by compelling Heldar's return to the army and Torpenhow. The spectacle of the grotesquely mutilated Sudanese soldier indicates the violence that is necessary to represent – and then annihilate – each 'opposition', whether it amplifies concerns about gender, race, or both. By adopting a principle of permanent antagonism, the 'Empire of the Selfsame' uses defensive structures to purify its center and unify its diffuse impulses. As *The Light That Failed* illustrates, however, this antagonism returns desire to itself, keeping it within the apparent safety and security of an enclosure that admits no alterity. Less by intent than by default, this enclosure also creates a reactive homoeroticism: the empire manifests an *erotics* of the 'same' rather than sexual desire for one man whom other men perceive differently. In this way, the novel promotes the idea that masculine imperialism glorifies phallic power and authority without resonating entirely of homosexuality. The novel eroticizes Torpenhow, for instance, because he represents an ideal whose physical realization never occurs. The narrative impedes the expression of Heldar's palpable desire for him, using the principle of de-eroticized friendship to withstand the pressure of this 'burden incommunicable'.[40] As the publication history of this novel testifies, however, the text could not sustain this ideal; it tried instead to resolve this ideal by writing first the suicide of its protagonist, then Maisie's marital conversion in a way that disbands Kipling's primary support for homophilia. Kipling's decision to leave *The Light That Failed* heterosexually 'secure' is thus contrary to the fundamental erotic path of this novel. Generally, however, he privileged the austere 'rigour' of colonial masculinity over the debilitating effects of marriage and the effeminacy he perceived the Victorian dandy as embodying. As he declared in the poem 'In Partibus', in a passage that attests to the impetus of most of his other writing:

> It's Oh to meet an Army man,
> Set up, and trimmed and taut,
> Who does not spout hashed libraries
> Or think the next man's thought
> And walks as though he owned himself,
> And hogs his bristles short.[41]

NOTES

This essay is reprinted with permission from chapter one of *The Ruling Passion: British Colonial Allegory and the Paradox of Homosexual Desire*, © (Durham and London: Duke University Press, 1995).

1. Rudyard Kipling, 'A Song of the White Men', *Rudyard Kipling's Verse:*

Definitive Edition (London: Hodder and Stoughton, 1943), p. 282.

2. Kipling, epigraph to 'In the House of Suddhoo', *Plain Tales from the Hills* ([1890]; Harmondsworth: Penguin, 1987), p. 143. All further references are to this edition and are included in the text.

3. Kipling, private correspondence to R. A. Duckworth Ford, 16 September 1907, qtd. in Lewis D. Wurgaft, *The Imperial Imagination: Myth and Magic in Kipling's India* (Middleton, Conn.: Wesleyan University Press, 1983), p. 151. I am indebted to Wurgaft's book for its thorough and astute research on Britain's imperialist relation to India.

4. Bosworth Smith, biographer of John Nicholson, the notorious colonialist of India, described Nicholson as driven by an 'ungovernable restiveness'. See R. Bosworth Smith, *Life of Lord Lawrence, Vol. II* (New York: Scribner's, 1883), p. 194.

5. Kipling, qtd. in Wurgaft, *The Imperial Imagination*, p. 169.

6. For examples, see Ronald Hyam, *Britain's Imperial Century 1815-1914: A Study of Empire and Expansion* (London: Batsford, 1976); Hyam, 'Empire and Sexual Opportunity', *Journal of Imperial and Commonwealth History*, 14, 2 (1986), pp. 34-89; Hyam, *Empire and Sexuality: The British Experience* (Manchester: Manchester University Press, 1990); Kathryn Tidrick, *Empire and the English Character* (London: Tauris, 1992); Lawrence Stone, *The Family, Sex, and Marriage in England 1500-1800* (London: Weidenfeld and Nicolson, 1977), pp. 52-54, 379-80; and Wayland Young, *Eros Denied* (London: Corgi, 1969), pp. 190-91. For a critique of these historians' assumptions about sexuality and sublimation, see the introduction to my *The Ruling Passion: British Colonial Allegory and the Paradox of Homosexual Desire*, pp. 1-8.

7. Lord Horatio Kitchener, qtd. in Wurgaft, *The Imperial Imagination*, pp. 10-11.

8. T. Rice Holmes described the British gratuitous assault on villages in India after the 'Mutiny' in 1857 as 'the infliction of punishment [that] was not a delight, but an awful duty' (Holmes, *A History of the Indian Mutiny* [London: Macmillan, 1904], p. 221). For further discussion of their model of chastity and askesis, see Joseph Bristow, 'Against the Double Standard: From the Contagious Diseases Acts to White Slavery', *Vice and Vigilance: Purity Movements in Britain since 1700* (Dublin: Gill and Macmillan, 1977), pp. 75-93.

9. I take this phrase from Hélène Cixons, 'Sorties', in Cixons and Catherine Clément, *The Newly Born Woman*, trans. Betsy Wing (Minneapolis: University of Minnesota Press, 1986), p. 78.

10. Robert Needham Cust, *Pictures of Indian Life; Sketched with the Pen from 1852-1881* (London: Trubner, 1881), p. 101.

11. Henry Lawrence, qtd. in Sir Herbert Edwardes and Herman Merivale, *Life of Sir Henry Lawrence*, Vol. II (London: Smith, Elder, 1872), p. 219. His equally fanatical brother, Walter, spoke of the delusion surrounding this self-aggrandizement, and the danger of its coercive practices: 'Our life in India, our very work more or less, rests on illusion. I had the illusion, wherever I was, that I was infallible and invulnerable in my dealing with Indians. How else could I have dealt with angry mobs, with cholera-stricken masses, and with processions of religious fanatics? It was not conceit, Heaven knows: it was not the prestige of the British Raj, but it was the illusion which is in the very air of India ... They, the millions, made us believe we had a divine mission. We made them believe we were right'. See Walter Lawrence, *The India We Served* (Boston: Houghton, Mifflin, 1929), pp. 42-43.

12. James Fitzjames Stephen, qtd. in Wurgaft, *The Imperial Imagination*, p. 71.

13. The term refers to drives that are ineffable, but still palpable, in these texts

because they are ontologically satisfying but subjectively destructive. My use of the term obtains from Jacques Lacan's designation for the combined un/pleasures of the drive and *objet a*. See Lacan, *Four Fundamental Concepts of Psycho-Analysis*, ed., Jacques-Alain Miller and trans., Alan Sheridan (New York: Norton, 1978), pp. 174-200.

14. Stephen, *Liberty, Equality, Fraternity* (London: Smith, Elder, 1874), p. 237.
15. Kipling, qtd. in *Kipling: Interviews and Recollections*, Vol. II, ed., H. Orel (Totowa: Barnes and Noble, 1982), pp. 256-57.
16. The reference is given by Jacques Derrida in *Of Grammatology*, trans., Gayatri Chakravorty Spivak (Baltimore: Johns Hopkins University Press, 1974), pp. 10-18, and would in this instance refer to Law, Nature, 'King and Country', and God.
17. Kipling, 'Working-Tools', *Something of Myself, for My Friends Known and Unknown* ([1936]; Harmondsworth: Penguin, 1988), p. 156.
18. Richard Holmes, 'Introduction', *Something of Myself*, p. 10. See also David Lodge, '"Mrs Bathurst": Indeterminacy in Modern Narrative', *Kipling Considered*, ed., Phillip Mallett (London: Macmillan, 1989), pp. 71-84.
19. Kipling, *Kim* ([1901]; Harmondsworth: Penguin, 1989), pp. 327-28.
20. Kipling, 'Working-Tools', *Something of Myself*, p. 154.
21. Benita Parry, 'The Content and Discontent of Kipling's Imperialism', *New Formations*, 6 (1988), p. 58.
22. Zohreh T. Sullivan, 'Memory and the Colonial Self in Kipling's Autobiography', *Prose Studies*, 12, 1 (1989), p. 83.
23. Kipling, *The Light That Failed* ([1891]; Harmondsworth: Penguin, 1988), p. 141. All further references are to this edition and are included in the text.
24. Kipling, *Kim*, p. 321.
25. Heldar's model, Bessie, is drawn to Torpenhow, though he does not reciprocate the interest; it causes him considerable discomfort. He later follows Heldar's advice and flees from her, only later returning to ignore her entirely:
    He went to the mantelpiece, buried his head on his arms, and groaned like a wounded bull ... 'Out you go immediately. Never resist the devil ... Fly from him. Pack your things and go'. 'I believe you are right. Where shall I go?' 'Pack first and inquire afterwards'. (p. 121)
26. For a comparable reading of failure, see Robert L. Caserio, 'Kipling in the Light of Failure', *Grand Street*, 5, 4 (1986), pp. 179-212.
27. See Adam Phillips, 'Plotting for Kisses', *On Kissing, Tickling, and Being Bored: Psychoanalytic Essays on the Unexamined Life* (Cambridge, Mass.: Harvard University Press, 1993), esp. pp. 96-97.
28. Kipling, 'With the Main Guard', *Soldiers Three: The Story of the Gadsbys in Black and White* (London: Macmillan, 1899), p. 72.
29. Kipling, 'Love-o'-Women' (1893), *A Choice of Kipling Prose*, ed., Craig Raine (London: Faber, 1987), p. 178. All further references are to this editon and are included in the text.
30. For elaboration of the concept of friendship as 'philia', and its distinction from 'eros', see Derrida, 'The Politics of Friendship', *The Journal of Philosophy*, 85,11 (1988), pp. 632-48.
31. Ibid., pp. 633-34. I discuss this argument of Freud's *Group Psychology and the Analysis of the Ego* (1921), *The Standard Edition of the Complete Psychological Works of Sigmund Freud*, ed., and trans., James Strachey (London: Hogarth, 1957-74), XVIII, p. 124n, more fully in 'Sublimation, Male Homosexuality, Esprit de Corps: Shattering the Dream of a Common Culture', *Homosexuality and Psychoanalysis*, ed., Tim Dean (London: Macmillan, 1996).

32. John M. Lyon correctly observes in his introduction to the Penguin edition that the passage is 'mawkish' – indeed all physical intimacy, and any formulation of sexuality by Kipling, shares this quality – though Lyon is strangely adamant that the relationship between Heldar and Torpenhow is 'not homoerotic' (p. xxiii). The passage, however, speaks for itself. Other Kipling critics, such as Mark Kinead-Weekes ('Vision in Kipling's Novels', *Kipling's Mind and Art*, ed., Andrew Rutherford [London: Oliver and Boyd, 1964], pp. 197-234) and Martin Seymour-Smith in his recent biography (*Rudyard Kipling* [London: Queen Anne, 1989], pp. 163-90) are less reluctant to consider its influence. Kinead- Weekes argues: 'In that most significant eighth chapter, male friendship and the life of action are directly opposed to the love of Maisie and the hope of marriage' (p. 206).
33. See chapter 7 of *The Ruling Passion: British Colonial Allegory and the Paradox of Homosexual Desire*, pp.176-92, and Emmanuel Cooper, *The Sexual Perspective: Homosexuality and Art in the Last 100 Years in the West* (New York: Routledge, 1986), pp. 63-111.
34. Lord Alfred Douglas, 'Two Loves', *The Penguin Book of Homosexual Verse*, ed., Stephen Coote (Harmondsworth: Penguin, 1983), pp. 262-64.
35. For an exposition of these codes, see Martha Vicinus, 'Distance and Desire: English Boarding School Friendships, 1870-1920', *Hidden from History: Reclaiming the Gay and Lesbian Past*, ed., Martin B. Duberman, Martha Vicinus, and George Chauncey, Jr. (Harmondsworth: Penguin, 1991), pp. 212-29; Carol Christ, 'Victorian Masculinity and the Angel in the House', *A Widening Sphere: Changing Roles of Victorian Women* (Bloomington: Indiana University Press, 1977), pp. 146-62; and Jeffrey Richards, '"Passing the Love of Women"': Manly Love and Victorian Society', *Manliness and Morality: Middle-Class Masculinity in Britain and America, 1800-1940*, ed., J. A. Mangan and J. Walvin (Manchester: Manchester University Press, 1987), pp. 92-122.
36. Kinead-Weekes argues in 'Vision in Kipling's Novels': 'Kipling is making this male love a substitute and haven, and the very overtness of his worry over homosexuality shows the pressure that insists on risking it' (p. 208). See also David M. Halperin, 'Heroes and Their Pals', *One Hundred Years of Homosexuality, and Other Essays on Greek Love* (New York: Routledge, 1990), pp. 75-87, and Dorothy Hammond and Alta Jablow, 'Gilgamesh and the Sundance Kid: The Myth of Male Friendship', *The Making of Masculinities: The New Men's Studies*, ed., Harry Brod (Boston: Allen and Unwin, 1987), pp. 241-58.
37. Seymour-Smith, *Rudyard Kipling*, p. 188.
38. Though it is abhorrent to consider that Kipling's readers identified with their mirth, Robert Buchanan's famous indictment of Kipling shows there was dissent and reproach toward this violence at the time. See Robert Buchanan, 'The Voice of the Hooligan', *Contemporary Review*, 76 (1899), pp. 775-89.
39. See *The Ruling Passion: British Colonial Allegory and the Paradox of Homosexual Desire*, pp. 171-75.
40. Kipling, *Kim*, pp. 327-28.
41. Kipling, 'In Partibus', *Early Verse by Rudyard Kipling, 1879-1889*, ed., Andrew Rutherford (Oxford: Clarendon, 1986), p. 472.

CHRISTOPHER E. GITTINGS

'What are soldiers for?'
Re-Making Masculinities in
Timothy Findley's *The Wars*

The unnamed researcher-narrator of Canadian writer Timothy Findley's 1977 novel *The Wars* sifts through archival, and interview materials to reconstruct Robert Ross, a man silenced by received history, and court-martialled for his rejection of a martial masculinity. 'What are soldiers for?' asks Robert, initiating the novel's inquiry into empire and hegemonic formations of martial masculinity during World War One.[1] Robert Kroetsch suggests that when we read *The Wars* 'what we witness is the collapse, for North American eyes, of the meta-narrative that once went by the name of Europe. Europa'.[2] I would argue that we also witness Robert Ross's collapsing of a dominant and destructive master code of masculinity. Robert's response to his sister Peggy's uniformed fiancee – 'bastard! You bastard! What are soldiers for?' – prefaces his encounter with the brutal and unthinking masculinity of Teddy Budge, and Robert's entry into the highly masculinized territory of the wars.

Upon the death of Rowena, his hydrocephalic sister, Robert's mother decides that her son must execute Rowena's pet rabbits 'BECAUSE HE LOVED HER' (p. 24). Mrs. Ross attempts to discipline Robert's gender identity to prepare him for the violent world of men awaiting him outside the domestic sphere.[3] Robert considered himself Rowena's guardian and feels some responsibility for her death, as he was absent, masturbating, when her wheelchair fell over. To save his son the trauma of killing the rabbits, Robert's father conscripts Teddy Budge, a labourer in the family factory, to carry out Mrs. Ross's instructions. Robert attacks Budge to save the rabbits, and is met with a ruthless response; unaware of why he is under attack or who his assailant is, Budge beats Robert senseless with an Indian club. As Findley's narrator emphasizes, however,

> Teddy Budge was a large and mindless man. There was nothing unkind or cruel in his nature – that was not the point. It was just that he would do what he was told. (p. 24)

Soon after his fisticuffs with Budge, Robert must negotiate other dominating formations of masculinity; he enters the Canadian army to learn how to kill, to be disciplined, to do what he was told.

My discussion will focus on the British Empire's production of exemplary forms of masculinity such as the military, and boy's adventure stories as these are represented in *The Wars*. I will also investigate the metafictional play Findley's novel engages in to interrogate such fictional systems, thereby unmaking a hegemonic martial masculinity, and making alternative masculinities. As many critics have noted, *The Wars* enters into a self-reflexive and counter-discursive dialogue with prior representations of imperial conflict and masculinity.[4] The novels of G.A. Henty, and Benjamin West's painting *The Death of Wolfe* are cultural texts that produce an exemplary masculinity in *The Wars*. The work of Graham Dawson[5] and R.W. Connell[6] argues convincingly that the military has been of fundamental importance to the definition of the soldier hero as a hegemonic form of masculinity in European and North American cultures. Discussing the situation of New Zealand, Connell provides a useful conceptualization for the production of exemplary masculinity in British colonies during World War I:

> It was produced in an interplay between the changing social relations of a settler population, the local state, the British imperial system and the global rivalry of imperialist powers. (p. 213)

And as Connel notes 'the gender pattern was not a mechanical effect of these forces; it was nurtured as a strategic response to a given situation' (p. 30). The making and remaking of masculinities is an historical and political process (p. 44), they constitute gendered allegories of nation. Icons of British imperial identity such as General Wolfe, textualized by writers like Henty, come to define not only a masculinized concept of nation, but also the socially accepted definition for what constitutes a 'real' man. Dawson writes that British adventure/hero narratives impressed upon their readership that a real man 'was one who was prepared to fight (and, if necessary, to sacrifice his life) for Queen, Country and Empire' (p. 1). The horrors of the trenches brought these assumptions into question throughout the British Empire,[7] and marked an increased decolonization of Britain's overseas territories, processes delineated by Findley in *The Wars*.

Robert Ross, a young man who 'doubts the validity' of the 'martialling of men' (*The Wars* p. 13) before the death of his sister, and his encounter with Teddy Budge, considers enrolling himself in the hegemonic masculine by enlisting in the military immediately following her funeral (p. 24) and his altercation with Budge. Robert's experience, however is constructed by Findley as oppositional to the imperial soldiers represented by Henty and West. Marian Turner, the nurse who cares for Robert, marks his difference to conventional soldier heroes in an interview with the novel's researcher-narrator: 'he was a hero. Not your everyday Sergeant York or Billy Bishop mind you ... You see he did the thing that no one else would even dare to think of doing' (p.16). The thing Robert does is to disobey a direct order from his commanding officer in an attempt to save 60 horses and mules from destruction. A week later, Robert suffers severe burns when the army set fire to a barn in which he is sheltering 130 other horses he has liberated from a bombed out train (pp. 183-184).

Robert's enlistment, and the socialization of basic training lend insight into the imperial production of a colonial masculinity. At the Alberta training camp Robert discovers a 'model' he could emulate in Eugene Taffler, a decorated, and athletic war hero (p. 35). Taffler, has also been modelled; he is textually determined by the master code of martial masculinity as this is produced in publications such as *Boy's Own Annual* and *Chums*. He looks like 'a *Boy's Own Annual* hero' (p.96). Taffler, the colonial who is written upon by the empire, who is translated into imperial masculinity, displaces an alternative colonial masculinity for Robert. Whereas Robert had previously identified imaginatively with the Canadian Aboriginal athlete Tom Longboat (p.22), this identification is destabilized by enlistment. In the trenches, Robert hopes to escape the violence of war by dreaming of running like Longboat 'but he kept turning into Taffler. Throwing Stones' (p. 93). Robert's identification with Longboat, however, is not unproblematic, and could be read as a white-settler romanticization of the indigene.

The formation of military masculinity involves a bodily performance of gender, not just athletically, but also sexually. Robert must demonstrate heterosexuality in the ritual trip of the young recruits to a brothel. Robert is 'shamed' into going to the prostitutes; 'if you didn't go you were peculiar' (p. 37). The military culture disciplines gender identity and sexual orientation. Ironically, Findley's brothel is a space where prescribed gender identity and sexual orientation dissolve; Robert fails to have heterosexual intercourse with the prostitute, but through a peep-hole in the bedroom wall learns of Taffler's homosexuality (p. 45). Taffler's violent penetration of the Swede is echoed in Robert's pelvic thrusting against the mud of the battlefield to save himself from drowning: 'He began to push again and to lift – thrusting his pelvis upward harder and harder – faster and faster against the mud' (p. 80). Robert's penetration of the mud constitutes a life-affirming parody of the death-dealing phallic shelling of the mud by the hegemonic masculine.

The textual production of imperial British masculinities is further elucidated aboard the troop ship to England where Findley establishes an intertextual dialogue between the Robert Ross narrative and the texts of G. A. Henty. Captain Ord, one of Robert's cabin mates, claims to lose his voice and spends the entire voyage reading Henty. When informed by another comrade Clifford Purchass that such works are for young boys Ord responds ironically 'that since he was going to do a boy's work he must read the "stuff of which boys are made"' (p. 58). Ord's voice is lost, displaced by the narrating voice of British imperial masculinity, G.A. Henty, a voice that according to Ord's reading produces or makes boys. Clifford Purchass, however, does not appreciate Ord's ironizing of Henty. Perhaps this is because Purchass, who read Henty up until the age of twelve, has been determined by Henty's disciplining texts. For Purchass the war was:

> a serious and heaven-sent chance to become a man. Every night before he went to sleep he stood on the bridge with Horatio – brought the news from Aix to Ghent and smiling, fell dead. (p. 58)

The destructive ramifications of such glorified imaginings of masculinity – the painless and serene death in battle – are adumbrated in the fall of Henty's *With Clive in India* from Ord's bunk onto Purchass' head. Ultimately, Purchass' experience of war cannot be correlated with Henty's fictive heroic code and he is shot in the back while attempting to desert (p. 176). As the Kleinian concept of phantasy would suggest, Purchass's Henty-influenced phantasies are 'not merely an escape from reality but a constant and unavoidable accompaniment of real experiences, constantly interacting with them'.[8] Even Ord, who might seem to be reading Henty as a means of escape from the regimented reality of the troop ship (Brydon p. 69), and who self-consciously ironizes his reading, is engaged in the phantastic introjection of Henty, and a subsequent projection of that reading experience onto the external world. The political value of boy's adventure narratives, their disciplining and indoctrinating nature is evident in Ord's projection of Henty's *With Wellington at Waterloo* onto Ypres. While packing his books prior to disembarking Ord gestures to the Henty textualization of Waterloo and says to Robert: 'That's where we're going, you know. I mean – it's sort of the same thing. Ypres is only sixty miles from Waterloo. Makes you feel better, doesn't it ...' (*The Wars* p. 67). Robert, however, silently questions why this should make them feel better (p. 67). Although Ross is sceptical of Ord's projection of Henty, he also measures his experiences in the military against the empire's representations of military life. When scattering his friend Harris' ashes he thinks: 'I've never seen this done or read about its being done – not even in *Chums* or Joseph Conrad, so I don't know what to say' (p. 107). The recruiting texts of empire have selected out the burial of slain comrades, leaving their readers without a script.

Henty's *With Wolfe in Canada; Or the Winning of a Continent*, one of the texts read by Ord (p. 59), and a colonizing narrative of British imperialism is an important intertext for Findley's parodic and counter-discursive dialogue with Henty. If we read *With Wolfe in Canada* as the inscription of a hegemonic imperial masculinity on the colonial imagination, then Findley's narrative of Robert Ross undoes this authoritative writing. At this point I would like to delineate Findley's dismantling of Henty in a brief comparative reading of *The Wars* and *With Wolfe in Canada*. Henty's narrative tells the story of young Jim Walsham who becomes a man through his participation in British Empire's invasion of New France. The structure of Jim's journey is reflected in the distorting mirror of parody held by Findley. Similar to Robert Ross and some of his colleagues, Henty's Walsham is indoctrinated/recruited by glorified images of British imperialism. A retired officer's travelling peep-show affords the boys and girls of Walsham's village visions of 'great battles by land and sea, where the soldiers and sailors shed their blood like water in the service of their country'[9] for one penny (p. 19). Conversely, Robert Ross's glimpse through a brothel peep-hole reveals a war hero and role model practising a sexuality that interrupts and does violence to the metanarrative of a heterosexual martial masculinity encoded in Henty. Henty's exemplar of idealized masculinity, Jim Walsham, adheres to the Sergeant's advice that 'the bravest men are always the most courteous and gentle with women' (p. 22), and 'not to grumble whatever comes; we all got to do our duty' (p. 18). Jim rescues the sergeant's granddaughter from a near drowning. Upon his return from the British North American field of battle, where he distinguishes himself by following orders, Jim's wounds are rewarded by the hand in marriage of a wealthy young woman who has waited for him faithfully. Robert Ross fails to satisfy these tenets of the dominant masculinity. His experience is an inversion of Jim's. He fails to rescue his sister Rowena, is rejected by his girlfriend, falls in love with a fellow soldier, is raped by his comrades, disobeys and kills his commanding officer, is court-martialled, disgraced, and finally dies in ignominy.

Heather Lawson breaks with Robert because he does not adhere to the dominant understanding of what it is to be a man; he refuses to fight a rival who has professed his love for Heather (*The Wars* p. 18). Heather along with Barbara D'Orsey – who is only capable of having relationships with the socially scripted masculine of the athletic and handsome soldier hero – exemplify how women and gender relations are socially constructed by a dominating masculinity. Robert leaves the domestic sphere for the army and the world of men where instead of keeping a torch burning for Heather, he falls in love with a man, Harris (p. 103). Robert, although he allows himself to be recruited by the military, cannot be recruited by its code of masculinity. Findley remakes the dominant. The researcher-narrator reconstructs alternative masculinities with the assistance of female voices who testify to Robert's difference. In addition to Marian Turner's testimony to his difference from the conventional hero paradigm, Lady Juliet D'Orsey's words tell us about Robert's feelings for Harris. As Lorraine York has noted Robert's very name is a reference to 'one of Oscar Wilde's closest and most constant lovers' (*Front Lines* p. 39). Concerning the significance of female voices representing Robert, I agree with Simone Vauthier's suggestion that as 'the two interviewees never shared in the male code of war' they are well positioned to re-define Robert Ross's gesture (p. 15).

The codes of military honour, and brothers in arms exemplified by Henty's Jim Walsham are further challenged by Findley in the violent rape of Robert Ross by his own men in the baths at Desolé. Like Donna Pennee and others[10] I read this scene as the symbolic and literal rape of Robert by the 'conventional rhetoric of war' (Pennee p. 47), by the destructive rhetoric of the soldier hero. Findley's journal entries reveal his belief that 'Robert Ross and his generation of young men were raped, in effect, by the people who made that war. Basically, their fathers did it to them'.[11] When Robert surveys the carnage wreaked as a result of the insane Captain Leather's order he thinks 'If an animal had done this-we would call it mad and shoot it and at that precise minute Captain Leather rose to his knees and began to struggle to his feet. Robert shot him between the eyes' (*The Wars* p. 178). Robert's murder of Leather is tantamount to the symbolic destruction of his rapists and martial formations of masculinity. At this point Robert pulls the lapels from his uniform and leaves behind him both the battlefield and hegemonic masculinity (p. 178).

The deaths of Harris, Purchass, Leather, and others are a response to the romantic and heroic representations of death in Henty and Benjamin West. Findley's researcher-narrator conflates Henty's written text *With Wolfe in Canada* (Henty p. 373) with West's painting *The Death of Wolfe* to suggest how death might be imagined by young men like Ross and his comrades who have consumed the popular images of military martyrdom:

> Oh I can tell you sort of how it would be like to die. *The Death of General Wolfe.* Someone will hold my hand and I won't really suffer pain because I've suffered that already and survived. In paintings – and in photographs – there's never any blood. At most the hero sighs his way to death while linen handkerchiefs are held against his wounds. His wounds are poems. *I'll faint away in glory hearing music and my name. Someone will close my eyes an I'll be wrapped around in flags while drums and trumpets-bagpipes march me home through snow ...* (p. 49).

Henty's Wolfe is shot in the wrist, but continues to advance wrapping a handkerchief around his wound. He is struck twice more before he finally sits down. Informed that the enemy is retreating, he says 'Now, God be praised, I will die in peace!' (p. 373).

Findley's novel challenges established masculinity. Von Clausewitz's *On War*, a foundational text in modern masculinity (Connell p. 192) is shown to be ineffectual in the trenches, and is literally scorched by the flames of combat it inspires. Findley provides alternative masculinities to the dominant in characters like Robert, Harris and the artist/soldier Rodwell. These men are more concerned with nature and preserving the lives of animals than with the mass destruction they have been recruited to participate in. And yet the novel also represents the erasure of these men by the dominant; all of them die in the imperial enterprise. This it would seem is what soldiers are for: eradicating difference and preserving the status quo. Like a good deal of Findley's fiction the moral cores of his novel, Robert Ross and opposition to the brutish power struggles of empire, are figured as entities that are written out of our pasts, elements that must be recovered if we are to interrupt the production of death-dealing masculinities. One intertext left unexplored in this paper is Diana Brydon's reading of *The Wars* with Conrad's *Heart of Darkness* as a revelation of the 'irrational heart of European rationality and the violence marked by western civilization'. She writes that as a Canadian Robert Ross must travel to Europe to find his 'heart of darkness' (Brydon p. 75). Findley's 1993 novel *Headhunter* further explores Condradian constructions of masculinity and empire in Canada's invader-settler culture.

NOTES

1. Timothy Findley, *The Wars* ([1977]; Harmondsworth: Penguin, 1978), p. 25. All further references are to this edition and are included in the text.
2. Robert Kroetsch, 'Disunity as Unity: A Canadian Strategy', *The Lovely Treachery of Words: Essays Selected and New* (Toronto: Oxford University Press, 1989), pp. 21-33 (p. 23).
3. For more on the tensions between public and domestic spheres in *The Wars* see Lorraine M. York, *Introducing Timothy Findley's The Wars. A Reader's Guide* (Toronto: ECW Press, 1990), pp. 45-58.
4. See the following: Diana Brydon '"It could not be told": Making Meaning in Timothy Findley's *The Wars*', *Journal of Commonwealth Literature*, 21 (1986), pp. 62-79 (p. 64). All further references are to this issue and are included in the text; Martin Kuester, *Framing Truths: Parodic Structures in Contemporary English-Canadian Historical Novels* (Toronto: University of Toronto Press, 1992), pp. 56, 67. All further references are to this edition and are included in the text; Donna Palmateer Pennee, *Moral Metafiction: Counterdiscourse in the Novels of Timothy Findley* (Toronto: ECW Press, 1991), p. 47. All further references are to this edition and are included in the text; Simone Vauthier, 'The Dubious Battle of Story-Telling: Narrative Strategies in Timothy Findley's *The Wars*', *Gaining Ground,* eds., Robert Kroetsch and Reingard M. Nischick, (Edmonton: Newest Press, 1985), pp. 11-39 (p. 27). All further references are to this edition and are included in the text.
5. Graham Dawson, *Soldier Heroes: British Adventure, Empire and the Imagining of Masculinities* (London: Routledge, 1994), p. 24. All further references are to this edition and are included in the text.

6. R.W. Connell, *Masculinities* (Cambridge, U.K.: Polity Press, 1995), p. 213. All further references are to this edition and are included in the text.
7. See Lorraine M. York, *Front Lines: The Fiction of Timothy Findley* (Toronto: ECW Press, 1991), p. 34. All further references are to this edition and are included in the text. See also Sandra Gilbert and Susan Gubar, *No Man's Land: The Place of the Woman Writer in the Twentieth Century Volume 2: Sex Changes* (New Haven and London: Yale University Press, 1989), p. 263.
8. See Hanna Segal, *Introduction to the Work of Melanie Klein* (Oxford: Hogarth Press, 1973), p. 14. Also quoted in Dawson, p. 32.
9. G.A. Henty, *With Wolfe in Canada; or the Winning of a Continent* ([1886]; Glasgow and London: Blackie and Son, 1958), p. 20. All further references are to this edition and are included in the text.
10. See Kuester, p. 65 and Vauthier, p. 12.
11. See Timothy Findley, *Inside Memory: Pages from a Writer's Workbook* (Toronto: Harper Collins, 1990), p. 151.

DIANA BRYDON

'Rogues and Brutes ... in Pinstripe Suits': Timothy Findley's *Headhunter*

Timothy Findley's recurrent obsessions with the legacy of colonialism, new forms of Empire under capitalism, and the social construction of masculinity come together in his 1993 novel *Headhunter* in a particularly troubling fashion. The novel replays Conrad's *Heart of Darkness* during a terrifying time of an AIDS-like plague in the late twentieth century, sometime in the near future, relocating its characters and their obsessions in Toronto, Canada's financial heartland. This deadly disease proceeds by discoloured speckling of the body that could be termed 'speculation', the implicit pun signalling an intertextual relation with 1980s capitalism as much as with Camus' *The Plague*.

The Conradian frame is explicitly invoked in the title, 'Headhunter', the epigraph to Section One, which cites Marlow's famous beginning, '... this also ... has been one of the dark places of the earth' and the novel's delightful opening paragraph, which runs as follows:

> On a winter's day, while a blizzard raged through the streets of Toronto, Lilah Kemp inadvertently set Kurtz free from page 92 of *Heart of Darkness*. Horror-stricken, she tried to force him back between the covers. The escape took place at the Metropolitan Toronto Reference Library, where Lilah Kemp sat reading beside the rock pool. She had not even said *come forth*, but there Kurtz stood before her, framed by the woven jungle of cotton trees and vines that passed for botanic atmosphere.[1]

The whimsical parody is overt, simultaneously funny and serious: the jungle has been faked; the darkness is real. We begin in the library. The library is the institutional repository of the images that haunt us, the representations that have shaped our world, enabling and constraining our ability to imagine otherwise. The library has become the simulacrum of the jungle, a more appropriate symbol for the darkness of Western civilization: its colonizing modes of knowing, its classificatory ambitions (including its stereotypes of gender construction), and its commodification fetish. Lilah Kemp, the schizophrenic retired librarian who loves books, had, a few years earlier when inadvertently possessed by the fascist bookburner Otto, burned down her old workplace, the Rosedale Public Library, symbol in the popular imagination of everything that was most genteel about the colonial Upper Canadian tradition. (There is a bookstore cutely called 'Not the Rosedale Public Library'.) Now she has unwittingly, she believes, released Kurtz into her world. Her burning of the books reveals her own complicity in the horror she dreads from Kurtz. Their conflict is not posed in the simplistic oppositions of us and them, but rather through the tangled emotions of a character so involved in humanity that her rejection of Kurtz comes from intimate knowledge rather than any assumption of moral superiority.

Not so much an 'Intended' as someone chosen to focus the hauntings of our past, and to be perceived as out of the mainstream of capitalist logic, Lilah is the moral centre and the great triumph, in human terms, of the book. In living for her readers as Conrad's 'Intended' never could, she reverses the gendered focus of Conrad's tale. Herself a reader, she is for readers the most sympathetic focalized centre of consciousness in the book, although an omniscient narrator guides us through a maze of characters and their interconnected stories. It is typical of Findley's work to locate the moral centre of the text in feminine consciousness and for the masculine to represent evil and a lessened awareness. In this opening scene, Lilah experiences the horror attributed to Kurtz in Conrad's tale; Kurtz remains oblivious to her presence and the significance of their encounter.

The headhunter of the book's title is most obviously Kurtz, who works as Psychiatrist-in-Chief at the Parkin Institute of Psychiatric Research, but Marlow (introduced later) shares his profession if not his approach to it. In Findley's resituating of horror from the beginning to the end of the twentieth century, inner and outer worlds are more closely fused. In the invader-settler context of Canada, the colonial encounter has usually involved settler attempts to appropriate the native, as Conrad does the African, to a European agenda. But in *Headhunter*, the focus clearly falls on the self-interrogation of the settler psyche. In Walter Benjamin's terms, the practice of psychiatry supplies the documents of civilization that simultaneously encode an ultimate barbarism.[2] Just as Conrad's Kurtz's idealistic memo includes its coda to 'Exterminate the brutes', so Findley's Kurtz has produced a memo documenting his search for *'absolute power'* via the motto: *'psychiatry is my mode, psychiatric research is my delivery system ... Under my guidance, they will soon enough become the willing addicts of desire'* (p. 426). Brutes and rogue traders are the same people in Findley's Toronto, and they are engaged in exterminating one another, egged on by the power-hungry Kurtz.

Findley is romantic about madness. He sees madness testing and revealing the limitations in psychiatry's modes of knowing. Madness opens imaginative possibilities psychiatry tries to close down. He shares a female character's perception of Kurtz as 'everything she feared. Authority with an armed guard' (p. 249). If we are to define madness as a sickness to be cured, then for Findley the sanctioned violence and miseries of our present system are the true insanity. In Conrad's text, his madness constitutes Kurtz's charisma. Marlow is seduced by that madness, and critics have been too, seeing Kurtz as the moral centre of the book for exposing the logical extreme of imperialism. Findley reverses this dynamic. His Marlow is seduced, not by Kurtz, who seems chillingly sane and businesslike, but by a series of mad and anguished figures Marlow cannot save, although he tries. Most of them suffer, like Amy Wylie, 'from a madness called *benevolence*' (p. 370). Several of them die because they get in Kurtz's way. Findley's Marlow seems to spend most of the narrative avoiding Kurtz and the discovery of his madness, which the text labels incomprehensibly evil in its quest for absolute power.

To blunt the insight of the clinically mad, psychiatrists prescribe drugs. Kurtz experiments with a new drug, called '*Obedian*', that creates absolute docility. It makes him the god he believes psychiatrists should be. His interest is power and he wields it ruthlessly. During the 1980s, the word 'headhunter' was widely used to describe corporate raiders, searching for the kind of executives who could make them the most money most efficiently. This use of the term best describes *Headhunter's* Kurtz, and others in his circle, who hunt, recruit, use, and even torture and kill people to advance their own wealth and power. It is as if Findley anticipated the Bernardo case in diagnosing the evils of our times.[3] These men, the executives and tycoons who would abuse their own children for a moment of fleeting gratification, embody Findley's own horror, made manifest for him through the Holocaust, that 'there is nothing people won't do' (p. 96). In earlier books, such as *The Butterfly Plague* and *Famous Last Words*, he explored this horror in its explicitly Fascist manifestations, what he calls the 'aggressive face' (p. 98) of this will to power at all costs. In *Headhunter*, he describes its 'corporate' (p. 98) face.

This face is masculine in modality, but can be assumed at will by men and women in Findley's world. Freda Manly, for example, is the kind of phallic mother to make one wonder about Findley's gender conservatism. Her son, Warren Ellis, makes his rejection of her and what she stands for, the 'manly', into a public gesture of defiance by appearing at his father's funeral in a Balenciaga dress, accompanied by her chief rival, his dead father's partner, whose cause he is now committed to serve. The gallery owner Fabiana Holbach (Kurtz's Intended in Findley's text) sums up the novel's position on gender construction: 'We're all in drag ... It's a drag act – men pretending to be men – women pretending to be women – but only the artists will tell us that. The rest of us cannot bear the revelation' (p. 239). In that sense,

Warren's cross-dressing marks his self-positioning as an artist. He has chosen the form of his complicity, refusing to become a 'manly headhunter', to highlight instead a self-construction that brings headhunter categories into question, while continuing to wear the class-marking Balenciaga. Warren also articulates the novel's equation of 'bedrooms and boardrooms' as places where 'someone is always getting bonked' (p. 94).

In Canada during the 1980s, the corporate face of power (Findley's horror), the headhunter or rogue trader, became associated, by Findley and eventually by the majority of English Canadians, most directly with the Progressive Conservative government of Brian Mulroney. The greed of the eighties has already become a legendary memory but few Canadian writers have attempted to understand it in their fiction. In a recent interview, Findley describes a hypothetical situation that I believe comments on the genesis of *Headhunter*, although he doesn't explicitly say this. What he says is:

> Let's say you state that Mulroney killed Canada – which I believe. How am I going to make that more than a mere rhetorical statement? I have to find a fictive way of proving that he did that – a believable way – by working that story through the lives of people and incidents in a way that is so engaging that you can't help but close the covers of the book and say 'It is all true'.[4]

'Mulroney', too, then, is the headhunter conjured by the book's title, as a potent symbol of the comprador class selling out the nation yet again within a neo-colonial world system, thus repeating the unimaginative ways in which Canada's elite has always operated under earlier forms of colonialism. This fusion of the corporatism of 'the new world order' hailed by George Bush, fascist ambitions for refashioning humanity, earlier forms of colonialism in Canada and imperialism in Conrad's text, creates a volatile, and self-condemning mix, in Findley's novel.

Findley's narrator uses a fashionable gallery opening to pull these threads together for his readers. On his arrival at the gallery, Kurtz muses that 'nearly everyone in this room ... has violence somewhere in the family background' (p. 59). The artist, Julian Slade, had been what Kurtz calls, in the currently dominant business-speak that Mulroney (and now Klein and Harris) have inflicted on the nation, 'a client' (p.59) of his at the Parkin Institute. Slade's paintings represent horror: 'Eyes that were blinded and mouths that were screaming' (p. 60); they are paintings that literally 'bled' (p. 60). Although he had wished to dedicate his paintings to Kurtz, to *'the man who released my demons'* (p. 60), as he put it, Kurtz had refused, finding the paintings 'too alarming' (p. 60). Griffin Price, one of the headhunting businessmen, thinks that Slade 'is the Mengele of art' (p. 61). He believes that 'The human race needs another Mengele to bring it up to date'; that 'we are ready for another version of the human race. The final honing' (p. 61).

Here, in this echo of Hitler's 'final solution', is the seduction associated with Conrad's Kurtz. Findley's Kurtz is not immune, hanging one of Slade's most horrific paintings in the lobby of the Parkin Institute.

Each character in the text is 'placed' by his or her response to Slade's paintings. Kurtz embodies the susceptibility of the scientific community; Griffin Price that of genteel old Toronto. Price hates his heritage, describing it as 'Like most pioneer colonial societies, [where] the rules of conduct were limiting and uncreative. *More British than the British had been the motto then ...* ' (p. 62). The narrator continues to paraphrase Griffin's thinking:

> Besides the old Toronto society there was the new. This ... is common in every culture – but the difference between one *new* society and another lies in the uniqueness of the given *old* society. It is the old society that is being aped – and what is being aped depends on where the old society got its values. In Toronto, Griffin said, they were got from snobs. So *snobbery* was aped – and, while snobbery itself is bad enough, the aping of it is vacuous. Money turned the key, as always – and what this produced, according to Griffin Price, was *a social class of rogues and brutes dressed up in pinstripe suits and screwing everything in sight. Metaphorically speaking, of course* ... (p. 62)

The irony here is that in the world of *Headhunter*, this metaphor is made literal, through the description of the sadistic rituals of a group of men, calling themselves the Club of Men, who recruit children (sometimes their own) to satisfy their various sexual fantasies, drugging them with *'Obedian'* to ensure their compliance. Their activities parallel the unethical experiments of Kurtz and a Dr. Shelley (echoing Frankenstein) with *'Obedian'*, creating a group of severely traumatized children at the Parkin. Kurtz 'raids' a colleague's list of 'clients' (many of them members of the Club of Men) so he can use their confessions to his own advantage. These stolen secrets join his other collectibles: ivory, pornographic photographs, and fetishized objects of sadism and misogny from around the world. Peggy Wylie seems right the first time when she misreads the sign 'THERAPIST' as 'THE RAPIST' (p. 322) on her visit to the Institute.

The metaphor of 'screwing' in its linking of money and sex through violent aggression toward others, defines the Torontonian world in this text as the late twentieth century inheritor of traditions of conquest begun much earlier, traditions embodied for Findley in the constructed masculinity of the rogue in a pinstrip suit. Findley's fictional persona, the Irish writer Nicholas Fagan, provides both the diagnosis and the cure for his protege, Lilah. Fagan's journey up the St. Lawrence River to Toronto makes him think of the colonizers who preceded him. He concludes:

> There is little beauty left – but much ugliness. Little wilderness – but much emptiness. No explorers – but many exploiters. There is no art – no music – no

literature – but only entertainment. And there is no philosophy. This that was once a living place for humankind has become their killing ground (p. 259).

So much for Canada. On a more general level, he writes:

> If I were to propose a text for the twentieth century, it would be Joseph Conrad's *Heart of Darkness*. As subtext, I would nominate Mary Shelley's *Frankenstein*. Nothing better illustrates than these two books the consequence of human ambition. On reading them again, I ... took up my current view that the human race has found its destiny in self-destruction (p. 98).

When Lilah says that she thinks this 'is the saddest sentence in all the world' (p. 260), Fagan responds that it is also 'a very angry thought' (p. 260). He sees some agency and some hope in the idea that every Kurtz 'has a Marlow' (p. 261) and both are conjured for us by literature. Fagan's Marlow, unlike Conrad's, is less a secret sharer and more an alternative – a model of integrity in a fallen world. Does this make Findley a naive or a resisting reader of Conrad? I'm not sure, but it does mean that he refuses to explore the homosocial implications of Conrad's text in his rewriting.

The destructive energies of Frankenstein and Kurtz's quests for forbidden knowledge find their counterpoint, in Fagan's reasoning, in the capacity of books to function as 'A way of singing our way out of darkness. The darkness that is night – and the darkness that is ignorance – and the darkness that is ... fear' (pp. 97-98). This is probably why Findley names the good psychiatrist who tries to save the children, only to be killed herself, Eleanor Farjeon, after the children's writer.

Findley's faith in the redeeming powers of literature, and in the ability of the Marlows of this world to bring the Kurtzes back into the fold of humanity, is both the charm and weakness of Findley's text. After successfully equating the evil of the members of the Club of Men, who are voyeuristic, greedy, and selfish, with that of the researchers tormenting children and animals in that spirit of objective enquiry our society has coded 'masculine', *Headhunter* retreats from its insights. Kurtz's role in linking the activities of the Club of Men and the Parkin Institute was in the service of a grand dream that there must be 'a new social contract' (p. 434). On his deathbed, he tells Marlow: 'of his immense plans. I was on the threshold of great things ... ' (p. 433), and later still calls them 'a business proposition ... The future is a business proposition' (p. 434). Marlow speculates that 'the absolute exercise of absolute power' has cut Kurtz 'loose from reality' (p. 433). Later, Kurtz offers another explanation, confessing, in halting, drawn out fashion, that when he was a boy at school, he had wanted 'not to be me ... I wanted to be ... my father' (p. 435). This is pure Findley: at the heart of all conflict lies the Oedipal struggle between fathers and sons. Although Kurtz's confession articulates a logic demonstrated throughout the narrative, most notably in the rewriting of *The Great Gatsby*, its statement here seems bathetic. In the end, the range of gendered subject positions explored in this text seems very narrow, the script already tightly written and unreceptive to substantial revision. Indeed, it seems to be in that generic contract that brings resolution at the end of a story that Findley pins his hope.

Fagan speaks the final, apparently authorized interpretation of the text we have just read, and his words seem complacent and insufficient. He writes to Lilah:

> Every Kurtz must have his Marlow – and Marlow will always come to take Kurtz home ... This process is played out over and over – and with every journey up the river, we discover that Kurtz has penetrated just a little farther than his counterparts before him ... why does [Marlow] always agree to go? ... I would guess it is because he is beholden to Kurtz for having provided him, after darkness, with a way to find new light. (p. 440)

After the desolation Kurtz has sanctioned, such consolation seems special pleading, an uncanny echo of the 'Sustaining fictions. Uplifting fictions. Lies' that Marlow tells Fabiana, Kurtz's 'Intended', after his death (p. 438). Lilah is left with Fagan's 'uplifting fiction', lying in bed 'with *Heart of Darkness* beside her', thinking no one would believe the story she has just lived: '*Its only a book*, they would say: *That's all it is. A story. Just a story*' (p. 440). Findley, of course, hopes he has convinced us to think just the opposite, that 'it's all true'.

In *Headhunter*, Findley explores the implications of the stories our culture tells itself about human limitations and possibility. The range of intertextualities is much vaster than those I have discussed here, but they all share, in Findley's retellings, an obsession with interpellated subjectivity and ways of living in bodies marked by gender, class and race. Perhaps his biggest innovation in rewriting *Heart of Darkness* is his reversal of Freud's equation of woman with that symbolic African darkness, reappropriating it instead for an analysis of the construction of masculinity and neo-imperialism in the late twentieth century. The aptness of his image of 'rogues and brutes in pinstripe suits' has been recently reaffirmed by media mythologizing of the latest celebrity 'rogue trader', Nicholas Leeson, who allegedly is responsible for breaking Barings Bank.[5] Nonetheless, some troubling questions remain. Marlow's complicity, retrieved by Fagan as part of the redeeming lie that men tell women to keep them quiet, links Fagan, Marlow, and Kurtz in the continuation of a civilization that the novel has exposed as morally bankrupt. Lilah embodies the idea that redeems the destruction, the values of Western Literature and the insights they provide, but she is effectively cut off from reality, living in her own schizophrenic world populated by ghosts and fictions. Marlow's lie to Fabiana, echoed in Fagan's reassurance to Lilah, suggests that the homosocial relationship of Kurtz and Marlow, unexplored in this text, remains nonetheless its own silent heart of darkness.

NOTES

1. Timothy Findley, *Headhunter* (Toronto: Harper Collins, 1993), p.3. All further references are to this edition and are included in the text.
2. Walter Benjamin, 'Theses on the Philosophy of History', *Illuminations*, by Benjamin, ed., Hannah Arendt, trans., Harry Zohn, 1968. (New York: Schocken, 1985), p. 256.
3. The Bernardo case was a sensational murder trial that dominated media attention for the first half of 1995.
4. 'Timothy Findley's True Fictions: A Conversation at Stone Orchard', interview by W.M.Mellor, *Studies in Canadian Literature*, 19, 2 (1994), pp. 77-101
5. 'How this man broke a bank', *The Globe and Mail*, Wednesday, 1 March 1995, p. A12.

JOHN MARTIN

Turning Boys into Men: Australian 'Boys' Own' Annuals, 1900 -1950

Over the past six years the works of Hall, Mangan & Walvin, Roper & Tosh, and Jackson have all illuminated the classed and gendered nature of history. Between 1900 and 1950 whiteness, superiority and solidarity were inseparable characteristics of the male middle classes.[1] Masculinity was shaped by the ideology of empire throughout the English diaspora.

This essay sets out to contextualize this middle class masculinity in Australia and to examine the shaping of Australian middle class masculinity over this period. The intent is to highlight the *changes* in representations of men and boys. The annuals used as a source were published especially for Australia. They were one way imperial ideology was circulated and the diaspora was maintained. It must be remembered that the readers of these annuals had dual identity. They were Australian and British.

Publication of these annuals was motivated by a widespread philanthropy directed to the betterment of boys.[2] In Australia as in England, these stories did not circulate through all levels of society.[3] There was a rejection by some boys of these masculinities.[4] Competing masculinities were recognised by the Directors of the Newsboys' Society in Sydney.[5] There would have been little identification or relevance in these stories for working class boys; this served to exclude some working class boys. Price of the annuals would have been a significant determiner of readership.[6] Ethnicity, religion, class and the rural/urban divide would have been factors in the consumption of these annuals. Readership of these annuals was confined to a small group of middle class boys.

Lyons (1992) argues that,

> In modern times and in a secular context, silent reading appears as a pre-requisite for the critical, individualist ethos of a liberal democratic society. Reading by one's self breaks down communal bonds of conformity or, in McLuhan's terms, it detribalises us.[7]

The readers of these books had an opportunity for individual reading. What they brought to the text and the meaning they negotiated with it were personal and private. They did not share the experience with others. The opportunity arose for a more private negotiation of at least some part of masculinity. Masculinity could be negotiated inwards, while at the same time but in other settings, it was being negotiated with and accommodated to the public sphere.

Poorer boys read textbooks and readers at school.[8] Their opportunity for privacy and personal introspection was restricted. Access to books, not just the annuals, may have been creating differences between boys. One group of boys developing an individualist ethos, the other group a communal one.These annuals were inheritors of a 19th century didactic tradition.[9] The stories were written in the third person. They appear more like statements of fact than works of fiction, with greater weight lent to the authorial voice. A heavy handed didacticism is apparent in every story.

Young Australia was published by The Pilgrim Press, the publishing company of The Religious Tract Society.[10] By the beginning of the twentieth century religion had been incorporated into imperial ideology, and they were promoters of patriotism.[11] The *Australian Boy* carried regular features and information for the Boys' Empire League in the first decade of the twentieth century. The motto of the Boys' Empire League was, 'To promote and strengthen a worthy Imperial spirit in British boys all over the world'.[12] The motive for the Boys' Empire League most probably lay in the general philanthropy directed toward boys.

The content of these annuals is wide-ranging. It is consistent over time, and does not differ greatly between the two annuals. Information and facts were presented in way which dictated to boys how they could come to know the world. There was suggested not only a clinical and objective way of knowing the world but an emphasis on the usefulness of objects and actions. The boys are cast as active participants in life.The broad genre of boys' story encompassed the same settings in both the 1905 *Young Australia* and the 1912 *The Australian Boys' Annual*. There were military and war stories, adventure, frontier, chivalric, sports, school stories and westerns. A variety of themes are then explored in each setting.

The 1928 editions of the same annuals changed only slightly in content. There had been a shift from handicrafts to science and technology which had a military application. The aspiring young scientist of a yet to arrive Cold War was being inducted. Factual articles of sporting advice appeared. They were part of a broader instruction on the importance of discipline and of obligation to one's group.[13] The settings of boys' stories remained much the same. The long tradition which saw westerns as especially useful in Australia[14] ensured that they continued.

The genre of boys' story was central. These stories were used as *devices* to convey masculinity.[15] Central to my argument is masculinity, the values associated with it and the way in which they changed over time. Manliness, in the tradition of these and similar annuals since the 1850s, had been represented as 'muscular Christianity'. In an effort to induce boys to become practicing Christians, godliness and manliness were combined.[16] At the end of the nineteenth century, athleticism grew out of muscular Christianity and began to replace it. Manliness was expressed through moral behaviour, manly love and sporting ability, rather than by spirituality, godly love and good health.[17]

Dan of Roper's Gully [18] is typical of the 1900 to 1914 boys' stories with a western/frontier setting. Indians are raiding white settlements. Dan, though we are told he is far too young, is sent out with the men and soldiers. Dan and a hunter steal away on a reconnaissance mission and are captured by the Indians. A signifier of manliness was taking action. Dan was defining himself as a man from the beginning of this story. The hunter is killed and Dan finds himself held captive with another young boy.

> Dan's horse had been confiscated, and both he and Chris had had to walk. Footsore and weary, it was a with a sense of inexpressible relief that they found the halt at last called. Under such circumstances to keep a brave heart was in no wise (sic) easy; yet Dan did it.

Endurance and courage in the face of impossible adversity were two hallmarks of the frontiersman. The Indians did not guard their captives carefully. Dan's horse, Grey Nell, refused to let the Indian braves ride her. The horse was hobbled and turned loose. Dan saw a chance of escape.

> A cloud was in the east, and with one accord the Indians observed it. They feared fire, the greatest prairie dread. For Dan the chance offered.

Dan's knowledge of the environment and the ability to read natural signs made him aware of the danger of fire. He displayed the frontiersman's resourcefulness, ready to take hold of the opportunity presented. The boys mounted the horse and fled.

> Dan would have magnanimously put Chris in front – the position of least peril – but Chris was no rider in comparison with himself, and to have done so would have been fatal, probably, to both.

Dan was willing to sacrifice himself to save Chris. He was a good enough horseman to see them back to safety.

All the admirable qualities of the frontiersman are illustrated, 'courage, endurance, individualism, sportsmanship, resourcefulness, a mastery of environmental signs and a knowledge of natural history'.[19] Dan asserted his masculinity by mastering his environment and by using cunning and guile to outsmart the Indians.

Plate VIII: "SNIFFING LIBERTY, SNORTING DEFIANCE, FORWARD SHE WENT."

> This lad had won his spurs, and the boy was of little worth who failed to own the fact. Favouritism was out of the question, and Dan was popular with all.

Hero worship was common in these texts. The more important function of hero worship for these stories was that it provided a context for manly love.[20]

> To Chris he was more than ever an object of admiration. Born anew in the stress of a great grief and peril, the bond of mutual confidence and love linked these two for life, and was the greatest result of that hazardous escape.

Here was formed a friendship which inherited a long tradition.

Relationships between men were represented as lifelong and characterized by love. There is a lack of unease in the description of intimate and intense emotional relationships between men. But life for men was about to be recontextualized. As was written by W.T. Stead (cited in Richards) at the time of Oscar Wilde's trial,

> A few more trials like Oscar Wilde's and we should find the freedom of comradeship now possible to men seriously impaired to the detriment of the race.[21]

As homosexuality has been constructed, fear of being labelled may have forced many heterosexual men to withdraw from close, emotional friendships.

Crooked Straight was published in 1927.[22] Rader and Blaine are two prospectors. They are partners. The traditional elements of friendship are present, a hostile setting, a common purpose and a common threat, but the relationship is one of suspicion. Rader was recognised by another miner who spoke to Blaine.

> 'He double crossed a partner in Idaho or Montana, ... I'm not advising you to call it off, but just watch him ... '.
> I've always maintained that an old-timer, with the experience behind him, can hold his own with any crooked youngster in this country; but watch.

This is a business arrangement and not a friendship. The discourse surrounding homosexuality had permeated society. The rupture this created in male friendships is apparent. There was no hint of emotion or intimacy between the two men. A tradition of male friendship had been broken.[23]

Typical of stories in the inter-war years is the reference to the authority and wisdom of elders.[24] A generational problem is emerging. The role of the older friend who is mentor and confidante needed to be redefined. Blaine and Rader eventually found gold after months of back-breaking toil. They barely had enough food to return to town to lodge a claim. They argued over the food and eventually agreed to split it 50 – 50. The younger man made his challenge. Rader suggested that rather than split the profits from the mine they race to town. The winner taking all. Blaine agree to the proposition.

> Then we'll put it in writing. That will be safest. Should either of us fail to make it, it will clear things up. This business of a man coming in without a partner causes people to ask questions. I'll draw up a writing, Rader;

The relationship was now contractual. There was no willingness to sacrifice all for the sake of one's partner, nor any sign of affection. They raced to town, Blaine, the older and more experienced winning. The men exchange letters. Blaine concludes his letter ...

> I was young once, and I learned my lessons at great cost. Now I'm old; I have experience; and I'm not too harsh in my judgement. Good Luck.
>   Blaine

> The reply came two days later ...

> Dear Blaine:
>   ... Yes, I was young and contemptuous of age. ... And because I have learned and am better for it, I stick by my bargain ...

> Rader

> Blaine carefully folded the letter. There is greater satisfaction in setting a young man on the right trail than in owning a hundred-thousand dollar mine.

There were still codes of behaviour to abide by. Experience was now a thing to be valued, as was a deference to elders. Rader was honourable and stood by the contract. And even if men no longer lived out the older values of friendship and self-sacrifice, in the end, they were paid lip service.

Crooked Straight takes the western of the period between the world wars to an extreme. The elements are essentially intact. The struggle is no longer between man and nature. The setting is only a backdrop.[25] The struggle is of a man who knows the codes of behaviour against a man or men who don't.[26] By deferring to the judgement of elders and betters, by adhering to codes of behaviour, boys would still be able to cope.[27] The typologies of friendship moved from the affective to the instrumental. In a less mobile world there is greater opportunity for the development of affective friendships between men. The instrumental friendship, based on contracted understanding is the friendship more likely in the commercial world.[28] This instrumental friendship stands in conflict with the ideal of mateship popularised by Henry Lawson. Mateship, though staunchly democratic could be accommodated within the established traditions of friendship. These were the male friendships which lasted until death, forged in times of danger or hardship and tolerant of affection between men.[29] Friendship was coming to be defined by what boys and men *must not* do rather than by what they *must* do. A tension was introduced into the representation of friendship which flowed into the representation of masculinity. Mateship was democratic and included the working class. The contractual friendships of a commercial world would not necessarily do the same.

The next four stories belong to the school setting and have a strong element of athleticism. In *Pilberry's Century*,[30] from *The Australian Boys' Annual*, 1912, the theme is of confronting the bully. Pilberry sends a younger boy to fetch a ball. The boy is caned by the Squire for trespassing. Pilberry did not hesitate to defend the younger boy.

> Like an avenging spirit he made toward them.
> 'Look here, you cruel bully! What do you mean by licking young Dodd like that?'

The comradeship and loyalty of the sports field, extended to action off the field. *Noblesse oblige* compelled him to act in defense of a weaker peer. Pilberry campaigned against the Squire. He was caught on every occasion.

> It was after the third caning that he had had for being in the orchard that he was observed by Douglas to chuckle to himself as he sat in the dormitory.

Attempts to revenge his young friend's caning through direct physical action all failed. He devised a plan to take effect at a cricket match. Before it could be put into effect the trickiness of the bowling had to be overcome. Pilberry had to have determination and endurance. Only when he had the support of the school and teachers and could not be stopped did he begin a demolition of the Squire's orchid house.

> Pilberry ... made the most of it, slashing with all his strength, and he watched the ball dropping over the Squire's hedge with a grin. The grin changed to a brilliant smile as its arrival was signalled by a crash of glass from the orchid-houses

It was not by brute strength that revenge could be exacted, it had to combined with the more important elements of guile and trickery.

This had changed by the time *The Last Lap* was published in 1925.[31] Camel, has a different experience when he confronts the bully, Bulgin. Camel was regarded by the school as an intellectual and represented as such.

> His shyness on some subjects was impenetrable. ... he had dreamed that he was winning a long-distance race, ... and never had his long legs performed in public. He hadn't tried them. He knew it would be no good. He shambled too much, he was too floppy for a runner.

Plate IX: "Get up, if you can, old man! There's another lap yet!"

It was impossible to be both an intellectual and an athlete. Time spent reading made boys introspective and stunted physical development.

Twice through trickery Camel humiliates Bulgin who keeps plotting his revenge. Other boys in the school do not take sides. Then Camel is tricked into a long-distance race against Bulgin who hopes to humiliate him. In the final lap of the race, Bulgin though well ahead, falls.

> 'Camel!' the onlookers roared, when they saw this disaster.
> Bulgin rose and limped on to the grass.
> The Camel staggered on.

Camel is exhausted and in pain, he can hardly walk to the finish line. The physical challenge drew the respect of the other pupils

> 'Twice', said Bulgin, 'you beat me by using your eyes –'
> 'But I didn't use them this time,' the Camel put in.
> 'No; this time, old man, you beat me by using your pluck'.

Camel gained respect by beating the bully in a physical challenge. Trickery and guile no longer worked. Pluck, a combination of courage, endurance and daring, was most valued.

Anti-intellectualism finds clear expression in *Not Out, Uncle!*, published in 1927.[32] If George's academic performance does not improve he will be taken from the school he likes. His uncle thinks he is spending too much time on sport.

> The truth was that George was not specially brainy, and that most of his class were; also he was growing very fast in all directions (he was nearly five feet eight in height, and weighed nearly ten stone)

Intellect and physical ability exclude each other. George has to obey his uncle and remain loyal to his team.

> 'Did I hear you say you were going to work!' repeated Jenkins, sitting down. ...
> 'if you're picked for the school first, you'll just have to play'

George's friend affirms the incompatibility of athleticism and intellect and reminds George of his obligations to his team-mates. For George, obedience to authority comes before loyalty and other values. George fails to win the History prize, as his uncle wanted. He is chosen to play for the school team the day the his uncle returns to speak to the Head. His anger can be expressed on the sporting field. George had submitted to authority. Self-assertion was to be permitted only after obedience to one's superiors. Loyalty to his team, spurred on his efforts. After winning the match for his team, George is praised by the Head.

> Your nephew is not one of the scholarly boys, but he is a *worker*, and that's the type of boy that succeeds – inevitably – where brains sometimes fail.

Plate X: 'George clinched the thing by punching another out of the ground.'

George's victory over his uncle's threat has a physical expression, though he does not challenge authority.

The last school story has been included because of its violent ending. In *The Mystery of Monk Island* published in 1948,[33] a group of school-boys discover a spy, track him to his hideout and capture him.

> 'Come on! Come on, everybody!' yelled Jerry, and the next instant Neal and Mr Tonkins were piling on to the killer. Even then it was a tough fight, and it was all the three of them could do to secure him ...
> But they succeeded at length and he lay swearing horribly, his eyes glaring fiercely in the torchlight.

In these stories there is a movement, across time, toward the solution of problems by resort to physical action and finally violence.[34] In the first, there was an element of trickery, which sanctioned the destruction of the green house. In the second story, trickery failed, and respect could only be gained through a physical deed. In the third, George could win with a display of aggression as long as authority was deferred to,[35] and by expressing this aggression acceptably on the cricket ground. The fourth solution is unashamed violence with no reconciliation between the adversaries.

The authors of these stories had created a problem for themselves. Intellectualism was represented as being undesirable and introspection as 'suspect'. Yet to reach their audience the boys had to read. To affirm the manliness of the reader, which the act of reading denied, the manliness of the text was strengthened. Violence became stronger and more direct.

The character building aspects of sports are evident. They remain fixed over time. Friendship does not enter into these stories so much as loyalty, pluck and team spirit. Obedience, too, was important. Pilberry and George could only successfully assert themselves after they had accepted authority, and shown they were prepared to put the team first.[36]

Athleticism was certainly preferable to intellectualism. At the turn of the century exercise was valued, reading and introspection were seen as unhealthy. As Kociumbas (1986) says,

> In older boys, tallness came to be seen as a sign of sexual purity, while short sightedness, a hunched back and hands deep in pockets were the mark of the bookworm and masturbator.[37]

The construction of homosexuality would have been good reason for boys to flee their study and seek acceptance on the sporting field. George was tall and growing. Camel was redeemed by the height implied by his long legs. They were a sign that he was not sexually impure.

Athleticism was used to assert superiority. It was not individual superiority, individualism was permitted among peers but loyalty between them came first. The obligations of loyalty, of *noblesse oblige*, were to one's class.[38] Asserting superiority through sport extended to a national level. Britain used its superiority at games to assert itself over its colonies. Eventually Australians were to use sport to assert their independence.[39] The importance of sport to the Australian reader, and his subsequent investment in it, encompassed class, gender, his particular type of manliness, his sexuality and a patriotism which did not encompass disloyalty to Britain.

There are other settings for boys' story in these annuals which have not been examined here. There is a great deal of repetition between all the categories of story, the core values associated with manliness being repeated over and over again. Reflections of each can be seen in the stories just visited, the chivalric code, identified by Richards, of 'bravery, loyalty, courtesy, modesty, purity and honour ... and a sense of noblesse oblige [sic]',[40] the comradeship of the war story and the 'pluck' and 'willingness to give it a go', of the adventure stories. In concert these values gave the British boy, even in Australia, an unshakeable moral superiority.[41]

The masculinities which the Empire offered were grounded in Social Darwinism. The notion that the Aboriginal population was bound to fade in competition with the white races was essential. The colonizing process in Australia had been very masculine, even though women were involved. These masculinities excused the bloody manner of colonization. But social Darwinism brought dangers. It was believed geologically older land was less capable of maintaining a more highly developed race.[42] The perception of the Australian landscape was reshaped. Where once explorers had spoken of Australia Felix the emphasis now fell on the harsh and confronting nature of the place. The danger was that the English living in Australia might degenerate. Impetus was added to the pursuit of athleticism. The vigour of the race could be maintained through physical exercise, arresting any degeneration. The intellectual, with 'stooped shoulders and arrested physical development', had the potential to pollute the race. He had to be excluded. By definition, the physically imperfect and the disabled, not to mention any boy who was not white, found this masculinity unattainable.[43]

It is clear that these middle class masculinities do not fit neatly into an Australian context. The specificity of Australian masculinities in the period 1900-1950 has not been established. Further investigation is required of athleticism, friendships, anti-intellectualism and group. There are many masculinities, all varying in relation to other masculinities, each dependent upon its context. Boys are not aware of where masculinity comes from in their own context of time, place and group. These annuals were a prescription for masculinity. They provided a space for the inward negotiation of masculinity. Their appeal is obvious.

Representations moved from the positive expression of male strength as *noblesse oblige* to defend the weak, to a more violent resolution of conflict. The male friendships represented became restricted in the range of emotions allowed. A strengthening interest in athleticism may have led to anti-intellectualism becoming more closely linked with Australian middle-class masculinities. Athleticism, with its push to maintain racial vigour and achieve a physical perfection, may have led to a greater intolerance of physical and intellectual disability. The origins of all these changes lie with social Darwinism.

For men, just as for women, the meaning of being differs over time and place, and is shaped by political and social forces. As this study has shown, even those men at the centre, the male middle classes which have traditionally recorded history and been responsible for the representation of those at the margins, are subject to these same forces.

NOTES

1. C. Hall, *White, Male and Middle Class* (Cambridge: Polity Press, 1992); J.A. Mangan and J. Walvin, eds., *Manliness and Morality: Middle Class Masculinity in Britain and America 1800-1940* (Manchester: Manchester University Press, 1987); M. Roper and J. Tosh, 'Historians and the politics of masculinity'. In M. Roper and J. Tosh eds., *Manful Assertions: Masculinities in Britain since 1800* (London: Routledge, 1991), pp. 1-24; D. Jackson, *Unmasking Masculinity* (London: Unwin Hyman,1990).
2. J. Richards, 'Passing the Love of Women: Manly Love and Victorian Society', in Mangan, & Walvin, p.107.
3. K. Boyd, 'Knowing Your Place: The Tensions of Manliness in Boys' Story Papers, 1918-39', in Roper, & Tosh, p. 149. One reader of these story papers, West, "was very aware of the differences in the papers he could buy, and astutely detected a marked difference in the class of the readers papers were meant for".
4. M. E. Hoare, *Boys, Urchins, Men* (Sydney: A.W. Reed, 1980), p. 30.
5. *Report of the Boys' Brigade 1914. Report of the Boys' Brigade 1917* (Sydney: Sydney Day).
6. J. Springall, [1987] 'Building Character in the British Boy: the Attempt to Extend Christian Manliness to Working Class Adolescents, 1880-1914', in Mangan, & Walvin, p .64.
7. Lyons, M. 'Texts, books and readers: which kind of cultural history?' *Australian Cultural History,* 11 (1992) p. 5.
8. J. Kociumbas, 'What Alyce Learnt at Nine: Sexuality and Sex Roles in Childrens' Literature to 1914', *History of Education Review,* 2 (1986) p. 30.
9. ibid., p. 19.
10. Springall, op. cit., p. 66.
11. J. Walvin, 'Symbols of Moral Superiority: Slavery, Sport and the Changing World Order, 1800-1950', in Mangan & Walvin.
12. *Young Australia.* (London: Pilgrim Press, 1902-3), p. 206.

13. Walvin, op. cit., p. 252
14. *Fortieth Report of the New South Wales Religious Tract Society for the Year Ending Sept. 30 1862.* (Sydney: The Religious Tract Society), p.7 M.L. 206/4 'The New South Wales Tract and Book Society is connected with the English and American Tract Societies, and many publications of the latter Society, are particularly suited for usefulness in the colony'.
15. K. Boyd, op. cit., p. 146.
16. Richards, op. cit., p. 103.
17. Ibid., pp 104-105.
18. 'Dan of Roper's Gully', *Young Australia* (London: Pilgrim Press, 1902-3), pp. 29-31.
19. J.M. MacKenzie, 'The Imperial Pioneer and Hunter and the British Masculine Stereotype in Late Victorian and Edwardian Times', in Mangan & Walvin, pp 177-78.
20. Richards, op. cit., p. 105.
21. cited in Richards, op. cit, p. 92.
22. 'Crooked Straight', *The Australian Boys' Annual.* (London: Amalgamated Press, 1927), p. 83.
23. Hammond, op. cit., p. 245.
24. Boyd, op. cit., p. 163.
25. MacKenzie, op. cit., p. 193.
26. Ibid., p. 194.
27. Boyd, op. cit., p. 146.
28. Hammond, op. cit., p. 244.
29. Ibid., pp 245-253.
30. 'Pilberry's Century'. *The Australian Boys' Annual.* (London: Cassel & Co., 1912), p. 173.
31. 'The Last Lap'. *The Australian Boys' Annual.* (London: Cassel & Co, 1925), p.52.
32. 'Not Out, Uncle!' *The Australian Boys' Annual.* (London: Cassel & Co, 1927), p. 175.
33. 'The Mystery of Monk Island'. *The Boy* (Melbourne: O.I.C., 1948), p. 129 Though this story is not taken from one of the two annuals it conforms to their type. Most tellingly, the school represented is a private boarding school.
34. Boyd, op. cit., p. 146.
35. Ibid., p. 163.
36. Walvin, op. cit., p. 249.
37. Kociumbas, op. cit., p. 27.
38. Richards, op. cit., p. 113.
39. Walvin, op. cit., pp. 242-245.
40. Richards, op. cit., p. 113.
41. Walvin, op. cit., pp. 242-245.
42. H. Mortimer, 'Will the Anglo-Australian Race Degenerate?' *Victorian Review,* 1 November 1879.
43. One interviewee from this time period in Penrith said, 'There were seven in the family, two girls and five boys. But he was crippled so I was the oldest boy'. The elder, crippled male was not classified as a male. Qtd. with permission from a forthcoming book by Peter West.

PETER WEST

Sons of the Empire: How Boys Became Men in one Australian Town, 1900-1920

As well as being the main actors of war, men have also been the main victims
R.W. Connell[1]

This article based on a project on becoming a man, in one town, Penrith (about which more later), started as an oral history of Penrith. Earlier, I had studied another major centre in Western Sydney, the settlement of Parramatta[2]. When I learnt that there was another major project based on a women's history of Penrith, I decided to take the unexplored territory of men's history. In short, I wanted to ask what it means to be a man – and how that has changed this century. As I examined newspapers and other sources, I became caught up in the men's movement and began re-examining my own life as a man, just as feminist friends were doing with their lives as women. I began to look at history in a new light. I recall the day I read, in the Australian National University's Library catalogue; 'for men, see sex'. That comment said a lot about how we expect men to behave.

Oral history is always a history based on people who volunteer to talk. In the period 1900 to 1920, there were no volunteers. A search of nursing homes produced very few men at all – for men die earlier than women, on average. No man was found who grew up before the twenties. So the project had to rely on written sources, primarily the *Nepean Times*. This newspaper was a vital way in which a small town found out about crop prices, and all kinds of events: local, national and international. It also enabled people to keep a check on other people's misdeeds.

It was unfortunate that nobody survived from the early period to interview; but a historian, however brilliant, cannot interview the dead. As data emerged, it was sorted by themes: Fathers, Being a Boy, Being Different, Men and Their Relationships to Women. I believe I am taking part in a personal exploration of masculinity. An acknowledged part of the process is my own being as a father, and as a man engaged in current debates about gender issues.[3] Every man – and woman – makes history in his or her own image.[4]

The Town

The research site was a town called Penrith, apparently after a town in England situated in a similar terrain on the river near the mountains in Cumberland.[5] Its appearance was clearly described by Miles Franklin, a well-known Australian female author:

> a few lackadaisical larrikins upheld occasional corner posts; dogs conducted municipal meetings here and there; the ugliness of the horses tied to the street posts, where they baked in the sun while their riders guzzled in the prolific 'pubs', bespoke a farming rather than a grazing district; and the streets had the distinction of being the most deplorably dirty and untended I have seen.[6]

Penrith was a railway town. It had been a set of farms scattered near the river, settled by families from the British Isles. The railway allowed residents to travel 50 kilometres east to the metropolis of Sydney. And it brought cattle from the vast western plains to cattleyards near Penrith. Boys grew up wanting to work on the railways, preferably driving a locomotive.[7] Most boys left school after a primary education to work, generally on the railway or on the many farms which surrounded the town of about 2,500. In time, the town became a city. After the second world war it expanded with immigration and natural population growth, along with Australia's population as a whole. It is now one of two main centres in Western Sydney. This region contains one-twelfth of the population of Australia. Penrith is the home of the Mighty Panthers, who won the Rugby League Grand Final in 1991. It also contains the University of Western Sydney, created in 1989 to spread over a number of sites scattered across the region. Many residents seem to think the first achievement more important than the second.

Boys and Empire

Penrith boys grew up as proud sons of the mighty British Empire. The Commonwealth of Australia had begun in 1901, but it was at first a weak form of government. State Governments remained strong, with the most powerful being New South Wales and Victoria. In many ways, the most important connections were with England. Documents and newspapers of the period are full of affectionate references to England, sometimes called the Old Country, or simply 'Home'.[8]

Much of the school day was spent reminding Penrith boys how lucky they were to grow up as sons of one of the greatest Empires the world had ever seen. In their classrooms, children looked at a map of the British Empire spread across the world. They were proudly told that it was an Empire on which the sun never set.

Then there was Empire Day. This was a day set aside from 1905 onwards for children to gather together to show their loyalty and appreciation for the Mother Country. Children sang 'The Englishmen', 'Auld Lang Syne', 'Dear Little Shamrock', and 'Rule Britannia', all of which reinforced the boys' determination to be ready to serve their Empire and their King. Religion also encouraged this devotion to the Empire. For instance, at the Empire Day service in 1909 the Rev. O. Jones reminded the children that 'if they believed in God they would sustain the Empire'.

Even an advertisement for the Dreadnought Fund played on this need to be loyal subjects

> to show our appreciation for the privileges and freedom we enjoy in this sunny land of Australia ... freedom given to us because of England's supremacy on the seas [9]

This constant emphasis on boys putting their masculinity in the service of the Empire would have brought before all boys the glorious life of the soldier or sailor willing to fight for England whenever the need arose.

War: August 1914

Thus when war broke out in August, 1914, the foundations for boys' enrollment as soldiers were already laid. Local newspapers carried news of a Recruiting Campaign by running an advertisement which proclaimed '50,000 Troops Wanted – BE ONE OF THEM'. The speeches and newspaper editorials played on the themes of the bonds of Empire and the scarlet thread of kinship. Young men were urged to be a man by fighting for hearth and home. A popular song ran

> Rally round the banner of your country
> Take the field with brothers o'er the foam.
> On land or sea, where ever you be
> Keep your eye on Liberty.
> But England, home and Beauty
> Have no cause to fear.
> Should Auld acquaintance be forgot?
> No! No! No! No! No!
> Australia will be there–
> Australia will be there.[10]

Young men who volunteered were highly praised. Masculinity was defined in terms of being the man the Empire needed, as we can see from this example:

> Private Reg McLean, who is in his twentieth year, is a typically athletic, valiant young Australian of the true Gallipoli standard ... who can be relied upon to do his part valiantly against the foe ... in vindication of the principles of Human Liberty which are those of the Empire.[11]

Men like this were good Australian boys, loyal to their wives and children, who came to aid brother Britons. Others were condemned as shirkers or poor types of men. Be a man in the desired way, or you're not a man at all, the propaganda seemed to say. There were many 'soldiers' send-offs' described in great detail in attempts to coax more men to join up.

Meanwhile, younger boys were not forgotten. The Boy Scouts movement helped to teach boys discipline through a military-style operation, particularly when participating in attack and defence games while camping. There was a constant reminder that England was the head of the glorious Empire, and boys must always be ready to defend her cause. Brothers, fathers, and uncles away at the war would have only served to heighten this awareness.

Several times the *Nepean Times* recorded the 'Unveiling of Memorial Tablets and Honor Rolls' by relatives of fallen soldiers. On 23 June 1917 the *Times* details the unveiling of a memorial tablet dedicated to the memory of the late Signaller A. Starling. The Rev. J.Tarn said of Signaller Starling

> he fought his way through life, and though his career had been cut short in his youth, he has, nevertheless, won through with honor, distinction and glory. In his youth, both at home and at school he was a pattern of neatness, gentleness and honor. As a comrade he was ever courteous, chivalrous and loyal to his mates ... his actions were brave, firm and decisive ... a real patriot – all the elements of goodness, greatness and heroism were well mixed in him.[12]

This description of courteous and chivalrous masculinity almost sounds medieval in comparison with the impoverished 'action heroes' portrayed by Schwarzenegger and van Damme on television and movie screens today. By praising such a fallen hero, authorities hoped other men would crowd in to take his place. But as more and more were injured, died, or occasionally came home with venereal disease, there were fewer and fewer Australians willing to volunteer. The authorities then decided to use force. The national government under Prime Minister Billy Hughes put two conscription referenda to the people, but they were defeated. Penrith voted against both. In a town like Penrith, men were needed on farms. A family which had sent one or two boys to the war could not afford to lose another. And so people began to question whether the town ought to sacrifice all its finest young men on the altar of the British Empire.

Problem Boys

Penrith's civic leaders expected that males of any age should play a role in running the family farm and upholding community standards. But some boys failed to live up to these stern expectations of masculinity.

The local paper printed several articles in 1909 and 1910 about the problems of youth. It was indignant when boys got drunk, played tricks on shopkeepers or festooned a bridge with toilet paper. Sir George Reid's 'manful protest against the undue devotion of Young Australia to sport' was noted on 22 January 1910. Sir George wanted boys to play sport, rather than standing on the sidelines and barracking, or yelling encouragement and boyish abuse:

> Muscular strength and physical address are invaluable endowments if worthily employed and directed. But everything depends on the 'if'. Moreover, it is difficult to see how even muscular strength or physical address are promoted by 'barracking' at a football or cricket or boxing match; and for one who plays or wrestles or boxes, there are hundreds who are simply limp and placid, though perhaps noisy, spectators. Devotion to mere pastime, when worthier work is called for, is bad enough. But merely to gaze at the pastime of others is a still lower depth of degeneracy. [13]

Sir George did not like boys who were limp and placid. Perhaps like many similar comments this would be interpreted by some modern readers as urging boys on to manic displays of heterosexuality. Unfortunately Sir George did not take his own advice, as so often happens with these types who exhort young people to do this and that. Indeed, one historian records Sir George as memorable for his fatness. On one occasion he lifted his vast stomach onto a balcony rail for support, probably on the upper storey of a country pub, often used for political meetings. A member of the crowd yelled 'What are you going to call it, George?'. He replied:

> If it's a boy, I'll call it after myself. If it's a girl, I'll call it Victoria, after our queen. But if, as I strongly suspect, it's only piss and wind, I'll call it after you. [14]

People spent a lot of time trying to make boys conform to their ideal of good sons of the Empire. In June, 1902 an article appeared in the *Times*, complaining of what boys did. Unfortunately, 'a harmful custom of sitting at street-corners, spitting and talking without object, except to kill time', was becoming apparent, resulting in 'mere lads, fresh from school' becoming 'careless in habit and speech, forsaking study ... classed as larrikins, ultimately becoming drunken and dissolute'. It would have been more profitable if these lads had spent this time in a more 'suitable place with dumbells or Indian clubs'. Like Sir George Reid, the author wanted strong boys who could be useful to the Empire in time of attack.

The local paper carried regular reports of young men being charged with drunk and/or disorderly conduct. In June, 1917, two youths, 17 years and 18 years respectively, 'were charged with having used indecent language within the hearing of persons passing by in Queen

Street', while a 21 year old was charged with being drunk.[15] In 1917 four young fellows were charged with having conducted themselves in a riotous manner in High Street, Penrith on the evening of 8 March 1917. The defendants 'were in town for the show and indulged in a bit of skylarking in High Street ... growing a bit too boisterous.[16] However, the semi-indulgent tone suggests that boys would always be boys. It might have been more upset if the boys had been effeminate.

Males and Females

Women in this era were seen mainly as spouses, wives and mothers. Girls and boys lived very different lives. A later generation still said 'Girls worked inside, boys worked outside'. An athletic sports gathering was held in Perry's Paddock at St. Mary's on Saturday afternoon, 3rd March, in aid of the Catholic church: '500 or more persons were present, and a real "bonsar" day's sport and competition resulted'. Men's sports on Boxing Day, 1905 were cricket, cycling, buck jumping, high jump and throwing at the wicket. Women and children were given less energetic sports to play: they guessed the weight of the pig, stepped 100 yards or took part in floral exhibitions.[17] Many races for boys and girls were held as well as 'Catching Rooster' and 'Throwing Sheaf of Hay' presumably for the men. Most sports days were affiliated with a local hotel where the sportsmen drank. The two sexes sometimes came together for a dance in the evening[18]

Miles Franklin's novel suggests that women still wanted men to be muscular. This female author wrote under a man's name. She suggests that muscular men make the best husbands in a comment on 'muscle' which seems to talk about a man's biceps and triceps, but might apply also to his penis:

> the wholesome athlete is generally more loveable [than an intellectual]. When his brawn is coupled with a good disposition, he sees in woman a fragile flower that he longs to protect.
>
> His muscle is an engine a woman can unfailingly command for her own purposes, whereas brilliance of intellect ... is too liable to be too sharply turned against wives, mothers and daughters to be a comfortable piece of domestic furniture. On the other hand, the athlete may have the muscles of a Samson, and yet, being slow of thought and speech, be utterly defenceless in a woman's hands. He cannot bring brute force to vanquish a creature so delicate.[19]

Today there would be a different view taken of brutal, muscular husbands, with references to domestic violence. Franklin was a feminist and wanted votes for women, but seems to admire men for their muscularity, and gives some erotic descriptions of the hero, Ernest, with his strong, beefy arms and powerful back. And in contrast, she portrays girls as soft, passive, almost weak. But there were some who asked if being a pretty wife was all a girl could be. In 1908 the *Times*

THE LIGHT THAT FAILED.   VOTE NO.

Plate XI: Claude Marquet (Worker c.1916)

published an article as to 'Why Don't the Men Propose?' The writer believed it was one of the signs of the times in that there was –

> an apparent superiority of the female sex. The girls are beating the boys in industry, in application, in good behaviour, and in general reliability. There are exceptions, of course, but they only prove the rule. Why should a self-respecting girl, who is able to earn her own living, take up with a young fellow who stinks of tobacco, whose language is bad, who seems to have no thought beyond his own diversions which range from picking the winners through every fashionable fad.

The article suggested that there was an artificial standard of living which was as much the fault of the girls as the boys. 'If the girls can't have a home of a certain style they prefer to remain single'.[20]

However, most sources suggest that people wanted women to complement strong men's muscularity, and support their role in the war. In the war years, women were enrolled in 'Win-the War-Leagues' and the Red Cross. There were women in the 'Would-to-Godders'. 'Would to God I were a man' and 'Would to God I were Strong Enough to Fight' were the slogans of this group.[21] Some women sent white feathers to men who would not enlist. There was the strong suggestion that girls would only consort with a man who would do his duty for King and Empire.

In sum, males of this time grew up in a society in which boys lived in one sphere, girls in another. Males were expected to be tough and physically strong; a male who did not test his strength was condemned by the usual array of do-gooders. In the war years these people were reinforced by urgers and 'Would-to-Godders'. Being a man meant you had to protect your loved ones and the Empire by going off – perhaps to get killed. Women watched their loved ones go, and sometimes gave them a white feather if they refused. They had the horrors of childbirth in a local hospital to contend with. Looking back, it seems amazing that so few men did refuse to die for loved ones and Empire. But Penrith was a place tightly bound by kinship and religion as well as affection for the Empire.

Conclusions

This essay has given us some glimpses of how boys became men in the period around the First World War in Penrith. It appears that males grew up with a strong sense of responsibility. They had to turn over soil, tend crops, and feed animals. Some had the privilege of working on the railway, which seems to have been an envied occupation, particularly for the locomotive engine-drivers. Boys were expected to care for mothers, other family members, and farm animals. When war came, there was little questioning of the idea that they would protect loved ones in the Empire's hour of need. We could call this a dominant or sanctioned masculinity. Men were liked if they were strong and muscular and took charge in a difficult situation. These were the men who would come to aid Mother England in her hour of need. As Bob Connell suggests in the quotation at the head of this article, some men might commit war atrocities, but many men also died on the battlefield. Men were both the majority of the killers and the killed. And men had little room to move – they had to go to war or face all the horrors that society could throw at them for daring to resist. It seems very few did.

There is another thread running through the sources studied, especially the newspaper. Boys played tricks, got drunk, acted as larrikins and scallywags. There seems to have been more tolerance of boys' misbehaviour than of girls. The phrase 'boys will be boys' captures something of the feeling expressed. The people of the town seem to have clucked their tongues, but were resigned to the idea that boys did get up to tricks. They received a good deal of education based on the premise that they were lucky to be sons of the mighty British Empire. In time these boys, too, would grow up to become her soldiers and sailors.

The biggest question has not been answered. What of the males who did not subscribe to dominant forms of masculinity? What did a male do if he found himself attracted to other men, or if he did not want to spend his weekend playing sport? There are no answers in the newspaper, nor in documents examined. We have to assume that there were men who for various reasons did not subscribe to dominant forms of masculinity. We might imagine that they could have become priests or clergymen. Perhaps they lived out their lives as bachelors attached to one of the family groups in the town. Some must have left for Sydney, where sources in a later era point to undercover sex among males. But history has never been good at describing the lives of people who live unobtrusively. Perhaps the answers might appear when masculinity becomes a more respectable field of study.

NOTES

The data for this project was collected with assistance from Andrew Martin, Sandra Rutter, and Kirsten West. Advice and encouragement were provided by Gar Jones and Jim Power.

1. [1] R.W. Connell, 'Masculinity, Violence and War', in *Men's Lives*, eds., Michael Kimmel and Michael Messner (New York and Toronto: Macmillan, 1992), p.182. This book is an excellent compilation of research and ideas on masculinities and is recommended to the serious researcher. The connell article is a thoughtful and compassionate piece worthy of attention by itself.
2. Peter West, *A History of Parramatta* (Sydney: Kangaroo Press, 1990).
3. An earlier report on the project is Peter West, 'Do Men Make the Rules or Do the Rules Make Men? Growing up Male in an Australian Country Town', *Masculinities* (USA), 2, 2 (1994), pp. 46-59.
4. Some of the expanding literature on masculinity can be seen from the following: Lynne Segal, *Slow Motion: Changing Masculinities, Changing Men* (London: Virago, 1990); Caroline Ramazanoglu, 'What Can You Do with a Man? Feminism and the Critical Appraisal of Masculinity', *Women's Studies International Forum*, 15, 3 (1992), pp. 339-50; Michael Messner, *Power at Play: Sports and the Problem of Masculinity* (Boston: Beacon Press, 1992).
5. Bronwyn Power, *A History of Penrith* (Sydney: Western Sydney Project, 1983).
6. Miles Franklin, *Some Everyday Folk and Dawn* (Sydney: Virago, 1986), p. 2
7. Unpublished interview with Ruth Paget. All names have been changed to preserve anonymity.
8. In 1905 the Sydney *Daily Telegraph* enthused about 'the great Empire which binds together in an Imperial brotherhood about one-fourth of the human race ... To the meanest man among the hundreds of millions who live under its world-embracing folds the British flag guarantees that full measure of rational freedom'. It went on to talk about the need for Australians to maintain the British connection as they were living next to a volcano. The rise of Japan and its success against Russia in the war of 1905 caused much anxiety in Australia. The Colonial Laws Validity Act of 1866 declared that British colonies could not enact a law repugnant to relevant laws enacted in England. Both documents are included in Peter West and Alan Dwight, eds., *Australia: From Empire to Asia* (Sydney: Science Press, 1980), p. 20 and p. 22 respectively.

9. *Nepean Times,* 10 July 1909.
10. West and Dwight, p.20.
11. *Nepean Times*, 8 January 1916.
12. *Nepean Times*, 23 June 1917.
13. Sir George Reid, cited *Nepean Times,* 22 January 1910.
14. Sir George Reid, cited in Humphrey McQueen, *Social Sketches of Australia 1888-1975* (Sydney: Penguin, 1991), p. 43.
15. *Nepean Times*, 15 June 1917.
16. *Nepean Times*, 31 January 1917.
17. E. Thompson, Growing Up in Penrith. Unpublished paper.
18. *Nepean Times*, 17 January 1917.
19. Franklin, *Some Everyday Folk,* p. 94.
20. *Nepean Times*, 11 January 1908.
21. Peter West and J.C. Bright, eds., *Australia: From Empire to Asia* (Sydney: Science Press, 1968) p. 33.

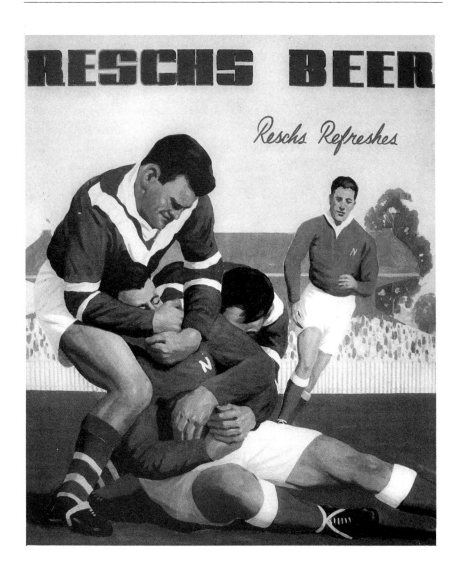

Plate XII: Blokes on the Bar Room Wall

BRIAN MATTHEWS

Casually Over the Balcony: Memoirs of a Bloke

It comes on to September of 1989 and Arthur's cows are out on the road again.

I've been looking after a dozen of them on my property (fifty acres of heavily mortgaged stringy bark scrub surrounding about ten acres of undulating pasture), but with the mellower airs of spring, the lushness underfoot, and the roaring of randy bulls each night in the perfumed darkness, two of these beasts have turned maverick and won't stay behind the wire.

It's very tiresome trying to make cattle go where you want them to. They are at least as dopey as sheep and, while capable of thundering sprints which reduce everything in their path to mulch and fractures, they resort at other times to a dogged four-square immobility, a heavy-lidded ruminating recalcitrance which neither well-aimed clods of dirt, alliterative obscenities nor the flailing of battered Akubras will easily overcome.

Once before I was reduced to pursuing them at Grand Prix pace down the track in my rattling old ute, heading off their lumbering charge and then high-speeding them back to my gate which they Light-Brigaded past with eyes red and mouths frothing and so I chased them down the other way.

This time it's all fairly routine. The two of them are sleepily swathed in languid camouflages of roadside banksia, half-grown wattle and native ti-tree. Their sleek, generous flanks are tight with the morning's illicit grazing. It is merely a passing and tolerable irritation for them when I insist that they lollygaggle home; so moodily back we all go, through the white-painted post and rail gateway where, having shooed them back down the paddock, I close off the entrance with a temporary gate. This is mostly for show because, while I have stopped their access to the road, only more robust and extensive fencing will keep them from random sallies into the 'home' paddock where they prune the roses, lean on and snap the young fruit trees, juice the burgeoning vegetables under dogmatic hooves, and shit everywhere with that lava spreading *plop* for which they are famous in joke and story.

As a city boy from the backstreets of Melbourne's West St Kilda, I brought no knowledge, experience or expertise whatsoever when I walked on to this wild tract of fragrant, flower-strewn wilderness twenty odd years ago ('One for the Conservationist' the advertisement had promised, with as much of a forlorn, defeated sigh as real estate prose can muster). It was beautiful, peaceful and cheap. It was a mad thing to do, buying this property, and ensuing experiences with house-building, neighbours' sheep and cattle, our sheep and cattle, sagging fences, disputed boundaries, blackberries, African Daisy, marauding foxes, garden-razing goats, cataclysmic storms, the worst drought on record followed by the worst fires in living memory all underlined the original lunacy. While keeping my day job, I worked on that farm till I had muscles of iron and skin like bark; my decrepit yellow ute could be seen waiting for me in the pub carpark on luminous Saturday evenings in summer while I, still grimy from the day's fencing or digging or woodcutting, yarned with the other rurals in the bar. When a shearer I'd hired looked me up and down and said, 'Well Brian, whadya do for a livin', mate? I've got you down as a long distance truck-driver', I felt I'd crossed some critical divide, and I was glad.

ll

Talk about down among the women. I grew up among droves of them, my mother and grandmother in the bustling foreground of a large, volatile group which in later life I would characterise as 'my innumerable aunts'. They weren't really aunts, not all of them anyway. There was my Aunty Jean – slim, dark and flighty – who was a real aunt, being my mother's younger sister. But then there was Aunt Bet and Aunty Tilly and Aunt Vina and Aunty Annie and Aunty Pat and Aunt Kitty and Aunty Letty and many others. All of these women were under the iron rule of two formidable matriarchs – Annie Murray, my maternal grandmother, and Agatha Cavanagh, her long-time best friend. They'd all grown up in Glasgow's infamous Gorbals where Annie, an Irish migrant who'd gone over to Scotland to marry, and Agatha were left to fend off the dangerous world after losing their young husbands in the trenches. With stunning resilience, they gathered up their few possessions and the nine fatherless children they had between them and went steerage on the SS *Balranald* to Australia.

Landing in Melbourne, they homed in on the cheapest rents and set up a little enclave in west St Kilda, a gangster ridden, smokey and furtive purlieu that seems in memory to have been always foggy and half-lit just as, on its boundary, the Esplanade and St Kilda beach seem always smiling with sun and blue sky and Port Phillip Bay's dazzle of flat water.

I was a small boy when all the males in this burgeoning Caledonian corner were suddenly drawn back into that same troubled Europe that

Annie and Agatha had fled. Along with them soon after went my
Australian father – to New Guinea. And there I was, among the
women, a Feather Boa of aunts. They cleaned offices, pulled beer,
worked in the Collingwood boot factory, sewed, mended, served
behind counters, polished and scrubbed. They would gather for a drink
and a smoke together in Annie's Havelock Street house, or at Agatha's
in nearby Clive Street; they laughed a lot and alternated between
spoiling me and treating me, unwittingly, like a flunkey. I remember
once, when I was about six or seven, confiding to a friend who lived
next door that I'd been 'born to run messages'. The shops were close
by – Rollason's for milk, bread, smokes (and a bet on the SP) and
Armstrong's ('the wee grocer's', as my Grandmother called him in
delicate reference to his hunchbacked stature) for just about everything
else. Up the other way, to Ackland Street and the beach were the
butchers and the Village Belle market – far more interesting but
forbidden territory for me until much later.

I was taught by nuns when I started school, had no brothers and,
effectively, no father. I saw few men and many of those I did see – the
drunks around the Prince Charles on the corner of Fawkner Street –
scared me witless with their shouting, swearing and random violence. I
followed the sad misfortunes of the St Kilda Football Club in the
Victorian Football League, but only from afar, having no one to take me
even to their home games at the Junction Oval. Mr Armstrong, the
'wee grocer', whom I got to know well because I ran so many errands,
was always threatening to take me to see Brighton in the Association,
but somehow we never made the trip.

I felt different, hard done by and – because I was a loudly reluctant
messenger boy frequently chastised for carelessness – I accepted I was
irredeemably 'bad'. I was embarrassed by the swarms of women who
seemed to be always buzzing round me. Other kids had their fathers
more or less at home. Dennis O'Reilly's father was in a 'reserved
occupation'; Keith Carter's was a drunk, Ray Waller's was in and out of
gaol and the Finnegan boys' father was a journalist. There was not
much cachet in having a father and uncles at the war because you
didn't know where they were or what they were doing; mail was
infrequent and the thud of a battered, much-travelled letter into the tin
letterbox on the gate was an occasion not for joy but tense anxiety
followed by tearful relief.

These misanthropies were exacerbated by my growing conviction
that, because I had temporarily no father, or anyone who could
possibly stand in for him (even if we *had* gone to see Brighton in the
Association, Mr Armstrong would never have done, he was too small
and too strange looking), I was somehow not as tough as the other
kids. When we played footy in the street with a 'ball' made of old socks
or tightly rolled newspaper held together by elastic bands, I seemed to

be more easily hurt than the others. I would crash to the ground or reel into the cobbled gutter or become espaliered on the Millers' front fence as the momentum of various ill-judged lunges, dashes and leaps carried me on to disaster. In summer, when our activities switched from kicking up and down the road to bowling as fast as we could across it, I would get hit in the testicles or on the nose – the latter producing merely lots of blood, the former an agony undreamt of in our philosophies. Worse, I would often cry after such encounters.

I see now that some of my more bizarre juvenile exploits were efforts to assert in some other, more manageable way, the emotionless grittiness the street required. One day when the great Joe Louis was in the news, I boasted to Ray Waller, as we dawdled outside Mrs Murphy's Penny Library in Grey Street, that I was tough enough to take any blow anyone could dish out. 'Go on,' I said, 'hit me on the jaw. It won't hurt *me*. Go on!' Waller, who was as tough as a jumps jockey's bum, obliged with a smashing thump that knocked me over and relieved my lopsided jaw of a couple of baby teeth. Another time, discovering that to jump off the high balcony at school was something even Waller jibbed at, I sauntered casually up to the rail and leapt over it. When I hit the ground with both feet, my legs doubled like lorry springs and rebounded me into a spiral of continuous somersaults that seemed to go on forever. I should have broken both ankles at least; but in fact I came eventually to sprawling rest and had the presence of mind to dust myself off with a great show of nonchalance, sensing as I did so the shrill note of sensation rising through the schoolyard babble. In the shelter shed at the other end of that pokey school playground behind Sacred Heart School, St Kilda, I fought Dennis O'Gorman, a rangey ten year old who, however, I intuitively knew was all talk and bluster. This fixture was precipitated by a clash in the yard at playtime and arranged during the day's lessons by means of clandestine notes, significant glances and sibilant whispers. As always, I went into the contest with such exaggerated determination and displays of force and will that I was beating the shit out of O'Gorman before his superior reach could avail him anything. Being basically a crybaby (it took one to know one), O'Gorman, bloodied and grazed, was capitulating early in the contest (though he landed two blows which respectively split my lip and blacked my eye) when his seconds, with a mastery of bureaucratic authoritarianism which I resent every time I think of it, had the fight stopped and a draw declared before my more plebeian backers realised what was happening. This all sounds very sturdy but I was crying at the end and shaking before it started. Ray Waller, conversely, shaped up to such encounters, which were much more numerous in his way of life, with a genuine insouciance which I envied, aspired to but would never attain.

'*Why do you always cry, Brian Matthews?*' This question was addressed to me by a girl in my class at Sacred Heart who even then I could see was hard and tartish. I can't remember her name and I have no idea what became of her, but it was a good question. She asked it just after I'd been hit square in the right eye by a rock-hard, ink-soaked paper pellet fired from a shanghai across the classroom, so maybe even she wouldn't have been so stoic if hers had been the eye in question. The pellet wasn't actually intended for me, but I'd turned round in my front desk to survey the pandemonium induced by the temporary absence of nuns and was characteristically just in time to cop the winging missile at the height of its velocity. It hurt like hell and I felt surely blinded. Possibly a glass eye looming. Nothing I could do – leaping publicly from no matter what heights, pounding no matter which better-equipped opponents, jumping from no matter what speeding trams – could apparently obscure the truth unerringly apparent to the tactless and precocious eye of youth: I was a crybaby; there was something suspiciously, well, *soft* in there.

About that tram: one day, Sister Mary Burkman deputed me to take a large, round biscuit tin full of unconsecrated hosts over to the convent on the Esplanade in Middle Park. She gave me the tram fare and off I went. On the tram, the conductor and one of his mates started teasing me. I was wearing my school blazer the breast pocket of which proclaimed, in heraldic mode, **SHS** for Sacred Heart School. 'What's that stand for?' asked the conductor, 'Sheila's High School?' You see! Somehow, he was on to me, instantly. I employed my usual physically exhibitionist method of countering reflections on my toughness. When the tram was approaching the convent stop, I jumped off with great bravado before it stopped. Long before it stopped, as it turned out, so that I went cartwheeling along the road while the biscuit tin, having survived a ricochet off the footplate, hit the tarmac and burst open like a grenade. Unconsecrated hosts, their original explosive momentum added to by a slick sea breeze, blew and wheeled and rolled over most of Middle Park. The conductor laughed and laughed and his mate, fascinated by my now revealed burden, said 'Those little buggers'd be bloody handy for cards, wouldn't they Bert!' I picked every last one of them up. The tram driver, though equally convulsed, graciously refrained from moving till I'd levered fifty or so out of the tramlines, thus avoiding blasphemy and eternal damnation.

At secondary school I started inventing brothers. My two best friends both had an endless supply of brothers. It took me no time at all to realise that, at my school, it was a huge advantage to have had an older brother, or preferably several, come through before you. This was a sign not only of a possibly large Catholic family – a sure way to pre-empt approval from a De La Salle Brother who'd never before set eyes on you – but also of a sort of male continuity and solidarity. I felt convinced then and I remain persuaded now that my inability to cite a brother or two was a severe drawback, a subversion of any chance I had to impress myself on that intensely male world. Though I could now endure as well as the toughest of my classmates and much better than some the hundreds of strappings that attended our efforts to master French and Latin vocabulary and geometric theorems and so on, I failed to make a rugged mark. Years among the women seemed to have placed an insignia on me as readily visible as the scarlet letter. So, to those who couldn't possibly know the truth I started to represent myself as having from two to four brothers, depending on need and what I could get away with at the time.

Gradually, it seemed to become less fraught. I turned out to be a more than handy cricketer, a pretty good footballer, later on, an excellent squash player, a finisher in five marathons, a part-time farmer who really did get his hands dirty. The need for conscious emphasis on physical attainment seemed to diminish; it was now coming naturally. A broad Australian accent, a capacity to mix as easily with the local farmers as with my academic colleagues and a penchant for old utes and fishing trips added the finishing touches to the picture I'd been trying to paint all my life. In the end, I went too far. Despite having a wide circle of women friends, I became known as an archetypal bloke.

The truth, I have now decided, lies as so often somewhere wimpishly in the middle. I'm utterly at home in the world of men but I'm not tough. I'd rather not go out in the boat in rough weather and I don't ever want to go too far, even in glassy calm. I'd run a mile rather than fight. When a commentator on my fiction and biography detected a 'strong feminine sensibility beneath the unmistakably male voice', I was momentarily shocked. But she was right and I took to accepting such insights as compliments. What else can a bloke do?

lll

I am winding along the track home admiring glimpses of the distant Southern Ocean flickering through the lattice work of roadside scrub. I'm thinking about running out the irrigation pipes because the weather's warming up, and I'm pondering a lecture I have to write on Gissing's *New Grub Street* and tutorials I have to give on Patrick White, and whether or not I should apply for a job at the Australian Studies Centre in London.

Round the last corner and – the narrow roadway is blocked by cows. Arthur's cows, looking as soulful and as loopy and as ponderous as ever. Nothing's changed.

Or has it?

NOTES ON CONTRIBUTORS

SUSAN BASSNETT is Professor in the Centre for British and Comparative Cultural Studies at the University of Warwick She has published extensively on Comparative Literature, Translation Studies, Women's Theatre Studies and British Cultural Studies. Recent books include: *Comparative Literature: A Critical Introduction* (Blackwell, 1993) and *Three Tragic Actresses* (CUP with J. Stokes and M. Booth, 1996). She has just edited the forthcoming *Studying British Cultures* for Routledge.

GARGI BHATTACHARYYA is a lecturer in the Department of Cultural Studies at the University of Birmingham.

JOSEPH BRISTOW is Senior Lecturer in the Department of English at the University of York, England, where he is also affiliated with the Centre for Women's Studies. During 1995-96, he is Senior External Research Fellow at the Stanford Humanities Center. His most recent book is *Effeminate England: Homoerotic Writing after 1885* (Open University Press/Columbia University Press, 1995). He is currently at work on a full-length study of sexuality and Victorian poetry.

DIANA BRYDON is Professor in the English department at the University of Guelph, Canada, has research interests in the fields of Canadian and postcolonial literatures, funded by grants from the Social Sciences and Humanities Research Council of Canada (1992-95) and the B.C. Matthews Fellowship (1994). She has written *Writing on Trial: Introducing Timothy Findley's 'Famous Last Words'* (ECW Press, 1995), *Decolonising Fictions* (with Helen Tiffin; Dangaroo Press, 1992), *Christina Stead* (U.K.: Macmillan; U.S.A.: Barnes and Noble,1987) has edited the Postcolonial issue of *Essays on Canadian Writing* (1995), and is currently writing a book on Timothy Findley for Twayne. She has served as editor of *World Literature Written in English* (1989-1993); research consultant and national Canadian editor for the *Encyclopaedia of Post-Colonial Literatures in English* (1994); President of the Canadian Association of Commonwealth Literature and Language Studies (1989-1992); and Administrator of the Commonwealth Writers Prize (1991;1992).

NICHOLAS J. CULL is Lecturer in American Studies in the Department of American and Canadian Studies at the University of Birmingham. His articles on propaganda have appeared in *The Historical Journal of Film, Radio and Television, The Journal of British Studies* and *Diplomacy and Statecraft*. He is the author of *Selling War: British Propaganda and American Neutrality in World War Two* (Oxford University Press, 1995).

GRAHAM DAWSON studied at the Centre for Contemporary Cultural Studies, University of Birmingham, and is now Senior Lecturer in Literary and Cultural Studies at the University of Brighton. His book, *Soldier Heroes: British Adventure, Empire and the Imagining of Masculinities* (Routledge, 1994), integrates Kleinian psychoanalytic theories of phantasy and identification into a cultural history of imperial adventure narratives and their heroes. He is currently researching English and Irish cultural memories of 'the end of empire' and 'the Troubles' focusing on the fiction of William Trevor.

MATTHEW FOX studied in Oxford and Berlin. He is Lecturer in Classics at the University of Birmingham. He is the author of *Roman Historical Myths* (Oxford, 1996), and researches gender, rhetoric, and historiography.

CHRISTOPHER E. GITTINGS is Lecturer in Canadian Studies in the Department of American and Canadian Studies at the University of Birmingham. He has published articles on postcolonialism and gender, and the cross-cultural dialogue between Canadian and Scottish literatures. Currently, he is preparing a study of alterity and the representation of nation in Canadian cinema for Routledge.

BRIAN HARDING is Senior Lecturer and Head of the Department of American and Canadian Studies at the University of Birmingham. He is the author of *American Literature in Context, II, 1830-1865* (1982), has edited *Young Goodman Brown and Other Tales* (1987) and *The Scarlet Letter* (1990) for the Oxford University Press World's Classics series, and the forthcoming *Nathaniel Hawthorne: Critical Assessments* (Helm Information).

SUSAN HAYWARD is Lecturer in French Studies at the University of Birmingham, U.K., with research interests in gender, and the *auteur* genre in French cinema. She is the general editor of Routledge's National Cinema series, and the author of *French National Cinema* (Routledge, 1993), and a forthcoming glossary of cinematic terms.

PETER HUNT is Reader in English Literature in the School of English at the University of Wales, Cardiff. He has lectured on Children's Literature at over sixty universities world-wide, and has written several novels. His academic works include *An Introduction to Children's Literature* (Oxford, 1994), *The Wind and the Willows: a Fragmented Arcadia* (New York, 1994), *Children's Literature: An Illustrated History* (Oxford, 1995).

CHRISTOPHER LANE is Assistant Professor of English and Comparative Literature at the University of Wisconsin-Milwaukee, and in 1995-96, a Mellon Fellow in the English Department at the University of Pennsylvania. He is author of *The Ruling Passion: British Colonial Allegory and the Paradox of Homosexual Desire* (Duke University Press, 1995), and of essays in *Raritan, ELH, Differences, Cultural Critique, Discourse, LIT, Contemporary Literature, Democratic Culture, Prose Studies, Literature and Psychology, American Literature, Critique* and *The New Statesman and Society*. He has also contributed to the collections *Writing India, 1757-1990* (Manchester University Press, 1995) and *Homosexuality and Psychoanalysis* (Macmillan, 1995).

JOHN MARTIN is Assistant Principal at Lawrence Hargrave School in Sydney, New South Wales, Australia. He gave the paper included in this collection at the Issues in Australian Childhood Conference at Queensland Museum in September 1993. He gave another paper 'Real Men Don't Read' at the First Australian Conference on Men's Issues in Sydney in December, 1993. His research interests include getting boys to read, developing empathy in boys and changing constructions of masculinity in Australian history.

BRIAN MATTHEWS is Professor of Australian Studies, London University, and Head of the Menzies Centre for Australian Studies. He was granted an Australian Council Writers Fellowship in 1989 and was Chair of the Literature Board of The Australian Council from 1990-92. He is currently on secondment for the five year duration of his London University contract. He is the author of many articles, essays and broadcasts on modern British literature and on Australian literature, culture, popular culture and sport. In 1988, his novel *Louisa* (Penguin, 1987), won The Victorian Premier's Award for Non-Fiction (The Nettie Palmer Prize); The NSW Premier's State Award for Literature; the Gold Medal of the Australian Literature

Society; and was joint winner of the John Hetherington Bicentennial Prize for Biography. In 1989, *Quickening and Other Stories* (Penguin, 1989), was runner-up for The Steele Rudd Short Story Award. In 1994 he was appointed to a Personal Chair in English – the first ever to be awarded at Flinders University, Adelaide – and in 1995 he was elected to Fellowship of the Australian Academy of The Humanities.

BARBARA RASMUSSEN is a lecturer in English at the University of Birmingham, with research interests in theories of gender, and psychoanalysis. She has published on Alice James, Henry James, and Jane Austen. She is currently editing a collection of essays on Virginia Woolf's *To the Lighthouse*.

ANDREW MICHAEL ROBERTS is Lecturer in English at the University of Dundee, with research interests in modern and contemporary literature and gender theory. His publications include *Conrad and Gender* (Rodopi, 1993) and *The Novel* (Bloomsbury, 1994). He is currently completing a book on Conrad and masculinity for Macmillan.

PETER WEST is Senior Lecturer in Education at the University of Western Sydney-Nepean in New South Wales, Australia. He wrote *A History of Parramatta* (Sydney: Kangaroo Press, 1990). He is interested in educational and historical aspects of how boys become men. He writes and speaks about a wide range of men's issues in the newspapers and on television. He is currently writing a report on boys, sport and schooling called *Wounded Warriors: Why Boys Are Turning from School to Sport* (UWS Nepean, Sydney, 1996).

ALAN F. WILLIAMS is a historical geographer with special interests in transport and Canada. He has been Head of the Department of American and Canadian Studies, and is currently Director of the Regional Centre of Canadian Studies, both in the University of Birmingham. He is author of a number of books and papers on northern regions, including *Scandinavia* (with B. Fullerton) and *Father Baudoin's War*. He has just completed *John Cabot and Newfoundland: 500th Anniversary of the Discovery* for the Historical Society of Newfoundland.